141 DIVES
in the protected waters
of Washington and British Colum.

SO-AUP-687

NEW UPDATED EDITION
The most authoritative guide to underwater fun in Washington and B.C.

Betty Pratt-Johnson

141 DIVES

in the protected waters
of Washington and British Columbia

Gordon Soules Book Publishers Ltd.
West Vancouver, Canada
Seattle, U.S.A.

First edition 1976
Updated edition 1977
Second printing of updated edition 1978
Third printing of updated edition 1980
Fourth printing of updated edition 1982
Fifth printing of updated edition 1985
Sixth printing of updated edition 1986
Seventh printing of updated edition 1988
Eighth printing of updated edition 1990

Canadian Cataloguing in Publication Data
    Pratt-Johnson, Betty.
    141 Dives in the protected waters of
    Washington and British Columbia

    Includes index.
    ISBN 0-919574-20-3 (Soules)

    1. Scuba diving.   2. Skin diving–British
    Columbia.   3. Skin diving–Washington (State).
    I. Title.

GV840.S78P73   1977   797.2'3   C77-002189-1
Library of Congress Catalog Card Number: 76-21055

Published in Canada by
Gordon Soules Book Publishers Ltd.
1352-B Marine Drive
West Vancouver, B.C.
Canada V7T 1B5

Published in the U.S.A. by
Gordon Soules Book Publishers Ltd.
620 - 1916 Pike Place
Seattle, WA 98101

Printed and bound in Canada by Hignell Printing Limited

Dedicated to. . .

All the divers who brought me
back to northwest diving
and gave me
some of the greatest pure joy
I've ever known. . .

CONTENTS

ACKNOWLEDGMENTS

Many old friends helped me with this book; and this book helped me find many new friends. Countless happy hours of shared diving and reflecting are collected on these pages. It is truly a joint effort. I want to thank every one for each special shared experience.

Particular thanks go to Neil McDaniel for reading and criticizing the entire manuscript; to Peter Vassilopoulos, Editor and Publisher of *Pacific Diver*, for constantly encouraging me by giving me a place to write for divers and for encouraging me to take pictures, pictures, pictures; to Bob Horton for teaching me how to use a photographic enlarger; to Lou Lehmann for lending me equipment to print photographs; to Paul Mockler for helping me select which of my photographs to include; to Alisen Brown for printing my photographs which appear in the book; to Raymond Hull for helping me to organize my thoughts as I started writing this book; to Gordon Soules for saying "Go ahead — write it!" and for giving me constant invaluable support throughout; to Gordon Elliott for creative and exciting editing; to my friend, Pené Horton, for starting me writing in the first place; to Gil Hewlett, Curator of Vancouver Public Aquarium, for initially encouraging me to write about diving when he pointed out that there is more camaraderie amongst divers than among any other group in the world.

More thanks go to those who have shared their knowledge and love of the sea with me in endless practical ways. For information, helpful criticism, driving of boats, and all the other essential acts that helped me to go diving and to write about it, thanks to Chris Angus, Executive Assistant of Vancouver Public Aquarium, Casey Arneil, Bill Bamford, Susan Biggs, Donna Blackwell, Marty Bonner, Gary Bridges, Bob Briggs, Bob Cant, Jim Cartwright, Dr. Larry Chen, Graham Christie, Mike Comeau, Brent Cooke, Jo-Ann and George Crawshaw, Patty-Ann and Geoff Cumpstone, Ron Czerniak, Lynn Daniel, Malena Davidson, Shirley Duncan and Dr. Kenneth Duncan, Gord Esplin, Horst Foellmer, Colin Foster, Art Gillies, Chic Goodman, Nancy Harwood, Arthur Hastings, Brenda Hourston, Neil Hurd, Norm Innes, Lon Kamann, Greg Kalyniuk, Mike Keepence, Gil Kneebone, Philip Lambert, Mike Lawless, Thelma Legge and Dr. Michael Legge, Ross Lind, Laura Lippert, Bob Logan, Marge MacFarland, Gaire McLean, Dave Manning, Colleen Millar, Eric Morris, Molly Murray, Terry Notley, Mike Pease, Jerry Penner, Tom Penner, Warren Peterson, Brian Pratt-Johnson, Doug Pratt-Johnson, Jim Price, John Quail, Paul Reeves, Elaine and Al Richards, Teri Roberts, Dr. Ted Robinson, Captain A. McPherson Ross, Bob Rouleau, Jerry Rowand, John Ruttan, John Seabrook, Mike Smith, Doug Sutherland, Tim Stevens, Dr. Max Taylor, Meryl Turner, Vancouver Public Library staff, Dave Wardell, Ralph Watson, Frank White, Jim Willoughby, Frank Wolff and Dick Yates. And I wish to thank the Canadian Hydrographic Service, Department of the Environment, Ottawa, and the United States Department of Commerce, National Oceanic and Atmospheric Administration, National Ocean Survey, Riverdale, Maryland, for allowing me to reproduce portions of their nautical charts throughout the book.

Many more thanks to to divers with whom I've shared those beautiful moments under water. For help, information and diving shared thanks to Bobbie Adkins, Daryl Aitkin, Ari Barck, Art Bennett, George Blackwell, Norm Brodie, George Brooks, Alisen Brown, Len Chambers, Dave Christie, Doug and Dolene Comstock, Laurelle Croteau, Duncan Cumming, Steve de Beer, Dan Eason, Phil Edgell, Jeremy Fitz-Gibbon, Ann Ford, Martha and Duane Goertson, Jim Goodman, Rick Harbo, Fred Hendrick, Ian Hornby, Marg Hortin, Barrie and Roy Innes, Rick Jones, Larry Kobetz, Gord Lavery, Jim Lee, Kevin Lehmann, Lou Lehmann, Norma Loughton, Tenny and Neil McDaniel, Larry MacFarland, Pat McKeown, Bill McLeod, Al McRae, Rick McTavish, Dave Macklin, Gary Mallender, Michael Marchant, Chuck Moore, Jock Morrison, Brian Morse, Lesley Munroe, Dr. J.P. Munroe, Richard Nakata, Dave Neises, Kjeld Nicolaisen, David Olafson, Rick Ostiguy, Reo Prendergast, Erik

Rasmussen, Mike Rawlins, Martin Roberts, Walter Rudek, Jan Rueger, Patti Seguin, Jim Shaw, Paulette and Tom Sheldon, Dave Short, Harvey Steen, Nancy Steinfort, Teresa Stoney, John Turpin, Danny Tucon, Carla and Peter Vassilopoulos, David Vincent-Jones, Marilyn Wolff and Dave Woodburn.

But most of all my thanks go to my husband for sharing many happy moments under water and for helping me in every way to make this book happen. Thank you, John.

Come Dive with Me

COME DIVE WITH ME

One overcast November day in 1967 I did my first — and almost my last — Pacific northwest dive. Nothing dangerous happened, but I just couldn't see why anyone would want to dive in these waters. Visibility was poor and I saw nothing that lured me back. In fact, I saw nothing. My husband and I had learned to dive because we were going to visit the tropics, and for seven years we confined our diving to brief holidays in faraway places.

I didn't dive in the Strait of Georgia again until the fall of 1974 when writing an article about scuba diving in British Columbia. The enthusiasm of every diver I met proved irresistible. By the time I'd completed a four-dive open-water refresher course — something I recommend for every returning dropout — I was a confirmed Pacific northwest diver wanting to plunge into every bit of water I saw.

Where to start? I wanted to dive during the week when clubs don't ordinarily plan dives. Boat trips were on weekends, too. I discovered no guide to follow, no book about local diving. Yet nothing could keep me from diving at this point. I'd been bitten. I therefore decided to write the very book I wanted to buy, a book containing basic information about facilities and sites.

Wherever there is water there is a potential dive site. This endless possibility for exploration is one of the great joys of diving. It also means I could not possibly list every location. However, this book offers something better than a mere list. It gives clues about how to dive different types of sites. And it offers a diverse sampling of various kinds of diving available, both from shore and by boat. It includes many of the better-known and more accessible dive sites, and some not-so-well-known spots in the protected inland sea which stretches from the top of the Strait of Georgia in British Columbia to the southern tip of Puget Sound in Washington.

To obtain information I have talked with local divers about each site. Then I went to look for it. I've had minor difficulties in determining whether some properties crossed in gaining access to diving waters are public or private property. Treat with respect, therefore, any new signs advising that property is private or stating that no trespassing is allowed.

My observations about marine life are the observations of an interested layperson. I refer to all animals by common names. In the absence of an authoritative common name I have used the common name most descriptive to me. As I completed this book I learned that throughout my entire diving and research I have been confused about dahlia and snakelock anemones. On this subject alone I have had to rely upon memory and consultation with others, rather than my logbook. I am sure that snakelock anemones occur much more frequently than they appear in this book, but I have mentioned their presence only where memory and consultation make me certain. On all other subjects I have kept careful records and I am confident that the dive descriptions do give photographers, hunters and sightseers a comprehensive idea of what to expect.

Though having personally dived every site in the book, I have not dived every site in every season, and thus may have missed some points. Many dives I've muddled through and I've become lost looking for some sites. Along the way I've made a lot of mis-

10

takes. But hopefully I've been able to write such accurate directions that you won't have to waste time making the same mistakes. You can make new ones!

This book is the right size to put in your pocket when you go off for a dive. But if you don't want to take the whole book, it is deliberately designed with each dive described on two opposing pages so that you can easily photocopy it for a dime and take just the photocopy when you go for your dive.

A portion of nautical chart in the actual chart size is included in each site description. These charts are for reference only and are not to be used for navigation. All soundings are in fathoms unless stated otherwise. The scale varies as the charts themselves vary. Therefore I have added a small scale bar under each chart.

Shallow wrecks are indicated on some charts by the symbol of a half-sunken hull: ◢ . Deeper wrecks are indicated on some by the word "wreck" and on others by a symbol: ⊹ . Some artificial habitats are marked "Fish Haven". Where no indication of a structure has been given and large fragments are present I have added a wreck symbol to assist in finding them. Roads, place names, and sighting lines have been added to some charts. An arrow has been added to all charts to indicate the entry point described.

All road signs in Canada are to be in metric by September 1, 1977, but because no dates have been set for American metric conversion I have included an abbreviated metric conversion table on pg. 393 to help with access directions during the changeover.

Each site description incorporates the best of current knowledge for your safety. All information has been checked by one or more experienced divers in addition to myself. But this book is not meant to teach you how to dive. Proper training and certification are required before you can rent or purchase equipment or obtain air fills. And you must have good equipment.

All dives are rated for the amount of skill and experience required. This cannot be measured by the number of years you have been diving. It can only be measured by the variety of diving situations you have encountered. Any certified diver should be able to attempt the dives classified "All Divers". Beginners and visitors should have experience with a number of these dives before doing any of the difficult ones. When a site has some complications but does not require intricate planning I have rated it for "Intermediate Divers". Dives which require precision and which present several difficult hazards are classified for "Advanced Divers". Many sites are suitable for snorkeling or skin diving as well as scuba diving. When this is so, I have mentioned it. I have tried to present a balanced number of dives for divers of all skills in each locale. The greatest number are in and around cities where there are the most divers looking for places to get wet.

141 Dives is a starting point for coastal divers who have just learned to dive, dropouts who are returning to diving, and visiting divers from around the world. It contains useful service information for all divers.

This book is an open invitation to enjoy some of the most varied and remarkable diving found anywhere. Writing this book has been like a holiday for me as I've re-lived every dive again and again. Come dive with me, with this book as a guide, and we'll go on and on and on discovering the colourful, still world known only to Pacific northwest divers.

WHAT'S DIFFERENT ABOUT PACIFIC NORTHWEST DIVING?

The waters are filled with life. You keep seeing things under the sea that you can't find in any book. Fascinating creatures, some still unnamed. It's fabulous to feel that you're on the edge of discovery on every dive.

Perhaps the second most striking feature of Pacific northwest diving is the sheer magnitude of protected coastline which makes this one of the safest and most accessible diving areas in the world.

Other features of this enormous inland sea are listed below, as well as some suggestions about how to use them to your advantage in pursuing a variety of diving activities. Details about local conditions are in the site descriptions which comprise most of the book. However, before you start selecting specific sites, read the following summary of basic information every diver will want to know. It includes a great deal of information:

General Conditions
1. Water Salinity
2. Water Temperature
3. Seasons
4. Visibility
5. Kelp
6. Currents and Rip Tides
7. Boats and Log Booms
8. Broken Fishing Line
9. Surge and Surf
10. Marine Life

Diving Activities
11. Underwater Photography
12. Spearfishing and Shellfish Collecting
13. Shell Collecting
14. Bottle Collecting
15. Wreck Diving
16. Night Diving

1. Water Salinity — All dives covered in this book are in salt water. Divers accustomed to freshwater diving will find they need to wear one to four pounds more weight when diving in the sea. Probably most divers should start by adding two pounds to accommodate for the increased density of salt water. Experiment until you find the right amount.

2. Water Temperature — Water temperature is affected by several factors, including depth and currents. Surface temperatures of Pacific northwest waters vary from 4 to 8° Celsius (39 to 46°F) in winter to 12 to 18° Celsius (54 to 64°F) in summer, depending upon location. However, below a depth of 30 or 40 feet the temperature varies little, winter or summer, from about 7° Celsius (45°F). It is just a matter of where the temperature drop, or thermocline, comes — at 30, 40, 50 or 60 feet, usually not deeper than that. Then if you are diving below the thermocline you will want to dress warmly year-round. Another factor to consider is that you will probably feel the cold more quickly when diving where there is a current. The current constantly forces a change of water under any gaps in your suit. And the water itself will probably be colder because shifting water never becomes warm.

Most local divers dive comfortably year-round in all locations wearing custom fitted wet suits of either ¼" or 3/8" neoprene. Many wear the "farmer John" or "farmer Jane" style of suit which covers the trunk of the body with a double thickness. Some divers obtain extra warmth for winter by wearing an Arctic hood with a large flange around the neck, by wearing a vest under their wet suit jacket, and/or by adding a spine pad to their suit. Others wear 3/16" neoprene five-finger gloves in summer and ¼" neoprene mitts in winter. Some — mostly commercial divers who spend hours in the water — wear dry suits. In future many sport divers too will be using dry suits, especially photographers who lie still in the water for long periods and need extra warmth because of their inactivity.

Many wet suits manufactured in California and other warmer parts are of 3/16" neoprene and will probably not be comfortably warm in winter waters of the Pacific northwest. Visiting divers may want to buy or rent a vest or an Arctic hood for added warmth while diving in Puget Sound and the Strait of Georgia.

3. Seasons — Year-round diving is enjoyed in the Strait of Georgia and Puget Sound and a variety of diving activities is possible. Winter is best for photography since low plankton activity and low river runoff levels make visibility best then. Spring and fall are spearfishing seasons. (See pages 21-24 for exact dates.) Because summer visibility can be poor, summer is a good time to combine a dive with a picnic on an unspoiled beach, or pursue some diving activity like bottle collecting. Because much bottle collecting is done at muddy sites by touch alone, visibility does not matter. Sunny September days are considered best all-round by some, as that season can be most beautiful both above and below the surface. I opt for year-round diving, choosing sites and diving activities suitable to each season.

4. Visibility — Water clarity is probably the most significant variable in Pacific northwest diving. It can vary from "faceplate" visibility when you cannot see 1 foot ahead, up to a crystal clear 100 feet. Poor visibility may be the result of several factors: the type of bottom, river runoff, industrial pollution, and plankton growth.

A. Type of bottom — Muddy substrates are liable to be stirred up when current is running, or when a lot of divers are swimming close to the bottom. In many locations, diving at the end of the outgoing tide will help you obtain the best possible visibility. A buoyancy compensation device, which gives neutral buoyancy at any depth, should be worn by all divers at all times. It is particularly useful when diving in muddy areas.

B. River runoff — Both melting snows and rainstorms cause murky surface water, especially near river and creek mouths. In the spring and early summer and after rainstorms, check your chart and avoid sites near large rivers like the Fraser or Skagit. A small, clear stream of fresh water flowing into the sea creates a shimmery appearance like scotch and water, but does not impede vision.

C. Industrial pollution — Effluents, tailings and other solid wastes from mines, factories and logging operations can impair visibility. Avoid these areas.

D. Plankton growth — Two "waves" of plankton growth or "bloom" come to protected waters of Pacific northwest seas each spring and summer. Prolonged sunny weather encourages these "blooms". The "spring bloom" invariably occurs each year throughout the Strait of Georgia and Puget Sound. It begins any time from March through April or May, and clouds the top 20 or 30 feet with a green growth of plankton making the water look like pea soup. Later, the plankton aggregates in white clumps and looks like a snowstorm in the water. This may last only two weeks or a month. However, often just as the plankton "bloom" fades away, river runoff comes to cloud surface waters. The second "wave" of plankton is less predictable and more localized. It may come in late summer, August through September or October, making the water look slightly red. This second "bloom" may come to one area and not to another, usually lasting a very short while. The water may be turbid one day and clear the next. Therefore, at easily accessible sites, it is always worth checking to see if the water is clear. The best summer visibility comes on a sunny day after a week of overcast weather.

Sometimes the only way to find good visibility in the late spring and early summer is to select a dive site deep enough that you can descend through the surface murkiness until the visibility improves. Swim with your hands touching and extended forward to protect your head and face, and take the precaution of surfacing with a good reserve of air so that you can meet any emergency poor visibility might create.

One of the most beautiful dives I ever made was on a sunny day in May at Lookout Point in Howe Sound. Fraser River runoff and a healthy "bloom" of plankton had combined to make the surface almost opaque. There was only "faceplate" visibility until my buddy and I reached 50 feet. Suddenly we were in a garden of fluffy white plumose anemones shimmering with phosphorescence. Spectacular! Like a night dive, only better, because it came as such a complete surprise. Is it any wonder I advocate diving year-round?

5. Kelp — Beauty or beast? If you have never been diving in kelp you should know something about it.

The large bull kelp is beautiful on its own as it streams above you like flags in the current. I love it just for that. Experienced Pacific northwest divers are lured to it for many other reasons, too: it can help orient you. It can show you the way the current is running and it can indicate depth. In the Strait of Georgia bull kelp usually grows in less than 30 feet of water. In areas where there are a lot of boats, kelp can indicate a relatively traffic-free place to ascend, if the kelp itself is not too thick to penetrate. It provides a rich habitat for marine life. You will often find crabs hiding under it and fish swimming through it. Urchins eat it as a favourite food. Kelp is interesting on its own, too. It is a seasonal plant which nearly dies off over the winter and grows again in spring and summer. It grows very rapidly, reportedly sometimes as much as six inches in a day. These facts are just a start. Interested divers can find a lot of fascinating information about kelp or marine algae.

It can be a hazard, though, if you are caught in it and then panic. When diving around bull kelp, be particularly careful at the surface. Kelp is easier to swim through under water. Enter the water by surface-diving down, feet first, to avoid entanglement. Always ascend with a reserve of air so that you can descend again, if necessary, and come up at another spot where the growth is not so thick. Bull kelp has a strong stem which is very difficult to break by hand. Wear a knife you can reach with either hand, so that if caught you can calmly cut your way free. A few unprepared divers have drowned as a result of entanglement, and most of these drownings were on the surface. Do not avoid kelp because of its dangers, but use the many positive points which recommend it. Be careful when diving in it, and respect its strength.

6. Currents and Rip Tides — Some of the largest tidal changes in the world occur in passages of the Strait of Georgia and Puget Sound. All of that moving water has to go somewhere. It is not surprising then that in some locations near islands and narrows there are strong tidal currents. You can glance at a chart and immediately predict areas where current will be a serious consideration. However, where there is current there is also abundant marine life, because the moving water provides food for many animals. It is well worth learning to dive safely in currents in order to enjoy the rich scenes that open to you:

A. Always ask local divers for advice about sites and times.

B. Learn to use your tide and current tables and charts and plan each dive carefully. Have your buddy make a dive plan, too. Then check to see if you have planned for the same time. Remember to account for daylight saving time when it is in effect. Wear a good watch.

C. When diving in an area subject to strong currents, a fairly safe rule for timing your dive is to get wet 30 minutes before slack tide, the period when the water is still and the tide is neither coming in nor going out. Remember that tides and currents do not always fit with the tables. Depend upon your common sense. Look at the water and sum up the situation visually before entering the water. For instance, at Campbell River be ready at the site 1 hour before slack, watching and waiting for the water to slow down. Then complete your dive shortly after the tide has turned.

D. When diving where the current is not too strong, you do not necessarily have to dive precisely on the slack, but somewhere near slack. Hold onto rocks and pull yourself along. Crawling up-current saves a lot of energy and air. Then when half of your air is gone, drift down-current until you have returned to your entry point.

E. When diving in a very strong current, plan to have a "live" boat ready to pick up all divers, if necessary. Your boat should be ready with motor running and an experienced skipper/diver at the helm.

F. Or, you can deliberately plan a "drift" dive. If there is no kelp in the area, mark each diver with a floating buoy so that the boat can follow easily. A white plastic bottle makes a good marker.

G. When diving from a boat in current, plan to ascend at the anchor line and surface near the bow. Leave a floating line trailing behind so that if you miss the boat you can catch onto the line. Attach a plastic bottle float to the end of the line, or use a polypropylene line which floats.

H. Wear a small volume mask. It is less likely than a large mask to be dislodged by the current.

I. If caught in a rip current, do not try to swim against it. Swim across it and gradually work your way out.

J. Do not dive at night in currents.

K. Learn to cope with current and then discover some most rewarding diving.

7. Boats and Log Booms — Thousands of boats also use the inland sea waters described in this guide. Areas where boat traffic is particularly heavy are noted in the detailed site descriptions, and you should be especially careful at these places. But remember, a boat could appear at almost any time over any site. Dive defensively:

A. Fly your diver's flag. In most crowded areas, the law requires divers to fly a diver's flag. In remote areas, your diver's flag will tell any passersby not to worry about your empty boat. A diver's flag is a hindrance instead of a help only when you are doing a "drift" dive.

B. When ascending, spiral and look up in order to see as much of the surface as possible.

C. Listen for boats, dive with a compass and, if possible, ascend close along the bottom all the way to shore. Or ascend near a rock face, up your boat or dive-flag anchor line or in a kelp bed, being careful not to become caught in the kelp. Larger vessels usually steer clear of kelp.

D. If you cannot ascend close along the bottom all the way to shore, listen for boats and ascend with a reserve of air. If you hear a power boat stay down until it passes. If you hear a really big ship, wedge yourself between rocks or hang onto a boulder on the bottom.

E. When diving near log booms, ascend with a reserve of air so that if you arrive immediately under the log boom you will have time to descend and come up again at another place. Spiral, look up, and extend one arm above you as you ascend.

8. Broken Fishing Line — Beware of broken bits of fishing line under water. It is very strong and difficult to see. Look for it where you know there are lots of fishermen and at rocky points near heavily populated areas. Carry a diver's knife; if you become entangled you can cut yourself free.

9. Surge and Surf — Since the scope of this guide is limited to inland sea and inlets protected from the open ocean, surge and surf are not factors to consider at the sites described.

10. Marine Life — The colour and variety of marine animals living in the Strait of Georgia and Puget Sound is astonishing. I carry an underwater light on every dive in order not to miss any of that colour. Marine algae or kelps are abundant, as well. Over 500

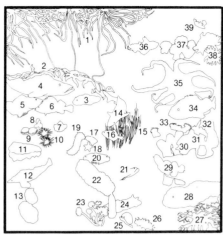

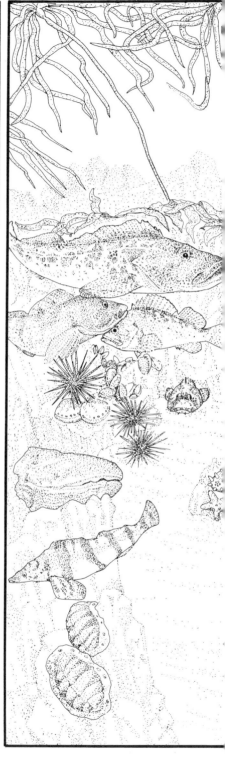

WHAT TO LOOK FOR

Rocky Reef
1. Bull kelp
2. Bottom kelp
3. Cabezon
4. Lingcod
5. Kelp greenling
6. Black rockfish
7. Red Irish lord
8. Swimming scallops
9. Abalones
10. Giant urchins
11. Rock scallop
12. Painted greenling
13. Chitons

Sand
14. Dogfish
15. Eelgrass
16. Seaperch
17. Striped seaperch
18. Leather star
19. Sea cucumber
20. Dungeness crab
21. Flounder
22. Sea pen
23. Plume worms
24. Orange peel nudibranch
25. Moon snail
26. Alabaster nudibranch

Rock Wall
27. Basket star
28. Wolf eel
29. Chimney sponges
30. Grunt sculpin
31. Giant barnacles
32. Sailfin sculpin
33. Dahlia anemones
34. Copper rockfish
35. Octopus
36. Ratfish
37. Plumose anemones
38. Sunflower stars
39. Sea peaches

Illustration by Greg Davies

species of marine algae have been recorded in British Columbia. The sea is teeming with life, all of it fascinating, and practically none of it dangerous to the diver.

At shallow sandy sites you will probably find delicious large Dungeness crabs revealed only by a pair of eyes and a slight indentation in the bottom. Moon snails that look like something from another planet. And sometimes the bottom itself takes off like a flying carpet — starry flounders in flight!

When diving deep you may find prawns or discover ancient ghostly clumps of cloud sponges with a small rockfish peeping from each tuberous appendage. No one knows how to gauge for sure, but some say a clump as tall as a man must be hundreds of years old. Some say thousands.

Among rocky reefs you will find red Irish lords, kelp greenlings skittering away spookily into crevices, and tiny grunt sculpins looking like precisely painted tropical fish. Popular food fish like lingcod sometimes grow to 30 or 40 pounds — and more — in the rocky current-swept depths. Over 325 species of fish live in the Eastern North Pacific. And Pacific northwest waters are unrivalled for colourful invertebrates. Over 90 species of sea stars — the greatest number of sea stars found in any one area of the world — inhabit these waters. Gorgeous red nudibranchs, delicate as tissue paper, waft through the water near newly laid eggs cascading over rocky cliffs like an intricate lace shawl. Many small nudibranchs live in these waters.

And the Pacific northwest is home to some of the world's largest octopuses. For many years octopuses had the reputation of being dangerous to divers, but this is myth. The octopus can be handled quite easily. If one grabs onto you, simply tickle him and he will release you and slip away. Octopuses are much more frightened of you than you are of them.

What animals *are* potentially dangerous in Pacific northwest waters? The following creatures are sometimes considered dangerous, or simply bothersome, by divers:

A. Wolf Eels — The wolf eel with its very strong teeth and jaws can inflict a bad bite. These eels are not known to attack without provocation, and if you avoid sticking your hands into holes and crevices you will probably never tangle with one.

B. Lingcod — Though not generally considered dangerous, the lingcod has a formidable set of teeth and has been known to attack divers. Males may be aggressive when guarding eggs during winter.

C. Sea Urchins — Urchins have sharp spines and can cause nasty puncture wounds.

D. Jellyfish — More of a nuisance than a hazard, the red, brown and yellow jellyfish can leave a painful sting. Even a severed tentacle can still sting. If you have seen any red, brown or yellow jellyfish, you and your buddy should check one another for stinging tentacles before removing your masks and gloves. Jellyfish are seasonal and appear most often in fall and early winter.

E. Ratfish — The ratfish has a poisonous spine just in front of its dorsal fin. Avoid this spine.

F. Seals and Sea Lions — These animals are sometimes sought, sometimes avoided. One diver told me he saw a seal dislodge a diver's mask in play, and caused the diver to panic. Another told me of a friend whose daily dive companion is a seal. Sea lions may approach divers and some divers have reported injuries.

G. Killer Whales — Killer whales are not known to attack people, but most divers leave the water when killer whales appear.

H. Dogfish — Dogfish are not known to attack people, but most divers leave the water when dogfish start circling in a pack.

● **For More Information**

The Barnacles of British Columbia, Handbook No. 7 by I.E. Cornwall, British Columbia Provincial Museum, Victoria, 1970.

Between Pacific Tides by Edward F. Ricketts and Jack Calvin, Stanford Univ. Press, Stanford, California, 1968.

Common Seashore Life of the Pacific Northwest by Lynwood Smith, Naturegraph Co., Healdsburg, California, 1962.

Guide to Common Seaweeds of British Columbia, Handbook No. 27 by R.F. Scagel, British Columbia Provincial Museum, Victoria, 1972.

The Intertidal Bivalves of British Columbia, Handbook No. 17 by D.B. Quayle, British Columbia Provincial Museum, Victoria, 1973.

Invertebrates of North America by Lorus and Margery Milne, Doubleday and Co., Inc., New York, (n.d.).

Light's Manual: Intertidal Invertebrates of the Central California Coast, edited by Ralph I. Smith and James T. Carlton, Univ. of California Press, Berkeley, California, 1975.

Pacific Fishes of Canada, Bulletin 180 by J.L. Hart, Fisheries Research Board of Canada, Ottawa, 1973.

Sea Life of the Pacific Northwest by Stefani and Gilbey Hewlett, McGraw-Hill Ryerson Ltd., Toronto, 1976.

Seashore Life of Puget Sound, the Strait of Georgia and the San Juan Archipelago by Eugene N. Kozloff, J.J. Douglas Ltd., Vancouver, 1973.

Some Common Marine Fishes of British Columbia, Handbook No. 23 by G.C. Carl, British Columbia Provincial Museum, Victoria, 1973.

11. Underwater Photography — "If you have a camera the very worst dive site is a good one," says one enthusiastic underwater photographer. Because of an awakening of ecological awareness and conservation, and because of improved equipment and camera housing, underwater photography is becoming more and more popular. Now when the word "shoot" is used in diving, it connotes the idea of capturing a subject on film, rather than on the end of a spear.

What's different about underwater photography in the Pacific northwest? Winter is the best season for it because visibility is then at its best. Artificial light is usually required, as available light is almost always insufficient to produce good photographs. Endless subjects are at hand, particularly to photographers interested in close-up work, as there are so many colourful invertebrates in these waters. Even after years of photography, an enthusiast may find new subjects on every dive.

12. Spearfishing and Shellfish Collecting — Underwater parks have been created in some areas of both British Columbia and Washington, largely because of pressure from concerned divers who want to preserve our fantastic underwater heritage. Today more and more conservation-minded divers restrict their hunting to hunting with a camera. It has even been suggested — by divers — that the entire Strait of Georgia be made an underwater park. Restrictions are necessary in highly populated areas if we are not to denude our seas. In future we may need more controls, or even a ban on hunting. The scuba diver may not take fish, shellfish nor any other marine life from areas designated as underwater parks at any time. These sites have been noted on the detailed site descriptions.

However, at the moment there is still a place for properly controlled spearfishing and shellfish collecting. Spearing can be an art and a skill. There is something very basic and satisfying about stalking, catching and consuming your prey. Even just a shellfish! The following food fish and shellfish are found in the Strait of Georgia and Puget Sound and are sometimes hunted and collected by divers:

Fish	Other Seafood
Cabezons	Abalones
Flounders	Clams
Kelp Greenlings	Crabs
Lingcod	Octopuses
Rockfish	Oysters
Yelloweye Rockfish	Prawns
(commonly called	Scallops
Red Snappers)	Sea Cucumbers
	Sea Urchins

British Columbia
Subject to change. The following information is intended as a guideline, only. Before collecting any marine life check current regulations. Fisheries Notices are posted at marinas, launching ramps, post offices and other obvious public places.

●Fish

Cabezons
No limit.

Flounders
No limit.

Kelp Greenlings
No limit.

Lingcod
Season: Closed December 1st through last day of March.
Size: No limit.
Bag Limit: Three in one day.
Possession Limit: Shall not exceed two single day bag limits.

Rockfish
No limit.

Yelloweye Rockfish
No limit.

●Other Seafood

Abalones
Size: At least 4 inches across the longest width of the shell.
Possession Limit: Twelve.

Clams
Bag Limit: Twenty four per person per day for all species in the aggregate. Consult local Fisheries Office for closed areas. Also look for posted notices.

Crabs

Pacific or Dungeness Crabs
No person shall use jigs, gaffs, spears, rakes or any sharp pointed instrument in fishing for crabs. May not collect in English Bay, False Creek, Burrard Inlet and between First and Second Narrows Bridges.
Size: 6½ inches or more across the shell.
Possession Limit: Six, including red rock crabs.

Red Rock Crabs
Size: No limit.
Possession Limit: Six, including Pacific crabs.

Octopuses
No limit.

Oysters
Consult local Fisheries Office for closed areas. Also look for posted notices.
Possession Limit: 25 in the shell or one quart shucked per day.

Prawns
No limit.

Scallops
No limit.

Sea Cucumbers
No limit.

Sea Urchins
Size: 4 inches or more across the shell.

SEASON, SIZE AND BAG LIMITS

Washington State
Subject to change. The following information is intended as a guideline, only. Before collecting any marine life check current regulations.

●Fish
Cabezons
No limit.

Flounders
No limit.

Kelp Greenlings
Bag Limit: Fifteen fish in the aggregate, included with all species of rockfish, and true cod.

Lingcod
Season: Closed December 1st through March 31st in Hood Canal and Puget Sound water lying south of lines drawn from Olele Point to Bush Point, Whidbey Island and from Possession Point, Whidbey Island true east to the mainland.
Size: No limit.
Bag Limit: Three.

Rockfish
Bag Limit: Fifteen fish in the aggregate of all species of rockfish, true cod, and greenling.

Yelloweye Rockfish
Bag Limit: Fifteen fish in the aggregate of all species of rockfish, true cod, and greenling.

● Other Seafood

Abalones
Size: 3½ inches or more across the shell.
Bag Limit: Five.

Clams

Geoducks
Bag Limit: Three.

Horse Clams
Bag Limit: Seven.

Razor Clams
Since razor clams are most abundant on surf-pounded beaches, seasons and bag limits are not listed here.

All Other Clams
Season: Open all year in Willapa Harbor, Grays Harbor and Puget Sound east of Dungeness Spit.
Open November 1st through March 31st on beaches west of Dungeness Spit.
Closed all year at public beaches in Hood Canal area and at Hoodsport Salmon Hatchery.
Closed January 1st through July 31st on San Juan Island at state owned tidelands between Bell Point and a boundary marker about 560 yards south of Bell Point.
Closed all year on San Juan Island south of above marker to about 1060 yards south of Bell Point.
Bag Limit: Seven pounds in the shell, not to exceed a count of 40 clams.

Crabs

Pacific or Dungeness Crabs
Size: Six inches or more across the shell, immediately in front of the points.
Bag Limit: Six male crabs.

Red Rock Crabs
Bag Limit: Eighteen.

Octopuses
Unlawful to use any chemical irritant in the taking of octopuses.
Bag Limit: Two.

Oysters
Bag Limit: Eighteen. Oysters must be shucked on the beach and shells returned to the tide level where found.

Prawns
Bag Limit: Ten pounds or ten quarts in the shell.

Scallops

Pink (Swimming) Scallops
Bag Limit: Twenty pounds or ten quarts in the shell.

Rock Scallops
Bag Limit: Twelve.

Weathervane Scallops
Size: Four inches or more.
Bag Limit: Twelve.

Sea Cucumbers
Bag Limit: Twenty five.

Sea Urchins
Red and Purple Urchins
Bag Limit: Eighteen.

Green Urchins
Bag Limit: Thirty six.

●Hints on Where to Look for Fish

Cabezons
Usually found over gravel bottoms. Grind your teeth, or knock rocks together to attract cabezons.

Flounders
Found over sandy bottoms.

Kelp Greenlings
Usually found amongst the rocks and in kelp.

Lingcod
Usually found over rocky bottoms where there is current.

Rockfish
Found amongst the rocks and in rocky crevices, usually in 15 to 60 feet of water.

Yelloweye Rockfish
Commonly called red snapper, this fish usually occurs in 100 feet or more over rocky bottoms.

●Hints on Where to Look for Other Seafood

Warning: Shellfish may be made unfit for eating by
1. Feeding in waters polluted by sewage. Do not collect shellfish in highly populated areas.

2. Feeding on toxic organisms in the water, *Gonyaulax catenella*, commonly called "red tide". These microscopic one-

celled animals turn the sea a striking, reddish colour and may cause paralytic shellfish poisoning. If shellfish come from "red tide" waters, cooking does not reduce their toxicity. Do not collect shellfish if you see a "red tide". Consult local Fisheries Office for closed areas. Also look for posted notices.

Abalones
Abalones usually are found attached to rocks amongst kelp where salinity is high and water temperature is below 15° Celsius (59°F) in 15 to 30 feet of water. Look for a black fringe-like mantle. Pry abalones loose on your first try, or they get a very tight hold on the rocks and may be damaged upon removal. An abalone takes six years of growth to reach the minimum legal size limit.

Clams
Hardshell clams
Hardshell clams are usually found in the tidal zone between minus 3 and plus 4 feet in a porous mixture of gravel, sand and mud. They are usually within 6 inches of the surface.

Geoducks
Geoducks are readily found at the extreme low tide line: most shore digging is restricted to less than twenty tides a year. Scuba divers can dig geoducks year-round.

Crabs
Pacific or Dungeness Crabs
Pacific or Dungeness crabs have a pale pink or sandy coloured shell and their pincers are gleaming white. Usually found on sandy bottom, often in eelgrass. It is difficult for a diver to see the actual crabs, because they bury themselves in the sand. Look for a slight indentation in the sand or mud and for two eyes sticking out. Crabs are more easily spotted on a slight slope.

Red Rock Crabs
Red rock crabs can be distinguished from Pacific or Dungeness crabs by their black pincers and bright red colour.

Octopuses
Octopuses are territorial. Their rocky lairs can be located by the litter of crab or clam shells at the entry.

Oysters
Oysters are found between the tide lines. Prime oysters at the lowest tide, from the lowest possible point on the beach, at sites which are far from human habitation. No limited season for collecting oysters, but the best oysters are harvested in winter and early spring.

Prawns
Prawns typically live over rocky bottoms at great depths, from 150 to 300 feet. They come up shallower at night to feed. Divers collect them at 70 to 120 feet on night dives.

Pink (Swimming) Scallops
Swimming scallops, which look like the shell on the gas station sign, occur in rocky areas where there is current. Sometimes on gravel bottom. They may be found quite deep — 30 to 100 feet. You cannot miss seeing these unique bivalves when they are present. They see you first and swim upwards to escape, clapping their valves like a pair of castanets, raining upwards around you.

Rock scallops
Rock scallops are found mostly in rocky areas where there is a current, below tide line to 100 feet. It is difficult to distinguish rough-shelled rock scallops from the rocks. They are often covered with tube worms, barnacles and encrusting sponges. Look between rocks for a pale orange mantle that disappears when the scallop sees you and snaps shut. One group of divers could quickly deplete an area of scallops; therefore, be conservation-minded when you collect scallops and leave some for the next time.

Sea Cucumbers
Sea cucumbers are abundant everywhere in the Strait of Georgia and Puget Sound.

Sea Urchins
Sea urchins are found amongst kelp in salty, cold water.

● For Information on Cooking Seafood
Bottoms Up Cookery by Robert B. Leamer, Wilfred H. Shaw and Charles F. Ulrich, Fathom Enterprises, Inc., Gardena, California, 1971.

Crab and Abalone: West Coast Ways with Fish and Shellfish by Shirley Sarvis, Bobbs-Merrill Co., New York, 1968.

Edible? Incredible! by Marjorie Furlong and Virginia Pill, Ellis Robinson Publishing Co., Inc., U.S.A., 1972.

How to Catch Shellfish! by Charles White and Nelson Dewey, Saltaire Publishing Ltd., Sidney, B.C., 1972.

How To Cook Your Catch! by Jean Challenger, Saltaire Publishing Ltd., Sidney, B.C., 1973.

Sunset Seafood Cookbook, Sunset Magazine eds., Lane Books, Menlo Park, California, 1967.

Vancouver Aquarium Seafood Recipes—Tasty delights from the waters of British Columbia, Washington, Oregon, Northern California and Alaska, compiled by Ainley Jackson, Gordon Soules Book Publishers, Vancouver/London, 1977 and The Writing Works, Inc., Mercer Island, Washington, 1977.

13. Shell Collecting — More than 900 different species of marine shells can be found in the Pacific northwest area.

●**For More Information**

Marine Shells of the Pacific Coast by Tom Rice, Ellis Robinson Publishing Co., Inc., U.S.A., 1972.

14. Bottle Collecting — Bottle collecting can be a whole new venture on its own, and may be lucrative for the discriminating collector. It is certainly a diving activity worth trying at least once. If you want to avoid loading yourself down with a bunch of useless bottles, as I did on my first bottle dive, some basic pointers might be useful. Look for barnacled bottles, the most obvious sign of age. Also look for odd and unusual shapes, and bottles with no threads for screw tops. Black shiny bottles may be old and rare and therefore most desirable. Look for bottles that *do not* have a seam running all the way up the neck. These are the hand-finished ones. If you find a bottle with a rough bit of glass called a pontil stuck to the bottom, you have found a really old and rare collector's item.

For ideas to start off, look for "bottle dives" in the index at the back of the book. Then when you have tried some of the known bottle sites, start finding your own. Locate old logging camps and settlements by studying old maps and charts and by reading regional histories. Soon you'll be discovering new caches of old bottles.

Bottles and crockery may be cleaned by soaking in a solution of muriatic acid and water. Mix 40 ounces of acid with two or three gallons of water. Set bottles in the mixture. Take out occasionally and scrub. In two or three days your bottles should be clean.

●**For More Information**

Old Tyme Bottles by Don Harrison, Precise Instant Printing, Vancouver, 1973.

Western Canadian Bottle Collecting, Volume 1 by George Watson and Robert Skrill, The Westward Collector, Nanaimo, B.C., 1973.

Western Canadian Bottle Collecting, Volume II by George Watson and Robert Skrill, The Westward Collector, Nanaimo, B.C., 1973.

15. Wreck Diving — If you've ever seen the gleam in the eye of a diver who's discovered a wreck, you know what "wreck fever" means. And vast possibilities for exploration are available to insatiable wreck divers.

Thousands of historic shipwrecks both known and unknown, litter the sea floor of the Pacific northwest. Many have never been dived on. Opportunities for adventure and reward are almost limitless. Even a well-known wreck that has been stripped provides a special diving thrill. It harbours quantities of marine life, has a history all its own, and always offers the chance of discovering yet-one-more brass plate or bell or other long-lost treasure. Wreck diving is exciting. It can also be dangerous. But like all other areas of diving, if you start slowly, build up your experience and observe a few basic rules, wreck diving can be a most satisfying sport. Begin with some of the simple wreck dives.

Then progress to more difficult ones. Some suggestions for wreck divers in the Pacific northwest:

A. As always, dive with a buddy, and know your buddy very well. The two of you should review and practice "ditch-and-don" procedures and emergency ascents.

B. Don't overload yourself. When bringing up "finds" be sure that you can support them with the flotation devices you have with you; otherwise you might drop your "finds" on divers below. When working a wreck, collect all of your "finds" and put them in one place. Then bring them up with a "lift" bag.

C. Be extremely wary of entering any wreck. Be sure that it is stable and is not going to collapse on you. Be particularly cautious when diving on a rotting timber vessel. Check surfaces in the way you check handholds when mountain climbing, to be sure they are solid. Take two good lights and use a return line to follow out if both lights should fail.

D. Always ascend with a good reserve of air and remember a working dive requires more air. Consider the fact that you are working and decrease your bottom time.

E. Salvage laws in Canada require that you report the find of a recent wreck. Any wreck in the Vancouver Harbour area, from Point Atkinson to Point Grey and east, or in the Roberts Bank area, should be reported:

Port Manager
Port of Vancouver
520 Granville Square
200 Granville Street
Vancouver, B.C.
V6C 2P9
(604) 687-0474

Experienced wreck diver using regulator to fill "lift" bag

Report wrecks in the Mainland and Sechelt Areas:
District Manager
Canadian Coast Guard Base
Canadian Coast Guard
Toronto Dominion Bank Building
6th Floor
1405 Douglas Street
Victoria, B.C.
V8W 2G3
(604) 388-3292

Report wrecks in Victoria Area north to Duncan:
Receiver of Wrecks
c/o Area Collector of Customs and Excise
816 Government Street
Victoria, B.C.
V8W 1X1
(604) 388-3177

Report wrecks north of Duncan:
Receiver of Wrecks
c/o Area Collector of Customs and Excise
66 Front Street
Nanaimo, B.C.
V9R 5H7
(604) 753-4181

F. Salvage laws in the United States require that any wrecks in
the Seattle area should be reported:
Captain of the Port
U.S. Coast Guard
Pier 90
Seattle, Washington
98799
(206) 284-2361

All others in Washington State should be reported to the
nearest U.S. Coast Guard Station.

● **For More Information**

Disaster Log of Ships by Jim Gibbs, Superior Publishing Co.,
Seattle, 1971.

Exploring Puget Sound and British Columbia by Stephen E.
Hilson, Van Winkle Publishing Co., Holland, Michigan, 1975.

List of Shipping, Canada Department of Transport, Ottawa,
(published annually since 1890).

Lloyd's Register, Lloyd's Register of Shipping, London, (published annually since 1760).

Marine History of the Pacific Northwest by Lewis and Dryden,
edited by E.W. Wright, Superior Publishing Co., Seattle (1895),
1967.

Marine History of the Pacific Northwest by H.W. McCurdy, edited by Gordon Newell, Superior Publishing Co., Seattle, 1966.

Merchant Vessels of the United States, U.S. Department of Transportation, U.S. Coast Guard, Washington, D.C., (published annually since 1867).

Pacific Coastal Liners by Gordon Newell and Joe Williamson, Bonanza Books, New York, 1959.

Pacific Liners 1927-72 by Frederick Emmons, David and Charles: Newton Abbott, Devon, 1973.

Pacific Square-Riggers by Jim Gibbs, Superior Publishing Co., Seattle, 1969.

Pacific Tugboats by Gordon Newell and Joe Williamson, Superior Publishing Co., Seattle, 1957.

The Princess Story by Norman R. Hacking and W. Kaye Lamb, Mitchell Press Ltd., Vancouver, 1974.

Shipwrecks of British Columbia by Fred Rogers, J.J. Douglas Ltd., Vancouver, 1973.

Steamships and Motorships of the West Coast by Richard M. Benson, Superior Publishing Co., Seattle, 1968.

Whistle Up the Inlet by Gerald A. Rushton, J.J. Douglas Ltd., Vancouver, 1974.

West Coast Windjammers by Jim Gibbs, Superior Publishing Co., Seattle, 1968.

16. Night Diving — If you've been disappointed in the marine life in an area, or by the diving in any way, or if you're just looking for an extra thrill — a new dimension — then try a night dive.

Nothing else can match it for me. Many more animals come out at night. Some, like prawns, come up shallower and can be hunted more easily then. And the old, familiar life takes on a new look. The eyes of the ratfish glow like sapphires. When you switch off your light the smallest crab is magical in the fabulous phosphorescent night sea. It's fun diving under wharves and enjoying the play of your lights making shadows on the pilings. And you may find an octopus — fantastic in the phosphorescence — coiling and uncoiling in a shimmer of light. Some practical notes on night diving:

A. Stay right with your buddy.

B. Both divers carry an underwater light, but also try turning off both, sometimes, to savour the beauty of the phosphorescence.

C. Surface with a reserve of air.

D. Do not dive in currents at night in rocky areas, for the rocks come past too fast.

E. Don't wait — do it now. Why not tonight?

STRAIT OF GEORGIA AND PUGET SOUND
SECTIONAL MAPS

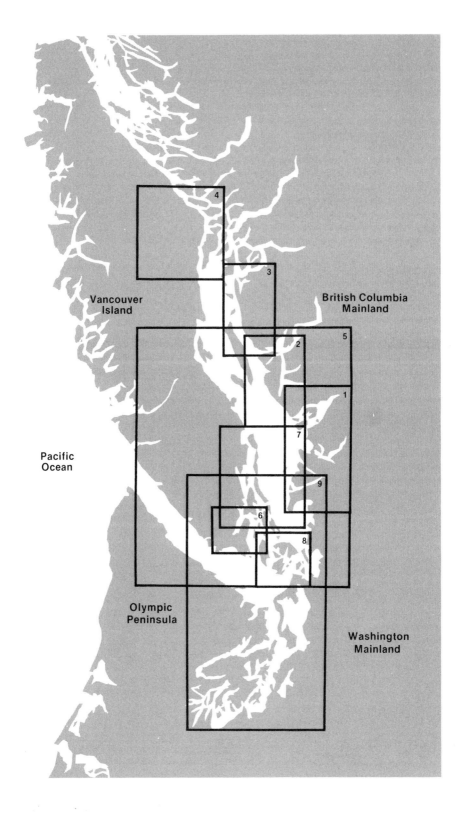

CHAPTER 1
Vancouver, Indian Arm and Howe Sound

Dives

1. Cates Park
2. Strathcona
3. Woodlands
4. Texaco Wharf
5. Belcarra Park
6. Whiskey Cove
7. Bedwell Bay Wreck
8. Jug Island
9. Racoon Island
10. Twin Islands
11. Buntzen Power Plant
12. Silver Falls
13. Croker Island
14. Caulfeild Cove
15. Lighthouse Park
16. Passage Island Reef
17. Larsen Bay Park
18. Whytecliff Park — Whyte Islet
19. Whytecliff Park — The Cut
20. Lookout Point
21. Copper Cove
22. Porteau Beach
23. Porteau ¼-Mile
24. Porteau ½-Mile
25. Christie Islet
26. Pam Rocks
27. Millers Landing
28. Seymour Bay
29. Worlcombe Island

Places

A. Second Narrows Bridge
B. Deep Cove
C. Rocky Point Park
D. Park Royal
E. Fisherman's Cove
F. Horseshoe Bay
G. Sunset Beach
H. Lions Bay
I. Squamish River Mouth
J. Snug Cove
K. Tunstall Bay
L. Keats Island
M. Langdale
N. Gibsons

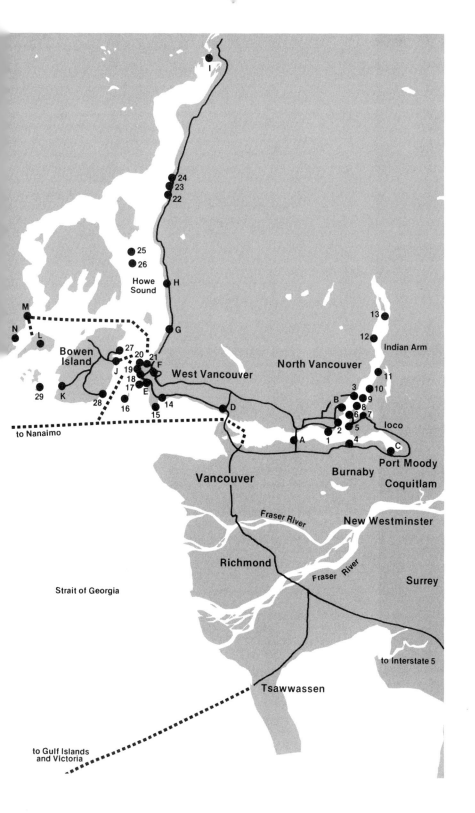

SERVICE INFORMATION*
Vancouver, Indian Arm and Howe Sound

Charts: Canadian Hydrographic Service
- 3435 Indian Arm
- 3481 Approaches to Vancouver Harbour
- 3484 Vancouver Harbour, Eastern Portion
- 3508 Plans in the Vicinity of the Strait of Georgia
- 3586 Howe Sound

Tide and Current Tables: Canadian Hydrographic Service
Tide and Current Table, Volume 5

Emergency Telephone Numbers
Rescue Coordination Centre (Vancouver) 732-4141

Vancouver General Hospital
(recompression chamber) 876-3211 ext. 2739

Marine Rescue 732-4242

Other Useful Numbers
Marine Weather Forecast 273-2373
National Harbours Board Office (weekdays) 687-0479
National Harbours Board Police (weekends) 689-3441

•Air Stations

Coquitlam
Pennant Marina
335 North Rd. at Lougheed Hwy.
Coquitlam, B.C.
V3K 3V8
(604) 936-9901

Gibsons
Smitty's Marina Ltd.
Box 96
Gibsons, B.C.
V0N 1V0
(604) 886-7711

New Westminster
Dive and Sea Sports
825 McBride Boulevard
New Westminster, B.C.
V3L 5B5
(604) 524-6444

North Vancouver
The Diving Locker
971 Marine Drive
North Vancouver, B.C.
V7P 1S4
(604) 985-1616

Points West Diving
1073 Roosevelt Crescent
North Vancouver, B.C.
V7P 1M4
(604) 980-6501

Watson Rentals
Panorama Park, Deep Cove
4511 Summerside Lane
North Vancouver, B.C.
V7G 1H4
(604) 929-5061

Richmond
All-Canada Diver's Supply
8133 River Road
Richmond, B.C.
V6X 1X8
(604) 270-3222 or
687-7711, local 2702
(Compressor rentals also.)

Richmond Diving Ltd.
6080 No. 3 Road
Richmond, B.C.
V6Y 2B3
(604) 278-7415

Rowand's Reef
5760 Cedarbridge Way
Richmond, B.C.
V6X 2A7
(604) 273-0704

Surrey
A.B. Sea R.V.
13211 King George Highway
Surrey, B.C.
V3T 2T3
(604) 581-3303

Olympic Sports
104th Ave. & Whalley Ring Rd.
Surrey, B.C.
V3T 1W5
(604) 585-1181

Vancouver
A.B. Sea Systems
1820 West Georgia S
Vancouver, B.C.
V6G 2W1
(604) 687-1028

The Diving Locker
2745 West 4th Avenue
Vancouver, B.C.
V6K 1P9
(604) 736-2681

Odyssey Diving Centre
2659 Kingsway
Vancouver, B.C.
V5R 5H4
(604) 430-1451

Rowand's Reef
2828 West 4th Avenue
Vancouver, B.C.
V6K 1R2
(604) 732-1344

•Boat Charters
Amphitrite
Scales Charter Boats
2021 Arbury Avenue
Coquitlam, B.C.
V3J 3K3
(604) 937-5226

Bayshore Inn Marina
North foot of Cardero
Vancouver, B.C.
V6G 2V4
(604) 689-7371

Charter Boat Pool
17 - 566 Cardero Street
Vancouver, B.C.
V6G 2W7
(604) 688-0481

Convoy Charters
6507 Sumas Drive
Burnaby, B.C.
V5B 2V1
(604) 299-8487

Danby Boat Charters
14716-55A Avenue
Surrey, B.C.
V3S 1B2
(604) 594-1263
(*Out of Sunset Marina.*)

Deep Cove Water Taxi
2890 Panorama Drive
North Vancouver, B.C.
V7G 2A4
(604) 929-3011

Eboness
Gambier Charters Ltd.
P.O. Box 5156
Vancouver, B.C.
V6B 4B2
(604) 688-4815

Granson Yacht Charters
North foot of Bute Street
Box 3056
Vancouver, B.C.
V6B 3X6
(604) 685-2226

Harbour Ferries Ltd.
#1 North foot of Denman
Vancouver, B.C.
V6G 2W9
(604) 687-9558

The Jib Set Sailing School
1020 Beach Avenue
Vancouver, B.C.
V6E 1T7
(604) 683-8819
(*Sailing charters.*)

M.R. Cliff
1021 Tuxedo Drive
Port Moody, B.C.
V3H 1L3
(604) 939-3987

M.V. Skeena
Nighthawk Enterprises, Ltd.
1946 West 4th Avenue
Vancouver, B.C.
V6J 1M5
(604) 926-6542

M.V. Tangle Fleet
All-Canada Diver's Supply
8133 River Road
Richmond, B.C.
V6X 1X8
(604) 270-3222 or
687-7711, local 2702

North Shore Sailing School
203 - 1139 Lonsdale Avenue
North Vancouver, B.C.
V7M 2H4
(604) 980-9116
(*Sailing charters.*)

Paradise Paquet Charters
1157 Melville Street
Vancouver, B.C.
V6E 2X5
(604) 688-5231
(*Sailing charters.*)

Proteus
Proteus Day Charters
Panorama Park, Deep Cove
2156 Banbury Road
North Vancouver, B.C.
V7G 1W8
(604) 929-7573

Santa Rita
Santa Rita Dive Charters Ltd.
3820 Francis Road
Richmond, B.C.
V7C 1J7
(604) 274-2760

•**Boat Rentals and Launching**
Gibsons
Smitty's Marina Ltd.
Box 96
Gibsons, B.C.
V0N 1V0
(604) 886-7711
(*Rentals only. Launching
nearby.*)

North Vancouver
Cates Park Public Ramp
Dollarton Highway
North Vancouver, B.C.
(*Launching only.*)

Deep Cove Marina
2890 Panorama Drive
North Vancouver, B.C.
V7G 1V6
(604) 929-1251
(*Launching only. Week-
days only.*)

Panorama Park Public Ramp
Foot of Deep Cove Road
North Vancouver, B.C.
(*Launching at high tide only.*)

Port Moody
Rocky Point Park Ramp
Port Moody, B.C.
(*Launching only.*)

Squamish Highway
Lions Bay Marina
Box 262, 7 miles north of
Horseshoe Bay
Lions Bay, B.C.
V0N 2E0
(604) 921-7510
(*Launching only.*)

Sunset Marina Ltd.
Sunset Beach
West Vancouver, B.C.
V7W 2T7
(604) 921-7476
(*Rentals spring through
fall. Launching year-round.*)

41   Pak-a-Boat Rental
       1601 Granville Street
       Vancouver, B.C.
       V6Z 2B3
       (604) 685-5738
       (Inflatable rentals.)

West Vancouver
Bay Boat Rentals
6395 Bay Street
Horseshoe Bay
West Vancouver, B.C.
V7W 2G8
(604) 921-7654
(Rentals spring and summer
only. Launching year-round.)

Whytecliff Boat Rentals
7120 Marine Drive
Whytecliff Park
West Vancouver, B.C.
V7W 2T3
(604) 921-7242
(Rentals spring and summer
only. No launching.)

●**Ferry Information**
B.C. Ferry Information Centre
1045 Howe Street
Vancouver, B.C.
V6Z 1P6
(604) 669-1211
(Ferries from Horseshoe Bay
to Bowen Island, Langdale or
Departure Bay; from Tsaw-
wassen to Swartz Bay.)

C.P. Rail Ferries
Foot of Burrard Street
Vancouver, B.C.
V6C 2R3
(604) 665-3142
(Ferries from Vancouver to
Nanaimo.)

Ministry of Highways Ferries
Langdale Ferry Terminal
Gibsons, B.C.
V0N 1V0
(604) 886-2242
(Pedestrian ferries from Lang-
dale to Keats Island.)

●**Tourist Information**
Department of Travel Industry
652 Burrard Street
Vancouver, B.C.
V6C 2L3
(604) 668-2300

National Harbours Board Regulations — No sport diving is allowed between First and Second Narrows Bridges or under them.
When planning a dive in any other waters of Indian Arm or
Vancouver Harbour west to Point Atkinson, telephone and obtain
permission from National Harbours Board. The telephone call is
really just a routine. If there are no unusual circumstances in the
harbour, permission to dive is granted easily.

The regulations are subject to change and may be altered as
necessary. At the end of July 1977 provisional regulations for
sport divers (By-Law A-1) were as follows:

1. A minimum of three people, two divers and one person on
the surface in case of emergency, must be at the site.

2. Diver's flag to be flown at all times.

3. Night diving from a boat must be from a lighted boat dis-
playing an illuminated dive flag.

All persons sport diving in National Harbours Board waters
should comply with National Harbours Board By-Law A1. Anyone contravening the regulations runs the risk of being prose-
cuted and upon conviction of being fined up to $500.

*All of this service information is subject to change.

Skill: Intermediate and Advanced Divers

Why go: Cates Park is close to the city. I still can't believe it's so easy to go out for a short dive on a rocky reef — a quick visit to another country! Red rock crabs and rockfish live on the reef. Dungeness crabs live around it. As we swam out through vast plains of bright orange sea pens we saw little snails scrambling all around. Snake pricklebacks, Oregon tritons and flounders are everywhere too. And grunt sculpins. Cates Park provides a pleasant morning or afternoon of sightseeing diving.

Access: Cates Park is 3 miles past Second Narrows. Heading *north* on Second Narrows Bridge follow signs towards Deep Cove. Three miles along Dollarton Highway you come to Cates Park. Park near the dock west of Roche Point. Suit up, and enter here. The reef is 200 yards offshore.

Bottom and Depths: Rocky reef, 200 yards southeast of the dock. It is 10 to 20 feet deep. Eelgrass around the reef. Silty sand, 20 or 30 feet deep, stretches from shore to the reef.

Hazards: Boats, poor visibility, shallow depths and some current. Be careful of hordes of small boats on summer weekends. For best visibility, dive one hour before low slack. It is shallow. Wear extra weight and use a compass so that you can stay on the bottom for the duration of your dive.

Telephones: 1. Cates Park, summer only.
                   2. Dollar Shopping Centre, on Dollarton Highway, ½ mile north of Cates Park.

Facilities: Large grassy area, picnic tables, large parking lot, dock and launching ramp. Restrooms in summer only.

Comments: Both beach and park are good for a picnic for the family or larger groups. However, this dive is safer in winter when fewer boats are on the water.
    Permission required from National Harbours Board to dive at Cates Park.

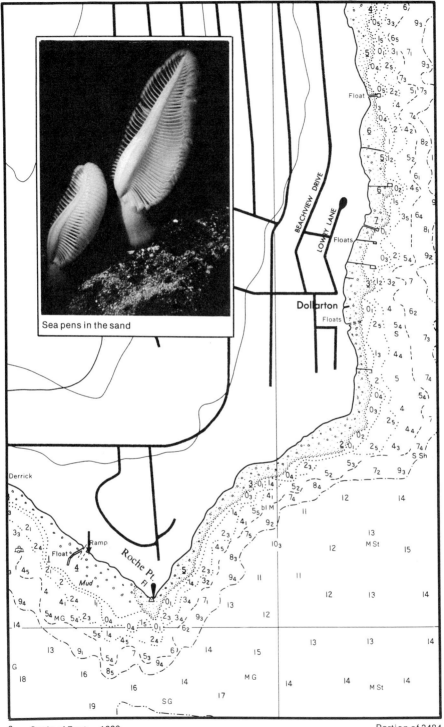

Sea pens in the sand

BEACHVIEW DRIVE

LOWRY LANE

Float

Floats

Dollarton

Floats

Derrick

Ramp

Float

Roche Pt.
Fl

Mud

Scale of Feet 1000

Portion of 3484

Skill: All Divers and Snorkelers

Why go: White Rock, commonly called Strathcona, combines sandy-bottom life and high-current life all on one dive. Diving on the inside of White Rock you'll see flounders, Dungeness crabs, Oregon tritons, alabaster nudibranchs and masses of sea cucumbers on the sand and hiding in the bottom kelp. On the outside current-swept channel we saw large purple stars plastered to the wall. Giant barnacles, plumose anemones, small tube worms, chitons and bright orange burrowing cucumbers. Rockfish hang by the wall. Orange sea pens and transparent filaments of burrowing anemones feather the flat sand in the channel beyond White Rock.
A "mixed bag" dive.

Access: White Rock is 5½ miles past Second Narrows. Heading *north* on Second Narrows Bridge follow signs towards Deep Cove. Five miles along Dollarton Highway, just past Mount Seymour Parkway, turn right down Strathcona Road. Go ½ mile to the water where two or three cars may park by the government dock. Snorkel 100 yards to White Rock, go down and dive right around the rock.

Bottom and Depths: Broken rock covered with bottom kelp is scattered around the base of White Rock. Along the channel side the rock wall falls to 50 or 60 feet bottoming out to flat sand in the channel. Sand and eelgrass in the bay between the shore and White Rock.

Hazards: Current. Red jellyfish, in the fall. Dive on the slack. If you have seen any red jellyfish, you and your buddy should check one another for stinging tentacles before removing your masks and gloves.

Telephone: Deep Cove, by government dock, less than 1 mile north of Strathcona Road.

Facilities: Government Dock.

Comments: Many private residences around this little cove and no place for a picnic. Good for the dive only. Then go to the park at Deep Cove.
    Permission required from National Harbours Board to dive at White Rock.

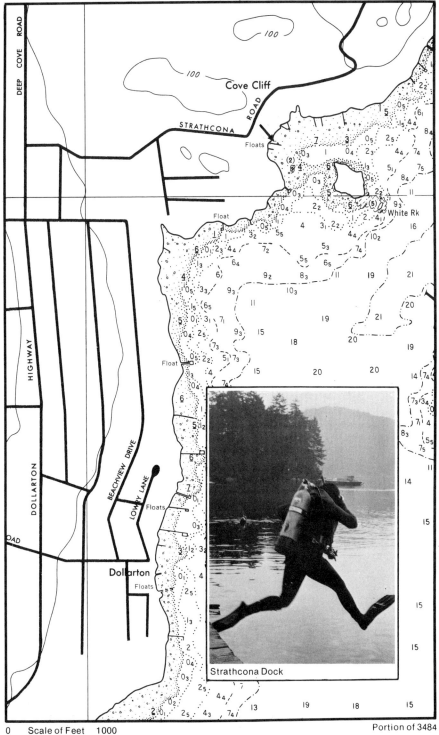

DEEP COVE ROAD

100

100 Cove Cliff

STRATHCONA ROAD

Floats

White Rk

Float

Float

HIGHWAY

BEACHVIEW DRIVE

LOWRY LANE

DOLLARTON

ROAD

Floats

Dollarton

Floats

Strathcona Dock

0   Scale of Feet   1000

Portion of 3484

Skill: All Divers

Why go: Woodlands provides opportunity for a deep dive or a shallow dive right at the one site. As the name suggests there's a real wilderness feeling both above and below water. Look for hairy lithode crabs which are not seen everywhere but are quite often seen in this part of Indian Arm. Lots of decorator crabs, rockfish and sunflower stars on the wall. Flounders on the flat sand. And an unequalled cascade of Johnnie Walker whiskey bottles kept me speculating for months about the kind of party once held at Woodlands!
Perhaps some old bottles here, too.

Access: Woodlands is 7½ miles past Second Narrows. Heading *north* on Second Narrows Bridge follow signs towards Deep Cove and Mount Seymour Park. One half mile past Second Narrows Bridge, just across a small bridge, turn left towards Mount Seymour Park, then right into Mount Seymour Parkway. Go east 2 miles to Mount Seymour Park turnoff. Turn north and go almost ½ mile. Just before the park gates, turn right and wind 3½ miles through the woods along Indian River Road, always keeping to the left, until you come to a "Stop" sign. You will have to park here. But first, drive down the hill to your left and unload gear at the end of the road. It is 50 feet from here to the government dock. Park back up the hill where there is room for two or three cars.
For a deep dive, swim from the dock to the marker on Lone Rock, descend and work your way around the wall to your left. For a shallow dive stay in the bay. But this is unsafe on a sunny summer weekend when boats are coming and going. Shallow dives at Woodlands are advisable only on a weekday in winter.

Bottom and Depths: Hard sand, 20 or 30 feet deep, slopes from the dock to the island. At the marker and around to the left, a rock wall drops off to 110 or 120 feet. The wall is covered with a cascade of small broken rock and rubble.

Hazards: Boats. Red jellyfish, in the fall. Poor visibility. Listen for boats and ascend with a reserve of air; if you hear a boat you can stay down until it passes. Or ascend close to the bottom all the way to shore. If you have seen any red jellyfish, you and your buddy should check one another for stinging tentacles before removing your masks and gloves. For best visibility dive on an outgoing tide.

Telephone: Mount Seymour Parkway and Mount Seymour Road, by the gas station.

Facilities: Government dock.

Comments: Good for the dive only. Even though in the wilds, private property surrounds the dock and there is no place for a picnic. Local residents bitterly resent divers who are thoughtless about parking and who do not stay under water when boats are around. Watch these two points and improve our image in order that divers will be welcomed at Woodlands.

Permission required from National Harbours Board.

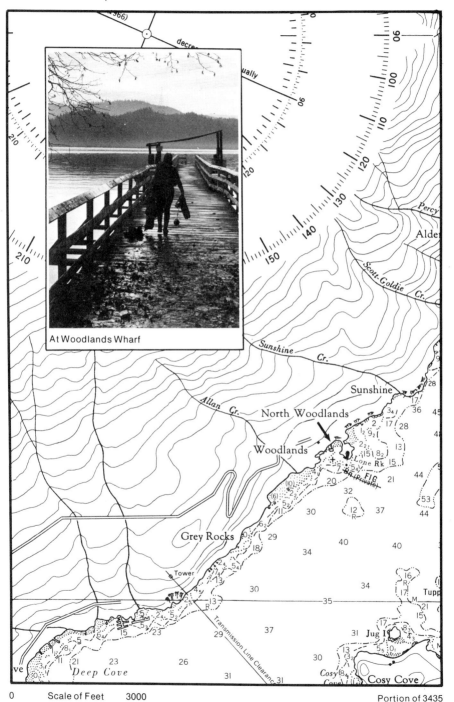

At Woodlands Wharf

Scale of Feet   0 — 3000

Portion of 3435

Skill: All Divers

Why go: Close proximity to the city, easy access at the site, sea pens, Dungeness crabs, flounders and old bottles are the attractions at Texaco Wharf.
If you've never seen the shimmering neon-green of a sea pen at night, you have a thrill in store for you. It's easy to dive here at night and sea pens are all over the place. Stroke the sea pen gently to make it glow.
Crabs at this site, too. And my buddy caught a flounder in her hands. After she examined it and put it down, the flounder seemed frozen with fear. We laughed when she had to gently push the fish on its way. We saw sea stars, Oregon tritons, widely scattered plumose anemones and small green anemones.
We also found old bottles at Texaco Wharf. This is an old part of town. A muddy bottom like this one is an excellent place for turning up old bottles, particularly when there is a back eddy by the shore as there is at Texaco Wharf.

Access: Texaco Wharf is 5 miles from Second Narrows. Heading *south* on Second Narrows Bridge turn left into Hastings Street and go east 3 miles to Burnaby Mountain. Bear left on Inlet Drive and go 1½ more miles to Texaco Drive which turns down to your left towards the water. Just before the railway tracks you'll find room for four or five cars to park. Walk across the tracks and follow the path around the left side of the fence 50 yards to the small sandy beach at the left of Texaco Wharf. Dive anywhere in front of the beach out towards the pilings.

Bottom and Depths: Gently sloping sand and rocky shore turns into eelgrass in about 10 or 15 feet. Then thick mud, levelling off at 30 or 40 feet, right out to the huge pilings. Sea pens are to the left.

Hazards: Poor visibility, shallow depths, and ships. Poor visibility, usually limited to 7 or 8 feet, inevitable with the mucky bottom. Also be careful of commercial ships coming into the wharf. Listen for ships, wear extra weight and dive with a compass so that you can stay on the bottom all the way back to shore.

Telephone: Inlet View Motel, 1 mile east on Inlet Drive.

Facilities: None at Texaco Wharf.

Comments: Surprising as it seems, there's a very pleasant small crescent of beach at the wharf.
Permission required from National Harbours Board to dive at Texaco Wharf.

Low tide at Texaco Wharf

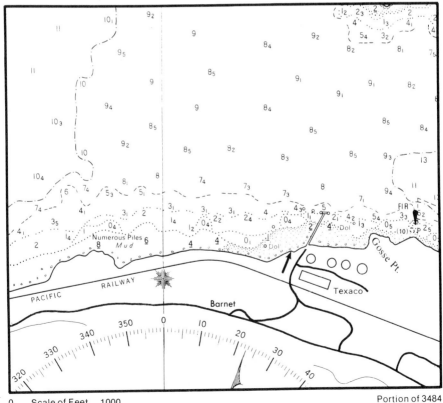

Portion of 3484

0   Scale of Feet   1000

BELCARRA PARK
Shore Dive

Skill: All Divers and Snorkelers

Why go: A scrambling good time can be had by all catching Dungeness crabs at Belcarra Park.

Look in the eelgrass and silty sand for nothing but a slight indentation in the sand and a pair of eyes. Because crabs bury themselves, they are difficult to see. When you spot one, catch hold of the front of it between the eyes. Pull it up, quickly take your hand away and grasp it from behind so that it will not pinch you.

At Belcarra there's a small rocky reef for sightseeing, too, with the easiest possible entry and the shortest possible swim. The area is small, but picturesque. Orange and white plumose anemones, chitons and calcareous tube worms cling to the rocks.

In another area — a long swim away — there are glorious two-foot sea pens.

Access: Belcarra Park is 19 miles from Second Narrows. Heading *south* on Second Narrows Bridge turn left into Hastings Street and go east 3 miles to Burnaby Mountain. Bear left on Inlet Drive which becomes Barnet Highway, and go to Port Moody. At St. Johns Street turn left. Continue through Port Moody, turn left at Ioco Road and go around the water 3 miles to a corner where there is a small church on your left, Ioco Elementary School on your right, and a park across the street. This is Bedwell Bay Road. Turn right and continue along this wooded road past Sasamat Lake to the end of the road. Just as you can see the water, turn left and you are at Belcarra Park. Plenty of parking at Belcarra, just a few feet from the beach. Easy entry over sand.

Bottom and Depths: Sandy, muddy bottom slopes gently to 40 feet. Look for crabs in 15 to 30 feet of water in the eelgrass immediately in front of the dock and to your left. The mini-reef 20 or 30 feet deep is at right angles to the end of the dock, 20 or 30 feet north. Giant sea pens in 25 or 35 feet of water near the day marker, 300 yards south of the dock.

Hazards: Small boat traffic and poor visibility. Red jellyfish, in the fall. Listen for boats and ascend with a reserve of air so that if you hear a boat you can stay down until it passes. Try not to stir up the silt. If you have seen any red jellyfish, you and your buddy should check one another for stinging tentacles before removing your masks and gloves.

Telephone: Belcarra Park.

Facilities: Large grassy area, parking, picnic tables, government dock and launching ramp. Restrooms and refreshment stand in summer only.

Comments: Based on 1977 regulations possession limit for crabs

is six crabs. Dungeness crabs must be 6½ inches or more across the shell.
Check current regulations before going crabbing.
 Permission required from National Harbours Board to dive at Belcarra Park.

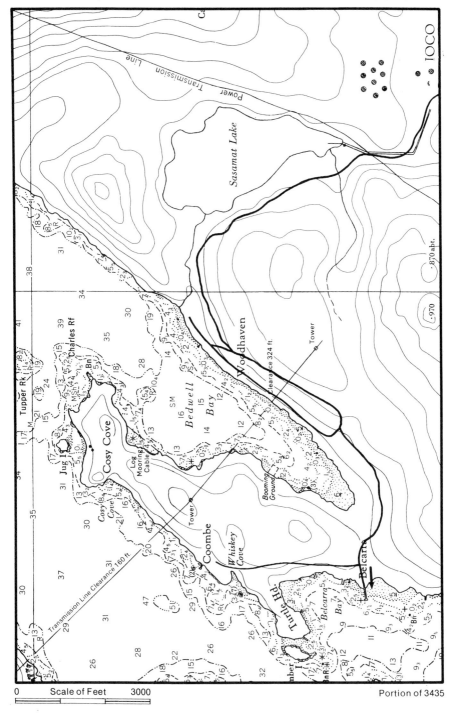

0   Scale of Feet   3000   Portion of 3435

Skill: All Divers

Why go: Whiskey Cove is a great lazy-day dive. The combination of an easy entry, short swim and shallow dive reward you with a wide variety of life. You'll see striped seaperch, rockfish and small lingcod. The fingers of bright orange burrowing cucumbers creep out of crevices. A rock face covered with transparent tunicates and tube worms. When diving here I stopped to look at them. Some tube worms waited until my finger was only an inch away before retracting. Then we cruised around past a wall covered with sea stars. A lovely sight — almost like cutout paper snowflakes, but in dark tones instead of white.
There's life on the sand, as well. Oregon tritons, Dungeness crabs and small snails scurry about. Suddenly the sea floor moves. It's a flounder before you. A field of sea pens stretches into Indian Arm.

Access: Whiskey Cove is 19 miles from Second Narrows. Heading *south* on Second Narrows Bridge turn left into Hastings Street and go east 3 miles to Burnaby Mountain. Bear left on Inlet Drive which becomes Barnet Highway and go to Port Moody, turn left at Ioco Road and go around the water 3 miles to a corner where there is a small church on your left, Ioco Elementary School on your right, and a park across the street. This is Bedwell Bay Road. Turn right and continue along this wooded road past Sasamat Lake to a place where you can see the water. Turn right down Belcarra Bay Road which becomes a rough gravel road. Go ¼ mile to the bottom of a very steep hill. Park and walk down a short, rough trail through the woods to the small log-covered crescent of beach. Snorkel to the rock on the left or the rock wall on the right of Whiskey Cove.

Bottom and Depths: The bay is rimmed with rocky walls, bottoming out to silty white sand at 30 or 40 feet. The wall on the right is undercut with small crevices and caves. A field of foot-high sea pens is in 40 or 50 feet of water straight out from the wall.

Hazards: Small boats and some current. Red jellyfish, in the fall. Listen for boats and ascend up the wall. If you feel any current pull yourself along the wall. If you have seen any red jellyfish, you and your buddy should check one another for stinging tentacles before removing your masks and gloves.

Telephone: Belcarra Park.

Facilities: Roadside parking for three or four cars.

Comments: Protected inlet dive for windy days.
Permission required from National Harbours Board to dive at Whiskey Cove.

Dungeness crab

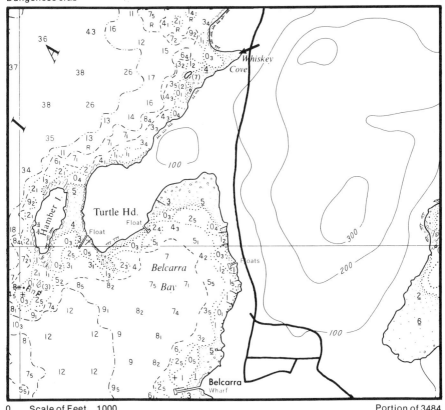

Skill: All Divers

Why go: The shallow wreck of the *H.M.S. Cranbrook*, a mine sweeper scuttled by the Canadian government in 1947 in Bedwell Bay, is beautiful for a first wreck dive!
Much of the wooden hull and steel superstructure remains intact in the shape of a ship, and it harbours so much life. When I dived here the *Cranbrook* was covered in five-inch lacy white nudibranchs tipped with blue. Calcareous tube worms and white and orange plumose anemones had attached themselves to the hull. Spider crabs crept over it. Seaperch, pile perch and rockfish, large and small, congregate inside the hull as though contained in a fishbowl. Swimming back to shore over sandy bottom crawling with Dungeness crabs, snails and flounders, galaxies of moon jellyfish billowed around us like a whole miniature universe under water. The experience was an eerie one.
A fabulous conclusion to the dive.

Access: The Bedwell Bay wreck is 18 miles from Second Narrows. Heading *south* on Second Narrows Bridge turn left into Hastings Street and go east 3 miles to Burnaby Mountain. Bear left on Inlet Drive which becomes Barnet Highway and go to Port Moody. At St. Johns Street turn left. Continue through Port Moody, turn left at loco Road and continue around the water 3 miles to a corner where there is a small church on your left, loco Elementary School on your right, and a park across the street. This is Bedwell Bay Road. Turn right and go along this wooded road ½ mile past Sasamat Lake to Kelly Avenue. Turn right and wind down a short way towards the water. At Kelly Avenue and Marine Avenue turn sharply left. Ten feet past the corner you will see a telephone pole on your right. Ten yards past the pole, a short and very steep path winds to the rocky beach. Enter and follow a 300-degree compass bearing to the wreck towards the middle of the opposite shore. One hundred yards offshore you should come to the wreck of the *H.M.S. Cranbrook* lying north to south.

Bottom and Depths: The wreck lies on gently sloping, muddy bottom. The bow is in 40 or 50 feet of water at the north end, the stern in 55 or 65 feet at the south end.

Hazards: The wreck itself, small boats and poor visibility. Waterskiers, in summer. Red jellyfish, in the fall. The wreck is intact — but crumbling dangerously — and should not be entered even by the most experienced wreck divers. Listen for boats and ascend with a reserve of air; if you hear a boat you can stay down until it passes. Allow time for a waterskier to pass, as well. Or use a compass and return to shore under water. Try not to stir up the silt. If you have seen any red jellyfish, you and your buddy should check one another for stinging tentacles before removing your masks and gloves.

Telephone: Belcarra Park, ½ mile farther along Bedwell Bay Road.

Facilities: None at the site. Even roadside parking is very limited. Picnic sites and pit toilets ½ mile back at Sasamat Lake.

Comments: Come and go quietly and be considerate about where you park. There is private property all around Bedwell Bay. Let's keep ourselves in good grace at this popular checkout site.

Permission required from National Harbours Board to dive at Bedwell Bay.

Looking north up Indian Arm from beach at Bedwell Bay

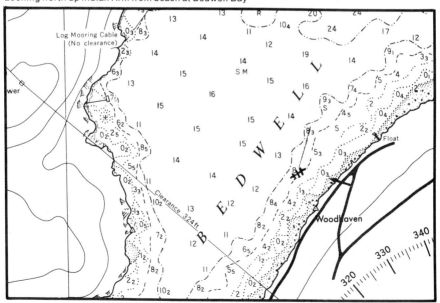

0   Scale of Feet   1000

Portion of 3484

Skill: All Divers and Snorkelers

Why go: "Crab City" is all you can call it! Red rock crabs hide amongst the rocks around the island. In fall and winter, female Dungeness crabs, bulging with bright red eggs, are eight inches apart all down the entire silty slope at Jug Island. This breeding ground for crabs is a phenomenon to see. But don't take any of them. Let them breed and continue to populate Indian Arm. There are lots of other places to catch them. Just come here for sightseeing. Anemones, lemon nudibranchs, sea stars and some rockfish hover around the rocky shores of the island. Flounders cover the sand.

Access: Jug Island is near the centre of the southern end of Indian Arm. It is like a piece broken off the peninsula which forms Bedwell Bay. Jug Island is 1⅓ miles east of Deep Cove and 3 miles northeast of Cates Park.
    From Deep Cove a water taxi can go to Jug Island in 10 minutes. Take a water taxi, a charter, rent an inflatable, or launch your own boat at Deep Cove or Cates Park. Anchor near the island or land on the small sandy beach on the mainland just south of Jug Island and snorkel 100 yards to the rocky point on the east end of the island. From here descend and swim east towards the point of mainland on your right. You'll soon be in the city of crabs.

Bottom and Depths: Rocky bottom with some lettuce kelp surrounds Jug Island and slopes gradually to silty sand. A small shallow reef, 10 or 15 feet deep, where small boats might go aground on a low tide lies between the beach and Jug Island. This is good snorkeling. From 20 or 25 feet on down, the gentle slope becomes very silty and suitable for crabs to hide.

Hazards: Boats. Waterskiers in summer. Red jellyfish, in the fall. On sunny summer weekends speedboats pulling waterskiers dash between the mainland and Jug Island. Since the site is so shallow these are real hazards. Wear extra weight. Listen for boats and ascend with a reserve of air; if you hear a boat you can stay on the bottom until it passes. Wait long enough for a water-skier to pass, too. If you have seen any red jellyfish, you and your buddy should check one another for stinging tentacles before removing your masks and gloves.

Telephone: Deep Cove, by government dock.

Facilities: None at Jug Island. At Deep Cove, a water taxi and launching ramps, one only available during the week and another useable only at high tides. At Cates Park, a launching ramp.

Comments: Lovely little sandy beach for a picnic opposite Jug Island, but often it's in the shade in winter and crowded on summer weekends. The best time for a dive and picnic at Jug Island is on a sunny fall day during the week.
    Permission required from National Harbours Board to dive at Jug Island.

Jug Island sprinkled with snow

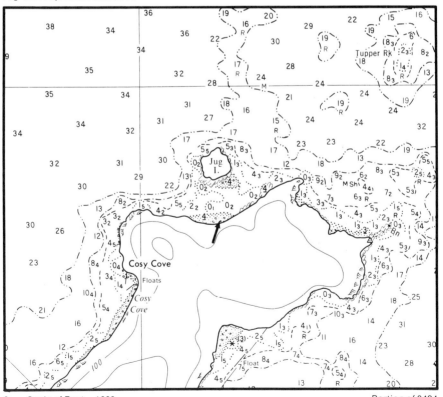

0   Scale of Feet   1000

Portion of 3484

RACOON ISLAND   **Tide Table:** Vancouver
       Boat Dive

Skill: All Divers and Snorkelers

Why go: Racoon Island is a picturesque undersea garden — ideal for checkouts and photography — and it drops off, too. A variety of both sand and rock dwellers live here.
    The first time I dived at Racoon Island we anchored over the white gravel bottom. As we jumped in a pair of harbour seals were playing, but they disappeared rapidly. We were soon into picturesque terrain with a rocky reef on either side. Gorgeous one- and two-foot tall white and orange plumose anemones cluster on top of each reef. We saw a few rockfish, one decorator crab, and a variety of other crabs. We looked over the edge of the dark drop-off and turned back towards the sand.
    Snails scurried away. Tube worms snapped in. We saw egg cases of moon snails, Oregon tritons and flounders. Millions of minute transparent fairy shrimp. Back at shore, beautiful little colourful anemones fill the tide pools.
    Racoon Island is a good experience. I'll go back anytime.

Access: Racoon Island is in the southern end of Indian Arm, 2 miles northeast of Deep Cove and 3½ miles northeast of Cates Park.
    From Deep Cove a water taxi goes to Racoon Island in 12 minutes. Take a water taxi, a charter, rent an inflatable, or launch your own boat at Deep Cove or Cates Park and go to Racoon Island. Anchor near the northwest shore, just north of the widest bulge of the island, in 30 or 40 feet of water. Or land on the island and enter from the pebble beach. Swim straight north and down to the two rocky reefs.

Bottom and Depths: Two ͏ ͏ ͏ ͏ reefs undulating from 30 to 40 feet deep parallel the northe. ͏ ͏ ͏ ͏ ore. At the eastern end of the reefs, a sheer drop-off to 275 feet. One of the darkest drop-offs I've seen. It stopped us at 80 feet. At the western end of the reefs, eelgrass and coarse white broken-shell bottom.

Hazards: Some boats. Red jellyfish, in the fall. Listen for boats and ascend with a reserve of air; if you hear a boat you can stay down until it passes. Or use a compass and ascend up the side of the island. If you have seen any red jellyfish, you and your buddy should check one another for stinging tentacles before removing your masks and gloves.

Telephone: Deep Cove, by government dock.

Facilities: None at Racoon Island. At Deep Cove, a water taxi and launching ramp, one only available during the week and another useable only at high tides. At Cates Park, a launching ramp.

Comments: The beach of this small, uninhabited island is a pleasant place for picnics.
    Permission required from National Harbours Board to dive at Racoon Island.

Looking south down Indian Arm towards Racoon Island

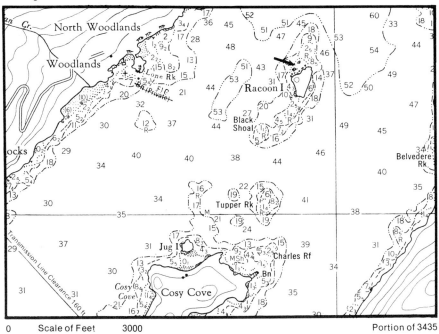

Portion of 3435

Skill: All Divers and Snorkelers

Why go: Twin Islands is particularly interesting in winter because it's a breeding ground for both crabs and lingcod. Also the place one of our local divers found a new species of chiton now named after him, *Tonicella goertsoni*. And many more beautiful animals are here. Gorgeous gardens of orange and white plumose anemones — so common in our waters but at all times beautiful — grace the southern end of Twin Islands. I gasp with delight when I see them clustered on the rocks. We saw large pink dahlia anemones, white nudibranchs with orange tips and heaps of Oregon tritons with yellowish rice-shaped eggs. Lots of shrimp and rockfish, a hairy chiton and a brown buffalo sculpin. Our dive was capped by the sight of two lingcod, one finning eggs, and by the sight of masses of crabs red and round with eggs.
A rich winter's day.

Access: Twin Islands is a quarter of the way up Indian Arm, 2½ miles northeast of Deep Cove and 4 miles northeast of Cates Park.
From Deep Cove a water taxi can go to Twin Islands in 15 minutes. Take a water taxi, a charter, rent an inflatable, or launch your own boat at Deep Cove or Cates Park. Anchor near the dock on the east side of the southern island. Enter here and dive south towards the tip of the island.

Bottom and Depths: At the dock the silty sand bottom, scattered with crabs, is 20 or 30 feet deep. Towards the southern tip the bottom is covered with loose rock, dropping gradually to 40 or 50 feet. Boulders are scattered about. At the north tip of the islands there is little marine life, but plenty of interesting rock formations.

Hazards: Red jellyfish, in the fall. If you have seen any red jelly-fish, you and your buddy should check one another for stinging tentacles before removing your masks and gloves.

Telephone: Deep Cove, by government dock.

Facilities: None at Twin Islands. At Deep Cove, a water taxi and launching ramps, one only available during the week, and another useable only at high tides. At Cates Park, a launching ramp.

Comments: A cabin on the southern island and no beach for a picnic. Twin Islands is good only for the dive.
Permission required from National Harbours Board to dive at Twin Islands.

Duane Goertson after whom *Tonicella goertsoni* was named

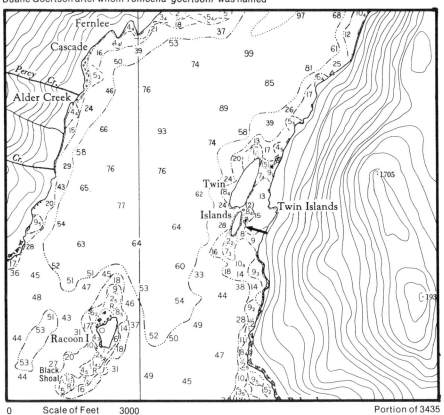

BUNTZEN POWER PLANT   **Tide Table:** Vancouver
Boat Dive

Skill: Intermediate and Advanced Divers

Why go: Beautiful rock formations plummet to 110 or 120 feet. The wall by Buntzen Power Plant is renowned as *the* drop-off of Indian Arm.
As we dived down through the shallows, schools of bright blue and yellow seaperch glinted in the sun. Millions of moon jellyfish throbbed through the water. Then there were no more. Spindly spider crabs and hairy lithode crabs — two specialties of Indian Arm — were clinging to the smooth rock wall. Little else. It felt barren. We saw a few scattered rockfish. At 80 feet, a pale white blenny. Suddenly a red jellyfish streaming ten-foot tentacles. Beautiful! And bright creeping pedal cucumbers decorating the dark wall sweeping down. . . down. . . down. . . to yelloweye rockfish deep along the wall.

Access: Buntzen Power Plant is half way up the east side of Indian Arm. It is 4 miles northeast of Deep Cove and 5½ miles northeast of Cates Park.
From Deep Cove a water taxi goes to Buntzen in 20 minutes. Take a water taxi, a charter, rent an inflatable, or launch your own boat at Deep Cove or Cates Park. Tie up by the big concrete power station, referred to by B.C. Hydro and Power Authority as Buntzen Number Two. There is another power plant slightly north, but Buntzen Number Two is the first one on your right as you go up Indian Arm. From the dock, snorkel north around the corner to the right and go down.

Bottom and Depths: Broken rock covered with lettuce kelp gives way immediately to sheer rock wall with loose gravel spilling over it. Beautiful rock formations drop to 110 or 120 feet. Slightly farther out it drops 300, then over 600 feet.

Hazards: Extreme depth and tail-race from the dam. Red jellyfish, in the fall. At any time, day or night, the power plant gates may be opened without warning to discharge a huge volume of water between the dock and dive site. The discharge is above the surface and is extremely turbulent. Because the gates are remotely controlled, divers will not be warned even when flying their diver's flag. Do not swim under water past the gates. Snorkel past. If you have seen any red jellyfish, you and your buddy should check one another for stinging tentacles before removing your masks and gloves.

Telephone: Deep Cove, by government dock.

Facilities: The dock and the land by the powerhouse are owned by B.C. Hydro and Power Authority. As long as we leave the property as we find it and use it at our own risk, B.C. Hydro and Power Authority will continue to allow divers to use the area.

Comments: On a sunny day the dock is a pleasant place for a picnic after your dive. Buntzen is brightest in the afternoon.
Permission required from National Harbours Board to dive at Buntzen Power Plant.

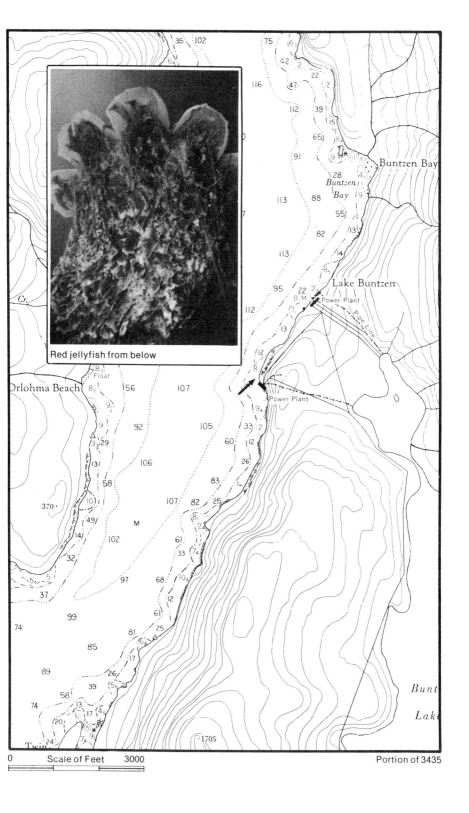

Red jellyfish from below

Cr.

75

63

42 2

22

47 2

2

116

112 39 1

15

65) 8₄

91 9 9

Buntzen Bay

4

28

Buntzen

Bay 19

113 88

55) 1

82 13₁

113 14

8₅

95 22 ₃ Lake Buntzen

B.M. Power Plant

112 2 Pipe Line

13

12

8

Orlohma Beach 8₅ Float

8₂ 156 107 9₄

9 33 2

92 105 60 12

106 26

58 83

370 · 107 82 25

10₁ 8₁

49 2

14 61 7₄

102 33 4

32

97 68 10₄

5₄ 5 12

37

74 99 61

85 81 25

6₁

17

89 26

39 5₅

58

74 13 17 4₅

20

5 *

Twin 24 7₄ 1705

Power Plant

Bunt

Lake

0   Scale of Feet   3000   Portion of 3435

Skill: All Divers

Why go: If, some morning, you want to dive over a drop-off go up Indian Arm to Silver Falls.

Silver Falls is on the west side of Indian Arm and morning sun shines through the water. As you descend through the shallows you'll see lots and lots of tube worms. Schools of seaperch range through the lettuce-kelp covered area to 20 or 30 feet. From there the bottom rolls down almost immediately into dark depths. An occasional boulder sits on the side of the steep slope. Crimson creeping pedal cucumbers stick to the rocks. Quillback rockfish and pale gobies hide in the crevices. Look for the weird hairy lithode crabs often seen in Indian Arm.

When diving at Silver Falls I saw my first ctenophores, or sea gooseberries. They look like free-floating walnuts with tails. A "first sighting" always marks a place, and makes it special for me.

Access: Silver Falls is three quarters of the way up the west shore of Indian Arm, 6 miles northeast of Deep Cove and 7½ miles northeast of Cates Park.

From Deep Cove a water taxi goes to Silver Falls in 20 minutes. Take a water taxi, a charter, rent an inflatable, or launch your own boat at Deep Cove or Cates Park. A small rocky beach where there used to be a loading conveyor, 200 yards north of Silver Falls, is a good place to land your boat. Descend and dive south towards Silver Falls.

Bottom and Depths: Small broken rocks covered with bottom kelp down to 20 or 30 feet. Then smooth silt-covered rock, a steep roll downward. An occasional big boulder perched on the edge of the drop-off.

Hazards: Depth. Red jellyfish, in the fall. If you have seen any red jellyfish, you and your buddy should check one another for stinging tentacles before removing your masks and gloves.

Telephone: Deep Cove, at government dock.

Facilities: None at Silver Falls. Small rocky beach. Land your boat and picnic after your dive at the old loading conveyor 200 yards north of Silver Falls. At Deep Cove, a water taxi and launching ramps, one only available during the week and another useable only at high tides. At Cates Park, a launching ramp.

Comments: From Silver Falls look across at a groove down the mountain from Buntzen Lake to the Buntzen Power Plant. That groove was made when the Buntzen Beasty — our own Ogopogo — slid into Indian Arm.

Permission required from National Harbours Board to dive at Silver Falls.

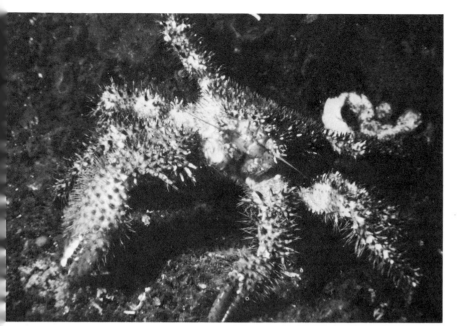

Lithode crab reaching its hairy claws

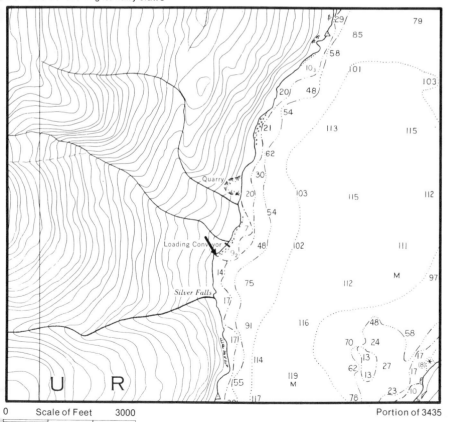

CROKER ISLAND
Boat Dive

Skill: All Divers and Snorkelers

Why go: "Paradise" one experienced diver calls this area, and maybe because you can find almost anything you can name somewhere around Croker Island. Clumps of anemones and sea stars overflow the south point. We saw small dahlia anemones, chitons, small green urchins, convict fish or painted greenlings, and burrowing cucumbers. Lingcod and rockfish haunt the ledges and the overhangs shelving down the western side under the bay. As you move around the tip to the eastern side below the light the water is thick with small shrimp. Tarantula-like crabs hang by a leg from the sheer smooth cliff that plunges 100 feet. On the northern end you'll see beautiful variety! Masses of cucumbers, stars, small barnacles, tube worms, seaperch, kelp greenlings and an occasional octopus and grunt sculpin. Spider crabs and bizarre-looking lithode crabs. A forest of sea whips. Huge schools of herring and salmon grilse sometimes, too.
There's no way that one tank is enough!

Access: Croker Island is at the northern tip of Indian Arm. It is 7½ miles northeast of Deep Cove and 9 miles north of Cates Park.
From Deep Cove a water taxi goes to Croker Island in 25 minutes. Take a water taxi, a charter, rent an inflatable, or launch your own boat at Deep Cove or Cates Park. A good place to start your dive is at the south tip of the island. Anchor west of the light in the bay on the southwest side of Croker Island.

Bottom and Depths: At the southwestern tip beautiful rock formations, large overhangs, caves and ledges drop to whatever level you choose, 100 feet and more. On the southeastern side, a sheer cliff plunges 100 feet. On the northern tip rocky bottom undulates to 60 or 70 feet. That is the best area for snorkeling. On the northeastern side, a 120-foot drop-off. Because little current stirs up the silt, visibility ranges up to 100 feet in winter all around Croker Island.

Hazards: Boats in summer. Red jellyfish, in the fall. Listen for boats and keep close to the bottom all the way to shore. If you have seen any red jellyfish, you and your buddy should check one another for stinging tentacles before removing your masks and gloves.

Telephone: Deep Cove, by government dock.

Facilities: None at uninhabited Croker Island. If the tide is out, maybe room for a picnic on the rocks by the light. At Deep Cove, a water taxi and launching ramps, one only available during the week and another useable only at high tides. At Cates Park, a launching ramp.

Comments: Excellent for photography in winter when visibility is best.

From Croker Island Light, looking south down Indian Arm

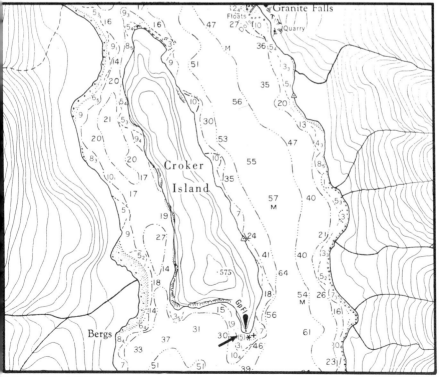

Skill: All Divers

Why go: Caulfeild Cove attracts divers because it's a good source of bottles — new and old.
First settled as a large private estate in 1899, there were no roads from West Vancouver to Caulfeild until Marine Drive was built in 1915. Ships called in frequently. Bottles and other things have been falling overboard for almost a century. Today there is still a dock at Caulfeild Cove, in the same spot as the original one. Old-time residents reminiscing about beach parties at Caulfeild recall valuable losses like diamond rings. The bottom is muddy and hides things well. You can always hope you will turn up something that's been buried for years.
   While diving here we saw flounders and Dungeness crabs disappearing in a cloud of "dust". Hermit crabs, blood stars and an occasional delicate nudibranch.
   But the site is best for bottles.

Access: From Park Royal in West Vancouver go 6½ miles to Caulfeild Cove. Heading west on Marine Drive go 6 miles until you see Tiddlycove Garage on your right. Turn left down The Dale and go 2/10 of a mile to the head of Caulfeild Cove. Walk down a short path to the water. Snorkel to the dock and go down.

Bottom and Depths: Near the dock the bottom is muddy and 15 to 25 feet deep, sloping to 35 or 45 feet at the mouth of the cove. Eelgrass, near shore.

Hazards: Poor visibility, shallow depths and boats, especially on summer weekends. Keep just off the bottom so that you do not stir up silt unnecessarily. Wear extra weight. Listen for boats and ascend with a reserve of air; if you hear a boat you can stay down until it passes.

Telephone: Cypress Park Shopping Centre, 1 mile east on Marine Drive.

Facilities: Government dock. Roadside parking is very limited; room for one or two cars. Nice beach for a picnic.

Comments: Easy access and entry make this a good dive for beginners, especially in winter when fewer boats are on the water.
   Permission required from National Harbours Board to dive at Caulfeild Cove.

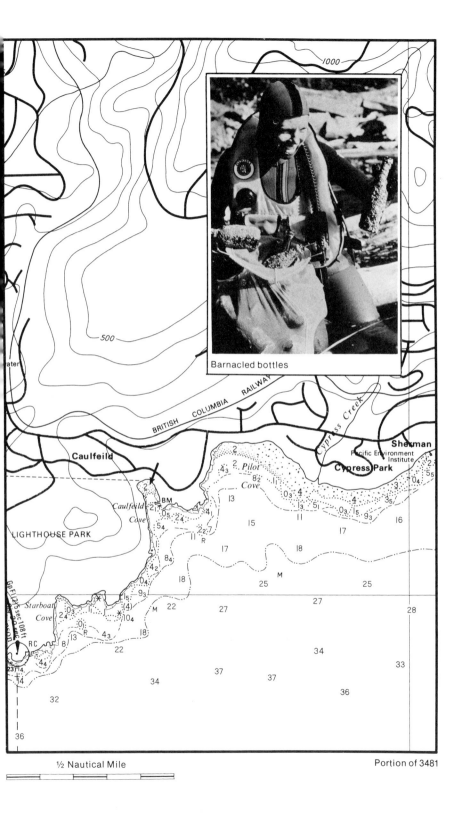

Barnacled bottles

½ Nautical Mile

Portion of 3481

Skill: Intermediate and Advanced Divers

Why go: Lighthouse Park has the wildest underwater seascape and the most fantastic variety of marine life in the Vancouver area. One dive at Lighthouse Park reveals an incredible amount of life. Large, grey warty cabezons and delicate shimmering kelp greenlings live side-by-side. Beautiful sea pens burrow in pools of sand between ledges covered with purple and pink sea stars. Schools of black rockfish swim past. Copper rockfish and lingcod live along the wall. We saw a huge octopus hiding under a ledge, little hairy lithode crabs, and small bryozoans that look like pale pink Christmas trees. Boulders smothered with small orange anemones so thick that you can't see the rock. One-inch creeping pedal cucumbers flame from the wall next to five-inch orange trumpet sponges and giant barnacles. Crevices overflowing with large white plumose anemones slice the dark slope. Cloud sponges start at 65 feet. There are green and red urchins, dahlia anemones and red Irish lords at Lighthouse Park. It's the richest dive in Vancouver.

Access: From Park Royal in West Vancouver go 7 miles to Lighthouse Park. Heading west on Marine Drive go 6½ miles to a sign pointing down Beacon Lane to Lighthouse Park. Drive to the parking area. Do not suit up yet, or you will be too warm before getting wet. Pack your gear for a hard hike, walk ½ mile down well-graded road to some park buildings and climb down one of the steep, treacherous rocky paths to a small bay just east of the lighthouse.
    Difficult access makes this dive feasible only for those who are really keen and physically fit. Allow at least an hour to walk from the parking lot to the water, and to suit up ready to dive.

Bottom and Depths: Flat sand scattered with rocks and brown bottom kelp gently tiers off, then drops in dramatic ledges with huge boulders poised at the edge. Light silt over all.

Hazards: Current, wind and broken fishing line. Small boats and poor visibility, in summer, because of Fraser River runoff. Plus the dangers of overheating and exhaustion if you do not allow plenty of time to hike to the site. Dive on the slack using current tables for First Narrows. Even though not seeming logical, it works. Enter 15 or 20 minutes before the turn of the tide. Do not dive at Lighthouse Park if a strong west wind blows up surf. Carry a knife. Listen for boats and ascend close to the bottom all the way to shore.

Telephone: Cypress Park Shopping Centre, 1½ miles east on Marine Drive.

Facilities: Lighthouse Park is large and forested with 9 miles of trails, a sign-posted circular nature walk, and wild, rocky beaches for picnics. In summer, conducted nature walks, films in the outdoor theatre and displays at Nature House. Restrooms and large parking area. For information, telephone Lighthouse Park at 922-5408 or West Vancouver Recreation Centre at 926-3266. For lighthouse tours, telephone 922-5702.

Comments: Lighthouse Park is great for a family outing — and a great dive! Permission required from National Harbours Board to dive at Lighthouse Park.

Copper rockfish bulging with eggs

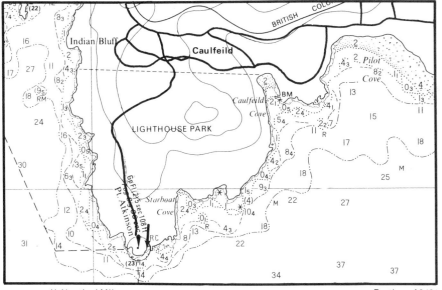

½ Nautical Mile   Portion of 3481

PASSAGE ISLAND REEF   **Tide Table:** Point Atkinson
Boat Dive

Skill: Advanced Divers

Why go: Passage Island Reef provides the best hunting in the Vancouver area and a magnificent underwater mountain for sightseeing.
Rising to within 20 or 30 feet of the surface this large mound covered with boulders lies in current-swept Queen Charlotte Channel. All of the water flowing between Bowen Island and West Vancouver pours over this large reef which snags nutriments to feed the fish.
Diving here you drop onto piles of white plumose anemones tumbling one over the other like a gigantic feather bed. I was tempted to lie in it and luxuriate in the fluffy white fronds. Moving down the side of the huge mound we saw lingcod lying on their chins looking out of dark seams in the rock. Each nook and cranny conceals another large fish or octopus. Transparent sea squirts hang from boulders like clusters of plastic grapes. Sea cucumbers, calcareous tube worms, burrowing cucumbers, sunflower stars and urchins are on the reef.
Skirting the southern end of the reef, we swam through a field of sea pens into a ghostly garden of long, slim white sea whips.

Access: Passage Island Reef is in Queen Charlotte Channel between Point Atkinson and Point Cowan on Bowen Island, less that ⅓ mile west of the southern tip of Passage Island. To find Passage Island Reef, line up the northern tip of Passage Island with a house (currently painted green) on the West Vancouver hillside, and another line sighting between the rocks at the southern end of Passage Island to Point Atkinson. Then plumb with a lead line until you find the reef.
Charter out of Vancouver or Whytecliff Park and go 2 miles south to Passage Island Reef, or rent or launch at Horseshoe Bay and go 4 miles around to Passage Island Reef.

Bottom and Depths: The reef rises like a huge mound scattered with boulders. Sloping muddy bottom surrounds the base of the reef at 50 or 60 feet. The top of the reef is always 20 or 30 feet below the surface.

Hazards: Current, small boats and wind. Poor visibility, in summer, because of Fraser River runoff. Dive on the slack, especially on large tidal exchanges. Ascend on your anchor line well out of the way of small boats, or listen for boats and ascend with a reserve of air; if you hear a boat you can stay down until it passes. Wind from almost any direction can make anchoring impossible at this very exposed site. Visibility best in fall and winter, and on an ebbing tide.

Telephone: Fisherman's Cove Marine Esso, parking lot.

Facilities: None.

Comments: If you can find it, Passage Island Reef is intriguing.

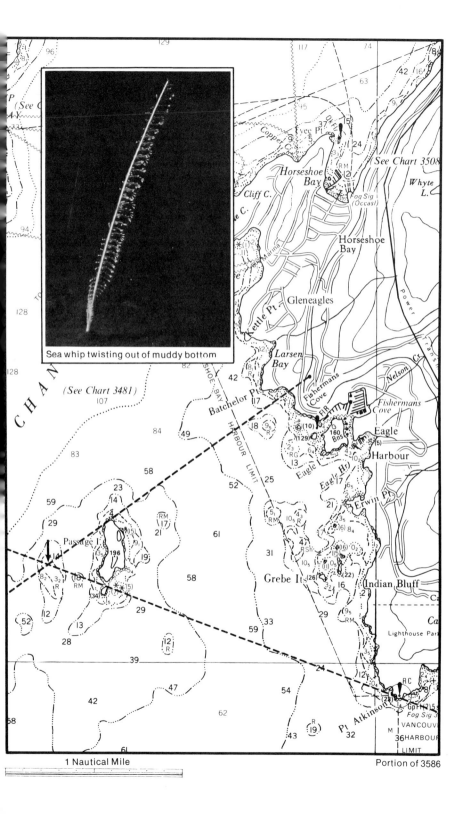

Sea whip twisting out of muddy bottom

1 Nautical Mile

Portion of 3586

Skill: All Divers and Snorkelers

Why go: Larsen Bay — often called Blink Bonnie — is as nice as its nickname. An ideal place for a pleasant shallow dive and family picnic. Rock walls rim the bay which bottoms out to flat sand at 20 or 30 feet. Small broken rock heaped at the bottom of the wall is covered with beautiful patches of purple-satiny kelp and scraps of emerald-green kelp. I've come nose-to-nose with a number of small lingcod, lots of rockfish, kelp greenlings and hundreds of spooky little blackeye gobies hanging in niches in the wall. And nearly trampled uncountable numbers of flounders beneath my fins. Look for sea peaches, urchins, decorator crabs, lemon nudibranchs, clouds of silver herring in summer, occasional plumose anemones and masses of purple stars. There's a shy octopus in residence, too, in a deep crack beneath the small private jetty on your right. Look for him, but leave him for others to enjoy at this popular checkout site. Look for Dungeness crabs in the eelgrass in the bay. Hermit crabs on the silty sand.
Basically this dive is a good shallow one, but you can go deep and into sponges if you swim far out over the sand. Prawns come up onto the sand at night. And I saw a snake prickleback for the first time while night diving at Larsen Bay Park.

Access: From Park Royal in West Vancouver go 10 miles to Larsen Bay. Heading west on Marine Drive go just over 9 miles to Gleneagles Drive where you will see a bus shelter. Turn left and wind down Gleneagles Drive for 2/10 mile. Then turn left into Blink Bonnie Road and go ½ mile to the end of the road where you will see Gleneagles Golf Course on your right and a tennis court on your left. Park, suit up and follow the wooded path to the left of the tennis court 200 yards to the beach. Snorkel to the point on your right and go down.

Bottom and Depths: Rock walls rim the bay bottoming out to silty sand at 20 or 30 feet. Bottom kelp covers small broken rock at the base of the wall. Deeper it is very silty. Eelgrass grows from the sand in the small bay.

Hazards: Boats and poor visibility in summer. Listen for boats and ascend with a reserve of air; if you hear a boat you can stay down until it passes. Because of silt, visibility is seldom good at Larsen Bay and in spring and early summer the water can become particularly murky with Fraser River runoff. However, the water may be turbid one day and clear the next, so that it is always worth checking to see if visibility is good.

Telephone: Fisherman's Bay Marina parking lot, south on Marine Drive.

Facilities: Small pocket park, crescent of beach, parking for ten cars and pit toilets. Swimming float, in summer. One public tennis court and Gleneagles Public Golf Course nearby.

Comments: Come and go quietly so that local residents will continue to welcome divers at Larsen Bay.

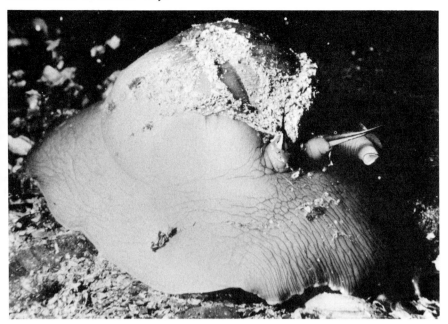

Moon snail creeping towards eelgrass

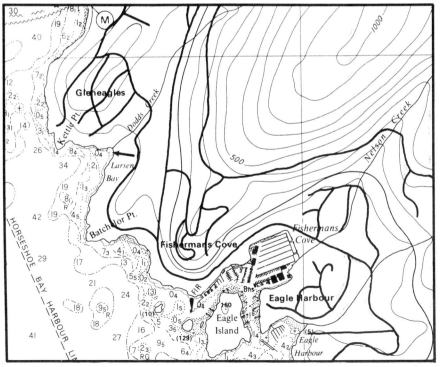

½ Nautical Mile

Portion of 3481

WHYTECLIFF PARK   **Tide Table:** Point Atkinson
WHYTE ISLET
Shore Dive

Skill: All Divers and Snorkelers — WINTER ONLY

Why go: Whyte Islet and the immediately adjacent marina area are popular checkout sites within Whytecliff Park Underwater Reserve where you can easily skin dive to see flounders and crabs, or enjoy a shallow dive.
Whyte Islet's smooth rock walls give homes to a variety of animals. You'll see lots of little things: calcareous tube worms attached to shallow rocks, lemon nudibranchs, leather stars and purple sea stars. Sea cucumbers all over the bottom. You may see an octopus. A couple of lingcod are usually cruising around the islet. You're sure to see orange plumose anemones tilting their ruffled fronds to the current. And I've even seen a feather star at Whyte Islet. If you see one, gently pluck it from the wall and watch it swim.
Whyte Islet offers a lot of interesting marine life coupled with very easy access. Is it any wonder many divers return here again and again?

Access: From Park Royal in West Vancouver go 13 miles to Whytecliff Park. From Park Royal head north on Taylor Way to Upper Levels Highway 1. Go west 10 miles to Horseshoe Bay. Then follow signs along the winding road to Whytecliff Park. Drive all around the park to the large parking lot near the refreshment stand. Walk down an easily inclined tarmac path to the water.

Bottom and Depths: Eelgrass and sand in 10 or 20 feet of water on your right near the marina and wharf. A rock groin, which dries on most low tides, leads out to Whyte Islet. Beside the islet a smooth rock wall drops to sand at 10 or 20 feet, sloping gradually to 50 or 60 feet at the tip of Whyte Islet.

Hazards: Small boats and poor visibility, in summer. Some current. Because of so much boat traffic this entire area is closed to diving all summer. *No diving permitted* between the marina and Whyte Islet from April 1st through September 30th. At other times wear extra weight, listen for boats and ascend with a reserve of air; if you hear a boat you can stay down until it passes. Current can be quite strong around the tip of Whyte Islet. If you feel current, stay under water and pull yourself along on the rocks.

Telephones: 1. Whytecliff Park, by refreshment stand in summer only.
2. Horseshoe Bay centre, by Troll's Restaurant.

Facilities: Whytecliff Park has a large grassy area, picnic tables, children's playground and restrooms. In summer, a refreshment stand, change rooms and boat rentals.

Comments: Spearfishing and removal of underwater specimens are forbidden in Whytecliff Park Underwater Reserve.

Feather star resting

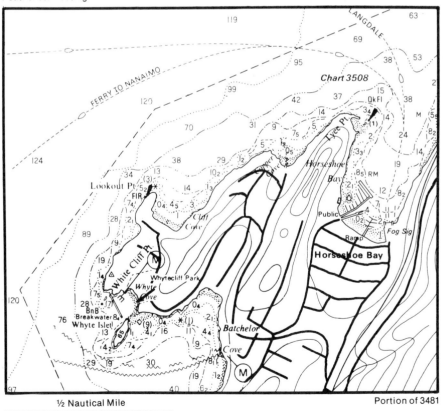

½ Nautical Mile

Portion of 3481

WHYTECLIFF PARK
THE CUT
Shore Dive

Skill: Intermediate and Advanced Divers

Why go: Amazing to have this fabulous underwater world always waiting in its wildness.
Incredible to think of all this wild and wonderful seascape being right in the city. Even more unbelievable to think that it will continue to be with us — forever we hope — because spearfishing and removal of marine life are forbidden at Whytecliff Park Underwater Reserve.
The reef by the day marker is home for several animals that are so familiar to divers they're like old friends. Two octopuses are well known. Almost every time I dive at The Cut I meet one old grandfather lingcod. You'll see rockfish, red Irish lords, seaperch, sea pens, urchins, grunt sculpins and sea stars. Sailfin sculpins, at night. Also on a night dive we saw a small stubby squid shimmer from blue to green to white like an opalescent teardrop pendant.
Masses of white plumose anemones cascade down the sheer rock wall. At 80 feet fluffy white cloud sponges lure you further, lighting up the dark cliff below. And as you drop into the depths lit with these puffs of white you think that Whytecliff Park must have been named by divers.
The most seasoned diver will enjoy the rocky reef and fantastic drop-off at The Cut at Whytecliff Park.

Access: From Park Royal in West Vancouver go 13 miles to Whytecliff Park. From Park Royal head north on Taylor Way to Upper Levels Highway 1. Go west 10 miles to Horseshoe Bay. Follow signs along the winding road to Whytecliff Park. Park near the pavilion and restrooms at the west end of the park. Then follow the steep steps and path south of the pavilion down the narrow ravine, or cut, to the sea.

Bottom and Depths: Rocky reef 20 or 30 feet deep, between the log-strewn beach and day marker, dropping off beyond the day marker. The wall on your right drops off to 700 feet.

Hazards: Depth, current and broken fishing line. Small boats and poor visibility, in summer, because of Fraser River runoff. However, the water may be turbid one day and clear the next; therefore, it is always worth checking to see if visibility is good. There can be considerable surface current past the day marker and along the wall. On large tidal exchanges, dive near the slack. Carry a knife and ascend with a reserve of air, so that if caught in transparent fishing line you will have time to cut your way free. Listen for boats and ascend along the wall all the way to the surface, well out of the way of those boats.

Telephones: 1. Whytecliff Park, by refreshment stand in summer only.
2. Horseshoe Bay, by Troll's Restaurant.

Facilities: Large grassy area, picnic tables, playground for children and restrooms. In summer, a refreshment stand, change rooms and boat rentals.

Comments: Spearfishing and removal of underwater specimens are forbidden in Whytecliff Park Underwater Reserve.

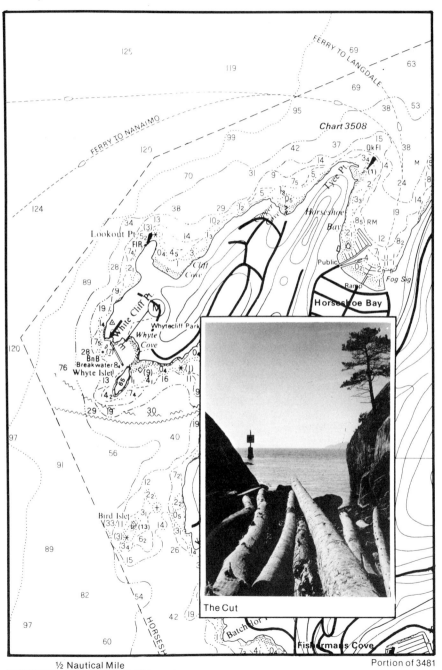

The Cut

½ Nautical Mile

Portion of 3481

Skill: All Divers

Why go: Lookout Point, the western extreme of Cliff Cove, commonly called Telegraph Cove, is ideal for checkouts, for photography, for night dives. Almost anything you can think of except spearfishing. It is part of Whytecliff Park Underwater Reserve.

So much life around Lookout Point that local divers keep coming back again and again. It's easy to choose your level and dive shallow or deep. When diving here I like to move down quickly to the second ledge at 50 or 60 feet where lovely clusters of white anemones are piled like mushroom caps on top of the rocks, spilling over into the valleys below. Walls are covered with small, anemone-like zoanthids. Octopuses live in the area. Lingcod, red Irish lords, urchins, rockfish, grunt sculpins, sea pens, ratfish, shrimp, sea peaches, hermit crabs and giant barnacles.

Once on a night dive at Lookout Point I even saw a vermilion rockfish, a fish more commonly seen on the west coast of Vancouver Island. Deeper, you will see cloud sponges and small solitary cup corals.

Access: From Park Royal in West Vancouver go 12 miles to Lookout Point. From Park Royal head north on Taylor Way to Upper Levels Highway 1. Go west 10 miles to Horseshoe Bay. Then follow signs along the winding road to Whytecliff Park. At Whytecliff Park take the road on your right. It is signposted to "Overload Parking". This becomes Cliff Road. Continue on Cliff Road as it bends around to the left. At the confluence of Cliff Road, Arbutus Road and Arbutus Place a narrow trail follows the telegraph line on your right down to Cliff Cove, 100 yards to the beach. Steep wooden steps make access easy. At the beach you may have to climb over logs to reach the water. Snorkel to the point on your left and descend.

Bottom and Depths: The point drops in rocky tiers. First a ledge at 30 or 40 feet, another at 50 or 60 and then at 110 or 120 feet. Bottom kelp covers broken rocks down to 30 or 40 feet. Pockets of sand in the ledges.

Hazards: Current, broken fishing line and small boats. Poor visibility in summer, because of Fraser River runoff. However, because the water may be turbid one day and clear the next, it is always worth checking to see if visibility is good. Visibility is best on a rising tide at Lookout Point. The ebbing tide can be overpowering; therefore dive near the slack, especially on large tidal exchanges. Carry a knife. Listen for boats and ascend along the bottom all the way to shore.

Telephones: 1. Whytecliff Park, by refreshment stand in summer only.
2. Horseshoe Bay centre, by Troll's Restaurant.

Facilities: None. Roadside parking very limited. Be considerate of local residents. If parking is full, unload your gear beside the path to Cliff Cove, park at Whytecliff Park and walk the short way back to Cliff Cove.

Comments: Beautiful beach and beautiful dive.

Grunt sculpin

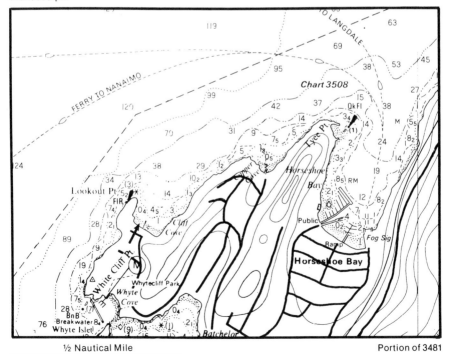

½ Nautical Mile

Portion of 3481

COPPER COVE
Shore Dive

Skill: All Divers and Snorkelers

Why go: Because of the easy entry, Copper Cove is especially good for night diving enthusiasts.

If you're in the mood for a relaxed dive you'll enjoy the shallow rocky shores rimming the cove where you can see a variety of life. Bright orange dead man's finger sponges poke from the bottom kelp. Huge sunflower stars and masses of smaller ones cling to the rocks. Pale orange sea peaches and small brown and beige anemones cluster under the overhangs. Sea cucumbers, rockfish, barnacles, burrowing cucumbers and lingcod live along the rock-rimmed cove.

Night diving over the sand yields a whole new experience. We saw a variety of flatfish: a mottled sanddab, lemon sole and C-O sole. Interesting small fish: a whiting, a small white curled up eelpout and a midshipman with golden eyes. And sculpins: a grunt sculpin, sailfin sculpins and a roughback sculpin, a small fish with an intricate dorsal fin that reminded me of a miniature lionfish. Spider crabs, prawns, hermit crabs, shrimp and lots of small ratfish come out on the sand at night.

And I love snorkeling back through the fabulous phosphorescent night sea.

Access: From Park Royal in West Vancouver go 10½ miles to Copper Cove. From Park Royal head north on Taylor Way to Upper Levels Highway 1. Go west 10 miles to Horseshoe Bay. Then follow signs towards Whytecliff Park. About ½ mile along the road to Whytecliff, shortly after a stop sign, you come to Copper Cove Road. Turn right and drive to the turnabout at the end of the road to unload your gear. Park back up the road a short way, walk down the steps to the beach and dive towards the point on your left.

Bottom and Depths: Rocks covered with bottom kelp rim Copper Cove bottoming out to smooth white sand at 20 or 30 feet. The sand slopes gradually to whatever depth you might want to go. There are three deep rocky reefs just left of centre of the cove, the first at 70 or 80 feet. To find the reefs go to the point on your left and follow the bottom down to the right.

Hazards: Wind. Poor visibility, in summer, because of Fraser/Squamish runoff. The water, however, may be turbid one day and clear the next; it is always worth checking to see if visibility is good. A Squamish wind from the north sometimes blows up surf, and makes entry and exit difficult. At Copper Cove divers often enter the water at mid-tides by jumping off the wharf without considering how they will climb out later. Before entering, be sure the tide will not go out leaving logs bobbing in the shallows which will make getting out impossible. Or you may have to wait for the tide to fall farther and the logs to drop so that you can walk over them.

Telephone: Horseshoe Bay centre, by Troll's Restaurant.

Facilities: Roadside parking very limited. Room for one or two cars.

Comments: The wharf is private and should not be used by divers.

Sunday afternoon at Copper Cove

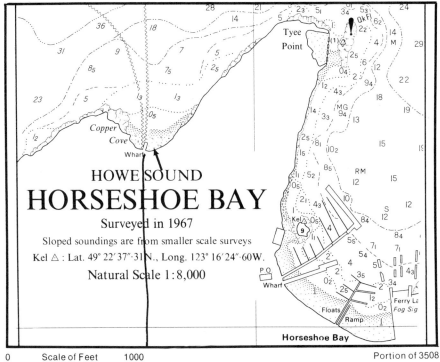

Tyee Point

Copper Cove

Wharf

HOWE SOUND

HORSESHOE BAY

Surveyed in 1967

Sloped soundings are from smaller scale surveys

Kel △ : Lat. 49° 22′ 37″·31 N., Long. 123° 16′ 24″·60W.

Natural Scale 1 : 8,000

P.O.

Wharf

Floats

Ramp

Ferry La

Fog Sig

Horseshoe Bay

0   Scale of Feet   1000

Portion of 3508

PORTEAU BEACH
Shore Dive

Skill: All Divers

Why go: Porteau Beach is easily accessible and is a super-safe shallow checkout site.
Sightseeing only is the order of the day at Porteau Beach. Not because it's a reserve, but because all rockfish, lingcod, shellfish and crabs in this area are contaminated with mercury and are considered to be unsafe for eating. In a way it's heartbreaking because Dungeness crabs scurry all around the pilings and it's hard to pass them.
But if you look around there are other things to see and do. Go 100 yards offshore and look for octopuses, seaperch, lingcod and hermit crabs. I'll never forget diving at Porteau Beach when for the first time I stroked a small red Irish lord. I couldn't believe it when this little fish stopped and wriggled appreciatively under my touch, just like a cat.
You never know what will make a dive — but I've found that every dive leaves me with something special to remember.

Access: From Park Royal in West Vancouver go 25 miles to Porteau Beach. From Park Royal head north on Taylor Way to Upper Levels Highway 1. Go west 10 miles to Horseshoe Bay. Then drive north towards Squamish on Highway 99 for 15 miles. When you see an arched sign over a road on your left saying "Porteau Camp", slow down. Less than 1 mile farther down the hill on Highway 99 you will see a small parking area on your left with room for several cars. Park here, gear up, walk a few feet to the beach and dive around and beyond the pilings.

Bottom and Depths: Sand scattered with small rocks slopes gradually out to old pilings in 20 or 30 feet of water.

Hazards: Sometimes poor visibility in summer because of Squamish River runoff. However, because the water may be turbid one day and clear the next, it is always worth checking to see if visibility is good.

Telephones: 1. Britannia, 4 miles north.
2. Lions Bay Store, 8 miles south.

Facilities: None.

Comments: Porteau Beach is so popular that you're certain to meet other divers around weekend bonfires on the beach.
From April 15th through October 15th telephone Squamish Forest Ranger, 898-3628, and ask if beach bonfire permit required.

Hermit crab reaching out its enlarged right claw

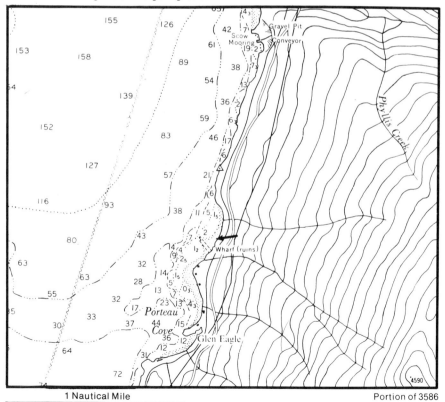

1 Nautical Mile

Portion of 3586

PORTEAU ¼-MILE   **Tide Table:** Point Atkinson
Shore Dive

Skill: Advanced Divers

Why go: Porteau ¼-Mile is a popular deep dive site. A crowd always collects here on Sunday. In addition to the usual sea life — anemones, octopuses, rockfish, shrimp, occasional lingcod and sponges — we saw five-foot sea whips at 80 or 90 feet. And something really unique at Porteau — a couple of railway cars that flew off the tracks and conveniently landed in 120 or 130 feet of water about 100 yards north of a very good entry point.

Because winter visibility is often excellent at Porteau — sometimes up to 100 feet — it's a popular place for photography.

But leave the fish and any crabs you find alone. All rockfish, lingcod, shellfish and crabs in this area are contaminated with mercury and are considered unsafe for eating.

Access: From Park Royal in West Vancouver go 25 miles to Porteau ¼-Mile. From Park Royal head north on Taylor Way to Upper Levels Highway 1. Go west 10 miles to Horseshoe Bay. Then drive 15 miles north towards Squamish on Highway 99. When you see an arched sign over a road on your left saying "Porteau Camp", slow down. Less than 1 mile farther down the hill on Highway 99 you will see a large parking area on your right with room for a lot of cars. Slightly farther, room for two cars to park on the left side of the road closer to the site. Park here or back at the large parking area. Gear up, cross the road and walk north along the railway tracks for about 100 yards, to a few trees and shrubs growing between the road and the tracks. Then follow a steep trail down to a big flat rock which is an easy entry point. To find the railway cars, snorkel 100 yards north from your entry point until you reach a tree which leans out over the water. Descend directly under this tree. In 120 or 130 feet of water you should find them.

Bottom and Depths: Smooth rocks drop off quickly to a rather featureless sand bottom at 100 feet. The sand continues dropping steeply. Very deep here. You could keep going and never hit bottom.

Hazards: Watch for trains — the track is still in use. The fairly difficult walk from the large parking area to the site can be tiring and dangerous before a deep dive. Sometimes poor visibility, in summer, because of Squamish River runoff. However, the water may be turbid one day and clear the next; it is always worth a check to see if visibility is good.

Telephones: 1. Britannia, 4 miles north.
              2. Lions Bay Store, 8 miles south.

Facilities: None.

Comments: Porteau ¼-Mile is a popular deep dive site for advanced classes, crystal clear winter waters are good for photography, and it's a great beach for bonfires. Always lots of divers at Porteau ¼-Mile.

From April 15th through October 15th telephone Squamish Forest Ranger, 898-3628, and ask if beach bonfire permit required.

Following tracks to site

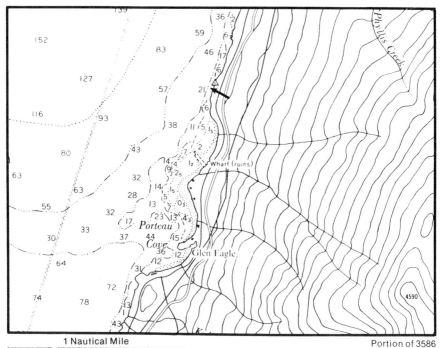

1 Nautical Mile

Portion of 3586

PORTEAU ½-MILE   **Tide Table:** Point Atkinson
Shore Dive

Skill: All Divers

Why go: Porteau ½-Mile is my favourite Porteau dive — despite all the silt and the hard climb down. Something about it feels wild and good — almost like a moonscape. Dungeness crabs everywhere stir up huge clouds of "dust". We saw a couple of large orange sunflower stars, lots of bright orange and white plumose anemones, and an abundance of white and orange dahlia anemones. Why all these animals don't smother in silt, I can't imagine. But they don't. Large boulders harbour life. We almost stumbled over a 1½-foot lingcod. Then saw a funny little decorator crab in the niche of a rock. He had decorated himself into the seascape and was almost impossible to see. Pale white, almost transparent, gobies are everywhere. They seem to have become the white of the whitish bottom silt. Starting back, we saw a foot-long kelp greenling dash off. Rockfish hide in nooks and crannies of the rocks. Attractive scenes in every direction.

Access: From Park Royal in West Vancouver go 26 miles to Porteau ½-Mile. From Park Royal head north on Taylor Way to Upper Levels Highway 1. Go west 10 miles to Horseshoe Bay. Then drive north towards Squamish on Highway 99 for 15 miles. When you see an arched sign over a road on your left saying "Porteau Camp", slow down. Two miles farther along Highway 99 is a small lay-by on the seaside of the road with room for six to eight cars to park. If you go as far as Britannia you'll have gone too far. From the lay-by, walk 100 yards down a fairly steep trail through the trees to the railway tracks. Cross the tracks, head south about 15 feet to another trail on your right down over the final rocks to the water. Climb across the rocks slightly to your left, enter and dive south.

Bottom and Depths: From the rocky shore, you can drop fairly quickly into 30 or 40 feet of water. Boulders are scattered along the sloping sand. Everything is covered with a very thick layer of silt.

Hazards: Watch for trains — the track is currently in use. The climb down the rocks can be tiring. Poor visibility, in summer, because of Squamish River runoff. However, the water may be turbid one day and clear the next; check to see if visibility is good.

Telephones: 1. Britannia, 3 miles north.
　　　　　　　2. Lions Bay Store, 9 miles south.

Facilities: None.

Comments: All rockfish, lingcod, shellfish and crabs in this area are contaminated with mercury and are unsafe for eating. Sightseeing only at Porteau ½-Mile.

Blackeye goby shyly peeping at divers

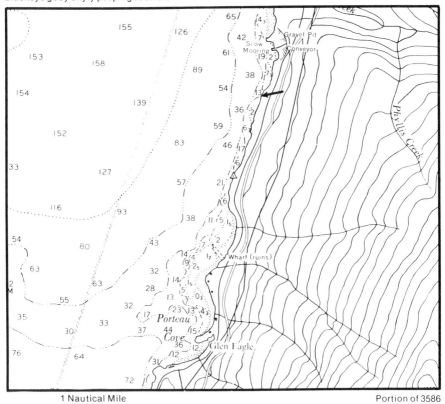

1 Nautical Mile

Portion of 3586

Skill: All Divers

Why go: Christie Islet, an ideal island to circle on one tank of air, provides some of the prettiest sightseeing in Howe Sound. On one dive here we saw everything from a small swimming scallop to hermit crabs, spider crabs and dogfish. Sprays of pink-and-white striped dahlia anemones bloom along the wall. Huge white and purple burrowing anemone tentacles pop out of the sand. Large orange and white plumose anemones are in profusion on the rocks. Lingcod and rockfish. You can go deep if you wish, but most of the life is shallow. Even cloud sponges and chimney sponges start at 50 or 60 feet.
Once around the island gives you a fabulous cross-section of life.

Access: Christie Islet is in Howe Sound ¾ mile south of Anvil Island and 7½ miles north of Horseshoe Bay.
Charter out of Vancouver, launch at Lions Bay, or rent or launch your own boat at Sunset Beach or Horseshoe Bay and go north to Christie Islet. Anchor close-in at the northeast side in order to hit bottom and dive once around the islet.

Bottom and Depths: A sampling of almost every kind of sea floor: sloping sand, rock walls and huge boulders tumbled on top of each other. Small caves in 10 or 20 feet of water. The southeasterly side of the islet descends like a huge underwater mountain. Most of the life is in 40 or 50 feet.

Hazards: Current, wind and broken fishing line. Boats and poor visibility, in summer, because of Squamish River runoff. Dive near the slack. If windy, plan to leave a boat tender on the surface. The water can become choppy quickly at this exposed anchorage. When wind is from the south, anchorage is better at Christie Islet than at Pam Rocks. Carry a knife. Listen for boats and ascend up the side of the islet, well out of the way of those boats.

Telephone: Lions Bay Marina.

Facilities: None.

Comments: Christie Islet is a Federal Migratory Bird Sanctuary. From May through July colonies of gulls and cormorants are nesting on Christie Islet. Do not land on the islet during this period because any disturbance could cause nest desertion.

Christie Islet with cloud-hung Anvil Island behind

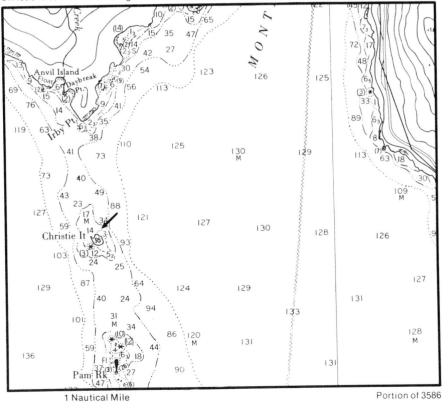

1 Nautical Mile

Portion of 3586

Skill: All Divers and Snorkelers

Why go: Pam Rocks flaunts flamboyant displays of oversized life starting with the seals usually lying on the rocks. Under water much of the life is oversized, too. Three-foot white plumose anemones, burrowing anemones with eight-inch purple plumes, big fat sea peaches and transparent tunicates are all over the place. Orange dead man's finger sponges poke from the bottom kelp-covered rocks in the shallows. You may see a rose star. In spring you'll see lots of nudibranchs. Fish life is not so big, but copper rockfish are abundant. Sometimes you'll see flounders, tiger rockfish, an octopus, lingcod and red Irish lords. Splendid cloud sponges start at 80 or 90 feet.

But the big thrill at Pam Rocks comes when you've been in the water a long while and the seals have forgotten you're there. Sometimes you can come up and be part of their group.

Access: Pam Rocks is just over 1 mile south of Anvil Island and 7 miles north of Horseshoe Bay in Howe Sound.

Charter out of Vancouver; launch at Lions Bay; or rent or launch your own boat at Sunset Beach or Horseshoe Bay and go north to Pam Rocks. Anchor southeast of the marker, between the two rocks, in 20 or 30 feet of water.

Bottom and Depths: On the east side of the marker undulating rocky bottom, clean-swept by the current, ranges from 20 or 30 feet deep to 90 or 100 feet. White sand between the rocks. In some places, deep canyon-like slots between the rocks.

Hazards: Current, wind, and broken fishing line. Boats and poor visibility in summer, because of Squamish River runoff. Dive near the slack. Use your compass, be aware of your direction, and watch the current. Be particularly careful if you go down into the deep slots, because the current can be strong. On the surface the water can become choppy very quickly at this exposed site. A difficult anchorage. It is wise to leave a boat tender on the surface. Carry a knife. Listen for boats and ascend with a reserve of air; if you hear a boat you can stay down until it passes.

Telephone: Lions Bay Marina.

Facilities: None.

Comments: Pam Rocks is a favourite site for underwater photographers in winter.

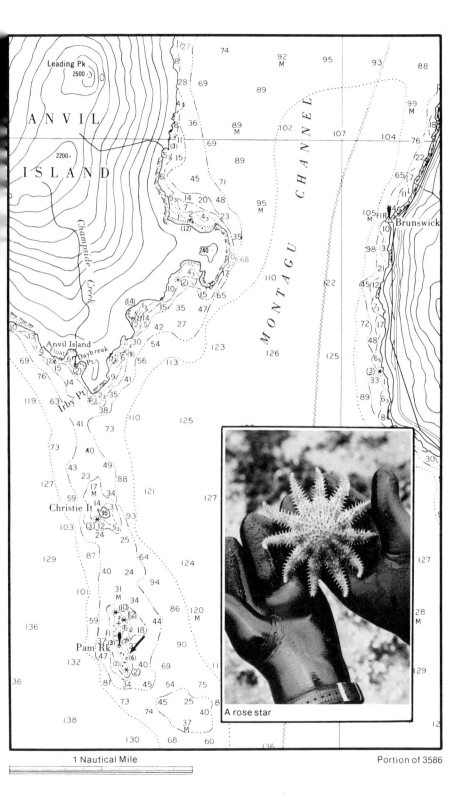

A rose star

1 Nautical Mile

Portion of 3586

MILLERS LANDING
Shore Dive

Skill: All Divers

Why go: Bouquets of white plumose anemones burgeon on top of the reef, cloud sponges billow below, and old bottles lie at the point on the right at Millers Landing.

But what I'll never forget about Millers Landing is the sight of a dahlia anemone trying to eat a coon-striped shrimp. As we came around a rock a lovely bright pink dahlia anemone held a 1½-inch shrimp with one of its tentacles and pulled the slender pink-and-black striped shrimp towards its flower-like mouth. The shrimp pulled back. The anemone pulled it forward again. The shrimp offered more and more resistance. Finally the anemone let go and the shrimp swam just out of the anemone's grasp and stopped. A strange life-and-death struggle.

More dahlia anemones were on the stark rock, bright yellow cup corals and tube worms with lovely spirals. Octopuses hid in the rocks. I swished my light in a swath through a cloud of silvery fish. They swung, dancing with my light. Then we went over the drop-off into cloud sponges so beautiful that I didn't want to come up. Millers Landing makes me understand why cloud sponges are considered a speciality of Howe Sound.

Swimming back we saw sea pens, kelp greenlings, burrowing anemones, vermilion stars with turned up toes and small pale orange nudibranchs in the shallows.

Access: From Park Royal in West Vancouver go 12 miles, 20 minutes by ferry, then 2 more miles to Millers Landing. From Park Royal head north on Taylor Way to Upper Levels Highway 1. Go west 10 miles to Horseshoe Bay and follow signs to the Bowen Island Ferry. On Bowen Island, you have to go 2 miles over fairly good tarmac and gravel roads to the site. Less than ½ mile off the ferry, turn right and follow signs to Millers Landing. Just over 1 mile farther, the tarmac turns left, but you continue straight ahead on the gravel road for another ½ mile to the turn-about at the end of the road. Walk 200 yards down a well-graded trail to a private wharf and the beach. Snorkel towards the rocks on your left. Shortly past the rocks, descend and follow a compass heading directly north to the reef.

Bottom and Depths: Rocky bottom, eelgrass, sand and silty white gravel slopes to the large rock reef 200 yards offshore in 40 or 50 feet of water. Beyond the reef, the bottom drops off sharply.

Hazards: Current and wind. Small boats and poor visibility, in summer, caused by Squamish and Fraser River runoff. But because the water may be turbid one day and clear the next, check to see if visibility is good. Some current around the point; dive the point on the slack. A Squamish wind can blow from the north and make entry and exit difficult. Listen for boats and ascend with a reserve of air; if you hear a boat you can stay down until it passes.

Telephone: Snug Cove Ferry Landing, Bowen Island.

Facilities: Roadside parking for ten cars. Nice beach for a picnic on a sunny day.

Comments: Come and go quietly and respect private property so that the residents continue to welcome divers.

A dancing cloud of silvery fish

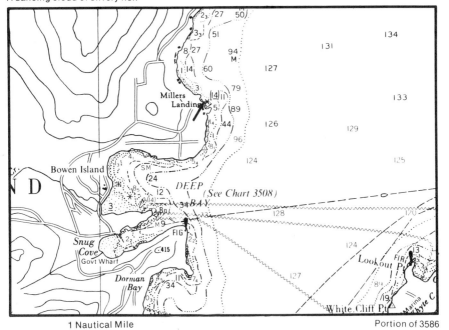

1 Nautical Mile

Portion of 3586

Skill: All Divers and Snorkelers

Why go: Seymour Bay is a low-key place where you don't have to do much planning to have a good dive. It's so pretty both above and below water that you should go when the sun is shining and plan to stay all day. Most life is in 20 or 30 feet. Swimming out over the sand we saw flounders, kelp greenlings and bright orange burrowing cucumbers flinging their fingers into the current. Sea peaches, tube worms and giant barnacles on the rock wall. Nudibranchs in the bottom kelp. An octopus curled up under a ledge in only 20 feet of water.
Deeper, dahlia anemones flow from the wall. Occasional bursts of large orange plumose anemones are attached to isolated rocks on sloping white sand below the wall. Thousands of miniature sea pens feather the sand. Copper rockfish and some lingcod live at the point.

Access: From Park Royal in West Vancouver drive 10 miles, ride a ferry for 20 minutes, then drive 6 more miles to Seymour Bay. From Park Royal head north on Taylor Way to Upper Levels Highway 1. Go west 10 miles to Horseshoe Bay and follow signs to the Bowen Island Ferry. Once on Bowen Island go 6 miles to Seymour Bay. Follow the road towards Tunstall Bay. At a sign to Cowan's Point, turn left and follow a rough, steep little road 3 miles farther, to an old orchard overlooking the water. Walk 300 yards down a rough trail to the beach. Snorkel to the point on your right and descend.

Bottom and Depths: Rocks covered with bottom kelp are scattered around the end of the point, dropping off in gentle tiers to a smooth white sand bottom. Most life is around the rocks in 20 or 30 feet.

Hazards: Some current and poor visibility, in summer, caused by Fraser River runoff. However, the water may be turbid one day and clear the next; it is always worth checking to see if visibility is good. Dive on the slack on large tidal exchanges.

Telephone: Snug Cove Ferry Landing, Bowen Island.

Facilities: None.

Comments: Seymour Cove, called Seymour Landing on charts, no longer has a wharf, or homes or other habitation. The orchard is a beautiful place for a picnic.

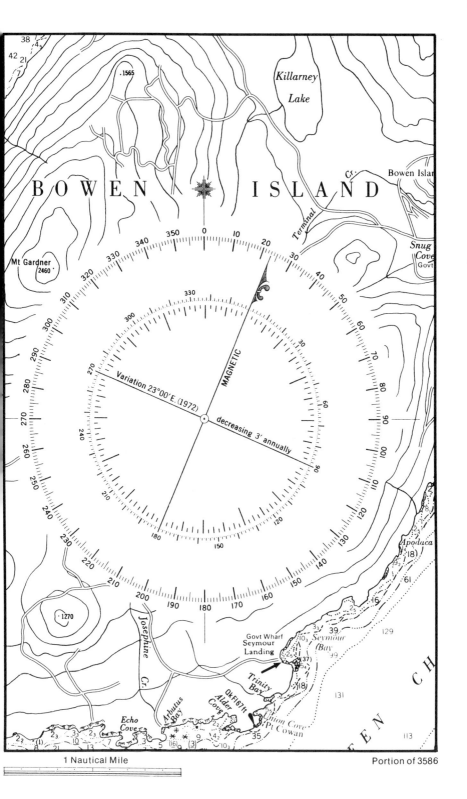

Skill: Intermediate and Advanced Divers and Snorkelers

Why go: It's a "holiday at home" for me to camp, dive and live off the wilds so close to the city. Worlcombe Island's great for photographers in fall and winter. It's the kind of place where you can take photographs all day, then pick up something for dinner at the end of your dive. Diving at Worlcombe Island we not only saw a wide spectrum of marine life, but also came up with a small but old and attractive anchor. Variety is the keynote.

Rockfish are so tame that you can tickle their chins and they don't move. We saw crabs in the eelgrass, giant nudibranchs on the sand, cabezons and kelp greenlings. You might see a salmon in the kelp and eelgrass. Moving around to the rock wall you'll find trumpet sponges, tube worms, lots of small solitary cup corals, shrimp, and sometimes an octopus or a wolf eel. We saw beautiful large dahlia anemones and a single swimming scallop. Cloud sponges and chimney sponges start at 60 feet. Small lingcod are abundant.

Access: Worlcombe Island is in Collingwood Channel, 1 mile west of Roger Curtis Point on the southwestern tip of Bowen Island. It is 1½ miles west of Tunstall Bay on Bowen Island; 4 miles southeast of Gibsons; 9 miles southwest of Horseshoe Bay.

Charter out of Vancouver, launch an inflatable at Tunstall Bay, rent at Gibsons, or rent a boat or launch your own at Horseshoe Bay and go to Worlcombe Island. Anchor where it is most sheltered. In fine weather this is usually on the north side. Just east of the marker on the northeast corner of the island there is a small bay conveniently near good diving. From here, dive around the southeastern tip of the island.

Bottom and Depths: The bottom varies. Eelgrass and sand in the small bay on the northeast shore. On the eastern tip, small rocks covered with bottom kelp are scattered over the sand. Around the corner on the southeastern side, a rock wall drops to 80 or 90 feet. An even deeper drop on the south side.

Hazards: Current, wind and waves. Small boats and poor visibility, in summer, because of Fraser River runoff. Dive on the slack. Worlcombe Island is very exposed. Be aware of wind and waves. If a strong west wind is blowing, you may have to leave someone in the boat, or you may not be able to anchor at all. Listen for boats and ascend along the bottom all the way to shore.

Telephone: Gibsons Government Wharf.

Facilities: None at privately owned Worlcombe Island. Plumper Cove Marine Park is in an apple orchard 5 miles away on Keats Island. The dock and anchorage are often crowded, but usually plenty of campsites are available at Plumper Cove. Running water, picnic tables and pit toilets.

Comments: Worlcombe Island is just one of many sites where you can dive and live off the land. Camp nearby. Look at your charts and explore; there are fabulous cloud sponges in Howe Sound.

Tube worm feeding from current, about three times life-size

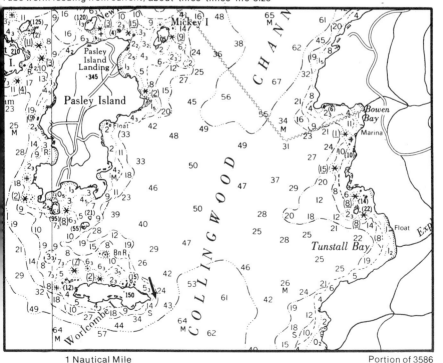

1 Nautical Mile

Portion of 3586

CHAPTER 2
Sechelt Peninsula

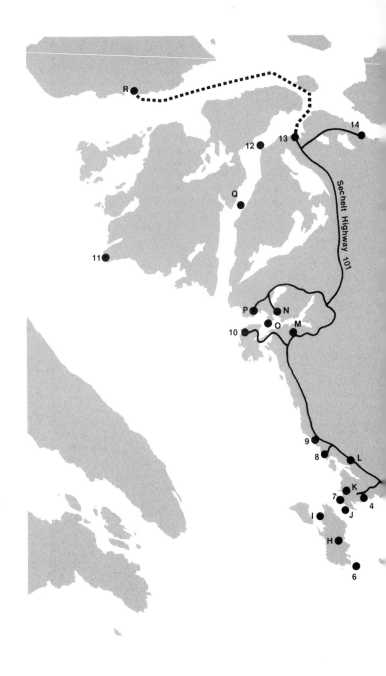

SECHELT PENINSULA

Dives

1. Tuwanek Point
2. Piper Point
3. Nine Mile Point
4. Brooks Cove
5. Merry Island
6. Pirate Rock
7. Grant Island
8. Oles Cove
9. Woods Bay
10. Francis Peninsula
11. Cape Cockburn
12. Caldwell Island
13. Earls Cove
14. Egmont

Places

A. Langdale
B. Keats Island
C. Gibsons
D. Sechelt
E. Porpoise Bay Park
F. Tillicum Bay
G. Halfmoon Bay
H. South Thormanby Island
I. Buccaneer Bay
J. Welcome Passage
K. Smuggler Cove
L. Secret Cove
M. Madeira Park
N. Garden Bay
O. Pender Harbour
P. Irvines Landing
Q. Agamemnon Channel
R. Saltery Bay
S. Skookumchuck Narrows

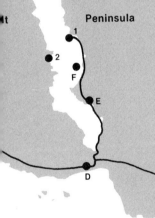

Sechelt Inlet

Peninsula

Sechelt Highway 101

SERVICE INFORMATION*
Sechelt Peninsula

Charts: Canadian Hydrographic Service
- 3509 Welcome Passage
- 3510 Pender Harbour and Approaches
- 3579 Burrard Inlet to Discovery Passage
- 3589 Jervis Inlet and Approaches

Tide and Current Tables: Canadian Hydrographic Service
Tide and Current Table, Volume 5

Emergency Telephone Numbers
R.C.M.P. Dial "0". Ask for Zenith 50,000

Rescue Coordination Centre (Vancouver) 732-4141

●Air Stations
Gibsons
Smitty's Marina Ltd.
Box 96
Gibsons, B.C.
VON 1V0
(604) 886-7711

Pender Harbour
Coho Marina Resort
Pender Harbour
Box 160
Madeira Park, B.C.
VON 2H0
(604) 883-2248

Egmont
Skookum Scuba
c/o John Seabrook
Egmont, B.C.
VON 1N0
(604) 883-2302

**●Boat Charters, Rentals
and Launching**
Sechelt Inlet
Tillicum Bay Marina Resorts
East Porpoise Bay Road
R.R. 1
Sechelt, B.C.
VON 3A0
(604) 885-2100
(Charters and launching only.)

Halfmoon Bay
Buccaneer Marina Resorts
Secret Cove
R.R. 1
Halfmoon Bay, B.C.
VON 1Y0
(604) 885-9563
(Charters and launching only.)

Jolly Roger Marina
R.R. 1
Halfmoon Bay, B.C.
VON 1Y0
(604) 885-3529
(Charters only.)

Lord Jim's Lodge
R.R. 1
Halfmoon Bay, B.C.
VON 1Y0
(604) 885-2232 or in
Vancouver 687-8212
(Charters only.)

Redrooffs Resort (Redroofs)
Redrooffs Road
R.R. 1
Halfmoon Bay, B.C.
V0N 1Y0
(604) 885-9432
(*Launching only.*)

Pender Harbour

Chinook Charters Ltd.
Box 77
Madeira Park, B.C.
V0N 2H0
(604) 883-2242
(*Charters only.*)

Coho Marina Resort
Box 160
Madeira Park, B.C.
V0N 2H0
(604) 883-2248
(*Charters, rentals and launching.*)

Duncan Cove Resort
Sinclair Bay Road
Box 18
Garden Bay, B.C.
V0N 1S0
(604) 883-2424
(*Charters, rentals and launching.*)

The Fisherman's Resort
Box 1
Garden Bay, B.C.
V0N 1S0
(604) 883-2336
(*Rentals and launching only.*)

Lowe's Resort
Box 81
Madeira Park, B.C.
V0N 2H0
(604) 883-2456
(*Rentals only.*)

Madeira Marina
Madeira Park Road
Box 189
Madeira Park, B.C.
V0N 2H0
(604) 883-2266
(*Charters, rentals and launching.*)

Whittaker's Garden Bay Res.
Garden Bay, B.C.
V0N 1S0
(604) 883-2282
(*Charters and rentals. Launching nearby.*)

Egmont

Bathgate's Store and Marina
Egmont, B.C.
V0N 1N0
(604) 883-2222
(*Rentals and launching only.*)

Egmont Marina and Resort
Egmont, B.C.
V0N 1N0
(604) 883-2298
(*Rentals and launching only.*)

Skookum Scuba
c/o John Seabrook
Egmont, B.C.
V0N 1N0
(604) 883-2302
(*Charters only.*)

● **Ferry Information**

B.C. Ferry Information Centre
1045 Howe Street
Vancouver, B.C.
V6Z 1P6
(604) 669-1211
From Sechelt Pen.: 886-2242
(*Ferries from Langdale to Horseshoe Bay and from Earls Cove to Saltery Bay.*)

● **Tourist Information**

Department of Travel Industry
652 Burrard Street
Vancouver, B.C.
V6C 2L3
(604) 668-2300

*All of this service information is subject to change.

TUWANEK POINT   **Tide Table:** Point Atkinson
Shore Dive

Skill: All Divers and Snorkelers

Why go: The shallow waters around three small islands at Tuwanek Point are like a large aquarium. It's beautiful for checkouts. Beautiful for fish. Beautiful for available light photography. Small fish are everywhere. You'll see schools of black-and-white striped pile perch. Lots of reddish pink and yellow-tinged rockfish apparently totally unafraid. I touched one with my light. Delicate yellow-and-blue striped seaperch school everywhere in the sunny shallows. Hundreds of pipefish, too. You're bound to see maroon-and-grey vertically striped painted greenlings, sometimes called convict fish. Lots of the very territorial and colourful four- or five-inch convict fish live here. They'll probably try to chase you from their particular portion of the sea.

There are many other creatures at Tuwanek, as well. Red hydroids that look like little tulips cling to the rocks. Small green urchins and lemon nudibranchs eat bottom kelp. Angular orange dead man's finger sponges twist out of the rocks. A small crab menaced me from under a leaf of kelp. Sea peaches and transparent sea squirts hang like grapes from the wall.

Sun shines through the shallow water and lights it all.

Access: From Langdale Ferry Terminal go 23 miles to Tuwanek Point on the protected waters of Sechelt Inlet. Tuwanek is at the end of the road going north. From Langdale drive northwest on Sechelt Highway 101 to the town of Sechelt. Just past the Ranger Station, where the highway turns sharply left, a sign on the right points to Porpoise Bay and Sandy Hook. Turn right and go along East Porpoise Bay Road for 6½ miles, past turnoffs to Porpoise Bay Provincial Park and Tillicum Bay. You are nearly at Tuwanek Point when you pass a small sign saying "Tuwanek Welcomes You". Continue ½ mile to where the road comes close to the water. Two or three cars can park at the side of the road. There's an archway over a couple of concrete steps to the beach, and in the concrete is written "Have a Happy Day".

Bottom and Depths: Shallow undulating rocky bottom encircles the islands. Large rocks and boulders are tumbled in 25 or 30 feet of water making marvelous hiding places for all kinds of life. At 50 to 75 feet the bottom turns to silty sand. South of the point near the creek the bottom drops off swiftly to muddy bottom scattered with a series of logs fallen to look like pick-up-sticks.

Hazards: Small boats in summer. Fly your diver's flag, listen for boats and ascend along the bottom all the way to shore.

Telephone: Tillicum Marina, 1⅓ miles back towards Sechelt.

Facilities: Sandy beach for a picnic at Tuwanek. Charters and launching at Tillicum Bay. Camping at Porpoise Bay Provincial Park 5 miles back towards Sechelt.

Comments: Let's leave this beautiful beach as clean as we find it so that the people who live in the small scattering of homes at Tuwanek Point will continue to welcome divers.

Preparing to dive at Tuwanek

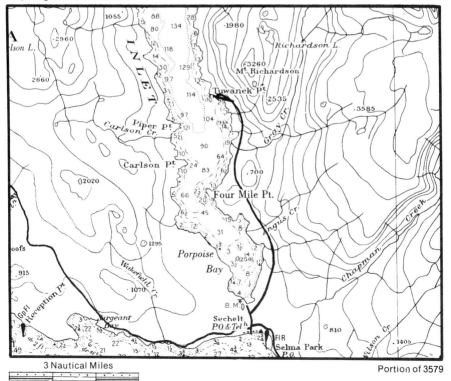

3 Nautical Miles

Portion of 3579

PIPER POINT   **Tide Table:** Point Atkinson
Boat Dive

Skill: All Divers

Why go: Piper Point is totally wild and unexploited feeling — yet so easy to dive.
There is no current in this part of Sechelt Inlet and the deep waters of the inlet seem crystal-clear year-round. Visibility is excellent — sometimes 20 to 50 feet in summer. Even more in winter. You experience a marvelous sensation of spaciousness when everything that's happening can be seen.
When I dived here I saw things I've seen nowhere else: a sea star consuming a sea pen; another sea star eating a clam; and a pair of wolf eels under the edge of a rock that looked as large as a house. Orange and white anemones and sponges shaped like little castles are scattered on top of the rock. Seaperch and rockfish hang like mobiles in the water all around.
Going up we saw a sleek ratfish. And a school of herring swept past making a silvery glint.

Access: Piper Point is on the west side near the southern tip of Sechelt Inlet. It is just over 1 mile across the water southwest of Tuwanek Point.
Charter or launch your own boat at Tillicum Bay or hand launch over the sand at the end of a gravel road just before Tuwanek Point. Tuwanek Point is 23 miles northwest of Langdale Ferry Terminal. From Langdale drive northwest to the town of Sechelt. Just past the Ranger Station, where the highway turns sharply left, a sign on the right points to Porpoise Bay and Sandy Hook. Turn right and go north on East Porpoise Bay Road along the east side of the inlet. Porpoise Bay Provincial Park is 1½ miles along this road. Tillicum Bay is 5 miles beyond Sechelt. Tuwanek, 6½ miles.
Launch, cross the water to Piper Point, and anchor in the bull kelp just south of the point. Go down and work your way west.

Bottom and Depths: Rocky bottom with some bull kelp drops quickly to a wide ledge at 60 or 70 feet where the big boulder lies. Over the edge of this ledge it's almost bottomless — 90 fathoms on the chart. Steep sides are typical of much of Sechelt Inlet.

Hazards: Depth and bull kelp. You tend to go deeper when the water is clear. Watch your depth. Carry a knife and surface with a reserve of air so that if caught in the kelp you will have time to cut your way free.

Telephone: Tillicum Bay Marina Resort.

Facilities: None at this wilderness site. Charters and launching at Tillicum Bay. Camping at Porpoise Bay Provincial Park.

Comments: Try diving Piper Point at night.

Swimming anemone

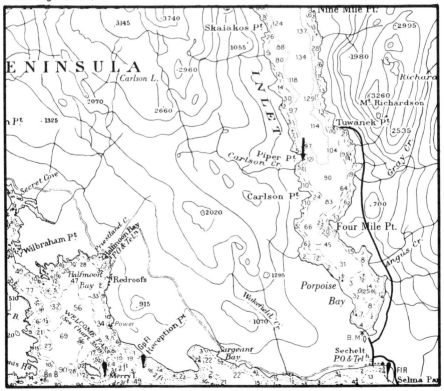

3 Nautical Miles

Portion of 3579

Skill: All Divers

Why go: If you want to go beyond the crowd to where there are still some yelloweye rockfish and lingcod, Nine Mile Point is a good place to go. Or try one of the other points up this way. It's best to spread out for hunting so that the fish population isn't shot out in one area. Lingcod and yelloweye rockfish are territorial. If overfished, they're gone. When my buddy shot a lingcod at Nine Mile Point another lingcod came up to watch the first one being removed from the spear. Spooky. Nine Mile Point is just one of many places to dive. The inlet is loaded. You'll have the best chance of finding fish if you pick your own point: "If I'm told a place is good for spearfishing," says one diver, "I go to another spot. I know it will be better!"

Nine Mile Point is good for sightseeing, too. Crabs and nudibranchs are in the kelp. Rockfish along the wall. Sponges down deep. And a fabulous feeling that this huge slope sweeps down to the bottom of the world.

Access: Nine Mile Point is halfway up Sechelt Inlet where the waters bend northeast into Salmon Inlet, 3 miles north beyond the end of the road at Tuwanek Point.

Charter or launch your own boat at Tillicum Bay or hand launch across the sandy log-strewn beach just before Tuwanek Point. Tuwanek Point is 23 miles northwest of Langdale Ferry Terminal. From Langdale go on Sechelt Highway 101 to the town of Sechelt. Just past the Ranger Station where the highway turns sharply left, a sign on the right points to Porpoise Bay and Sandy Hook. Turn right and go north on East Porpoise Bay Road along the east side of the inlet. Porpoise Bay Provincial Park is 1½ miles along this road. Tillicum Bay is 5 miles beyond Sechelt. Tuwanek, 6½ miles.

Launch and go by boat 3 or 4 miles north to Nine Mile Point. A small bay just south of the point seems made for you to beach your boat and go down.

Bottom and Depths: Large broken rocks slope rapidly to 30 or 40 feet to bottom kelp and bull kelp. Then the rocks sweep down into very deep water.

Hazards: Small boats and bull kelp, especially in summer. Listen for boats and ascend along the bottom all the way to shore. Surface with a reserve of air; if caught in the kelp you will have time to cut your way free.

Telephone: Tillicum Bay Marina.

Facilities: None at this wild, uninhabited site. Charters and launching at Tillicum Bay. Camping at Porpoise Bay Provincial Park.

Comments: "Shelter from the sea", the meaning of the Indian word for Sechelt, became a reality for me the day I dived here. The waters glistened, shining and still, like a mirage around Nine Mile Point.

North to Nine Mile Point

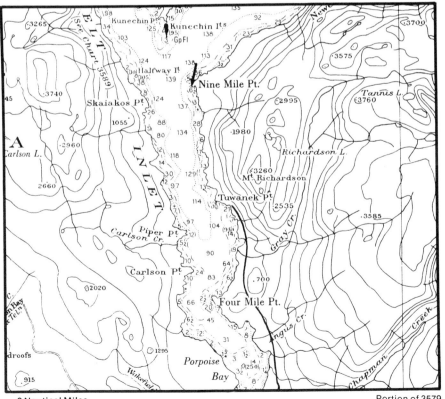

2 Nautical Miles

Portion of 3579

Skill: All Divers and Snorkelers

Why go: There's a lot of good diving in the Secret Cove Area —but mostly from boats. If you have no boat and you still want to dive, here's one place you can go. The price: one very long swim. What will you get for it? If you go far enough you'll come to a rock wall dropping to 80 or 90 feet. You'll see lingcod, rockfish, greenlings and sponges. Wolf eels, if you look hard. But save your air till you arrive at the site. Swim on the surface right around to the second point on your left. The water is usually clear at Brooks Cove with visibility up to 80 feet in winter. You don't have to go down to see what's there. While snorkeling out and while still in the shallows, we saw nudibranchs, small crabs, anchovies and perch. Slightly deeper we saw ratfish, dogfish, some medium-sized lingcod and countless schools of smaller fish. All this before we started our dive. And then down to the sponges.

Access: From Langdale Ferry Terminal go 30 miles to Brooks Cove. Heading northwest on Sechelt Highway 101, 10 miles past the town of Sechelt and ½ mile past Halfmoon Bay go to a small sign marking Brooks Road. Turn left and continue along this wide gravel road for 2½ miles. After 1½ miles a couple of dirt roads branch off. First take the right fork, then the first left and keep going until you come to the sea. There are a few homes along either side of the cove. And lots of parking space. Enter the water only a few feet from your car over the rocky log-strewn beach. Then a very long swim. I warn you! It is 350 yards around to the left before you arrive at the wall.

Bottom and Depths: In the bay, mud and eelgrass slope gently out to 20 or 30 feet. At the point 350 yards around the corner on your left, the wall drops to 80 or 90 feet.

Hazards: Long swim. For very fit divers.

Telephones: 1. B and J Store, near Halfmoon Bay Wharf, inside.
2. First Aid Station, Sechelt Highway, 1 mile south of Brooks Road, inside.

Facilities: None.

Comments: Great for a bonfire on the beach.
From April 15th through October 15th telephone Sechelt Forest Ranger, 885-2034, and ask if beach bonfire permit required.

Alabaster nudibranch laying eggs

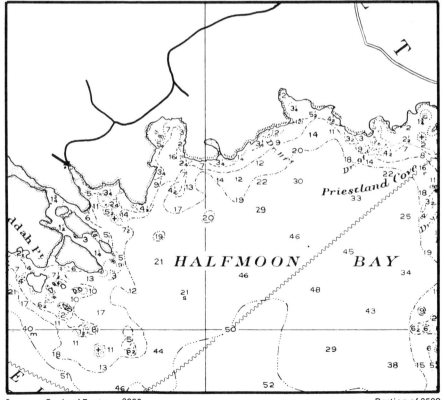

0   Scale of Feet   3000

Portion of 3509

MERRY ISLAND   **Tide Table:** Add 10 minutes
        Boat Dive   onto Point Atkinson

Skill: Intermediate and Advanced Divers

Why go: For some the scattered remains of the 58-ton *Salvage Chief* and the two 10-ton wrecks, *Linda-K* and *Carla-N*, are the big attractions at Merry Island. For others the many lingcod, the octopus that regularly suns himself on the 10-foot reef, or the wall thick with red dahlia anemones that drops down at the southeast end.

The steel-hulled *Salvage Chief* was stranded here on February 7, 1925. The *Linda-K* and *Carla-N* on April 29, 1962. All three have been dived on a lot, but a wreck always excites the imagination. Who stayed on her to the end? What did they do on the *Salvage Chief* when she was picked up by a swell, crashed onto the reef, and holed? And what loot has the current uncovered? You never know when the powerful sea will turn up something new.

Merry Island glows in my memory as the place with the best visibility I've experienced anywhere outside of the tropics. And I dived here on a day in May when most other places in the Strait of Georgia were blotted out by river runoff. Visibility sometimes does deteriorate here because of plankton bloom in summer, but this seems one of the last areas to be affected.

Wrecks, game fish and excellent visibility for photography are all part of the dive at Merry Island.

Access: Merry Island is in the southern end of Welcome Passage off the coast of Sechelt Peninsula, 3 miles south of Halfmoon Bay or 4 miles south of Secret Cove.

Launch at Halfmoon Bay or Secret Cove and head south. The reef is at the southern side of Merry Island. Be careful as you approach, especially on low tides. The reef dries on 2-foot tides. To find the reef, line yourself up on the intersection of two lines. One line runs from the south tip of Merry Island to the Merry Island light; the other from the south tip of the island just south of Merry Island to Reception Point light. At the pinnacle of the reef the *Salvage Chief* was holed. Scraps of all three wrecks have been found just to the north of this pinnacle.

Bottom and Depths: The reef is large broken rocks with bull kelp. It dries on very low tides and can be 10 feet deep on high tides. Heading southeast, the slope is gradual to 50 or 60 feet. Then the rock wall drops off sharply.

Hazards: Current, wind and bull kelp. Dive on the slack. Wind from almost any direction can be a problem at this very exposed site. If going in a small vessel, pick a calm day. Carry a knife and surface with a reserve of air; if caught in the kelp you will have time to cut your way free.

Telephones: 1. Merry Island Lighthouse radiotelephone.
2. B and J Store, near Halfmoon Bay Wharf, inside.
3. First Aid Station, Sechelt Highway, ½ mile south of Halfmoon Bay, inside.

Facilities: None at Merry Island. Launching at Halfmoon Bay and Secret Cove. A beautiful wilderness provincial campsite at Smuggler Cove at the northeast end of Welcome Passage. No drinking water, no restrooms or other facilities at Smuggler Cove. Just a place to pitch your tent.

Comments: Prime area for camping and boat diving.

Dahlia anemones

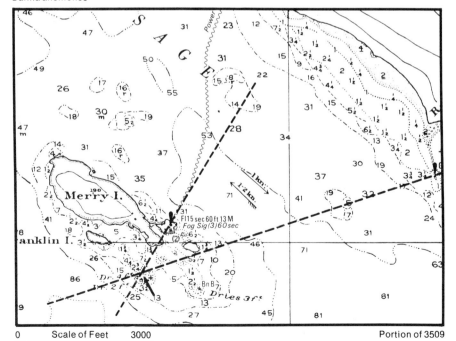

0   Scale of Feet   3000   Portion of 3509

PIRATE ROCK
Boat Dive

Tide Table: Add 10 minutes
onto Point Atkinson

Skill: Advanced Divers

Why go: Pirate Rock sits "king-of-the-castle" on top of a series of irregular ledges, boulders, and arches. It's the most dramatic pinnacle of rock I've dived.
And there's more than an average amount of life around it. Quillback rockfish — smallish to medium-sized — crowd the cracks of the rocks. Tube worms, sea peaches and plumose anemones hold tight under the overhangs. Sea pens tilt out of pools of sand between the ledges. Greenlings hide in the bottom kelp. Lingcod move in and out of the shadows.
Deeper, ratfish slide past big grey immobile chimney sponges. A wolf eel hangs back out of sight in a hole under the rocks, while snakelock anemones, thick like fringe on a Spanish shawl, test the current with sticky fingers. And foot-wide cloud sponges float below like fluffy summer clouds in a beautiful reverse world.

Access: Pirate Rock is ¼ mile off the southeast tip of South Thormanby Island near Welcome Passage, 3 miles southwest of Halfmoon Bay or 4 miles south of Secret Cove.
Launch at Halfmoon Bay or Secret Cove and head south. Anchor anywhere around the rock, but do not tie onto the marker. It is a federal offense to make fast to a marker or tamper with any aid to navigation.

Bottom and Depths: Bull kelp is attached to irregular 20 or 30 foot rocky bottom around Pirate Rock. Ledges, overhangs and arches which you can swim through surround the rock. The arches are formed by boulders tumbled one over the other. The north side drops off quickly. Narrow ledges tier down to 10 or 20 feet, to 60 and 80 and on.

Hazards: Current, small fishing boats, bull kelp and broken fishing line. Dive on the slack. Even then it is difficult. Currents come in streaks on the surface. One streak from Welcome Pass side. Then dead water. Then another streak of current from the west side of Thormanby Island. A pickup boat is advisable. Pirate Rock is popular with salmon fishermen; be especially careful of small boat traffic in salmon fishing season. Because the bottom undulates irregularly it is difficult to find your anchor line or to ascend along the rock all the way to the surface. Fly your diver's flag, listen for boats and ascend cautiously with a reserve of air; if you hear a boat you can stay down until it passes. Carry a knife.

Telephones: 1. Merry Island Lighthouse radiotelephone.
2. B and J Store, near Halfmoon Bay Wharf, inside.
3. First Aid Station, Sechelt Highway, ½ mile south of Halfmoon Bay, inside.

Facilities: Launching at Halfmoon Bay and Secret Cove. A beautiful wilderness provincial campsite at Smuggler Cove at the northeast end of Welcome Passage. No drinking water, no restrooms or other facilities at Smuggler Cove — just a place to pitch your tent.

Comments: One of the warmest sandy swimming beaches in British Columbia is only three miles north of Pirate Rock between the Thormanby Islands at Buccaneer Bay.

From South Thormanby, off to nearby Pirate Rock

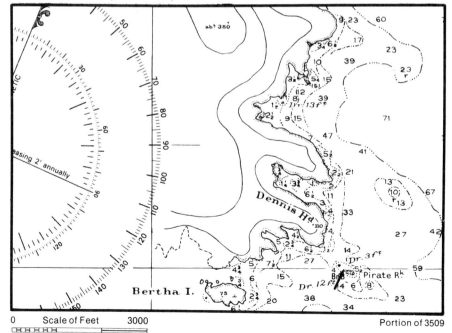

0   Scale of Feet   3000

Portion of 3509

GRANT ISLAND   **Tide Table:** Add 10 minutes
       Boat Dive   onto Point Atkinson

Skill: Intermediate and Advanced Divers

Why go: Grant Island Light marks the narrowest point, the
deepest drop-off and the place in Welcome Passage where you
will find the most of everything. The most large lingcod. The most
varieties of unusual animals. Plus old familiar ones like rock
scallops.
   When diving here my buddy shot a lingcod so huge that it broke
the line and swam off with the spear. We saw hard pink hydrocoral
and small bright red gorgonian coral — both "firsts" for me. And
the sponges were magnificent: chimney sponges, trumpet sponges and vase sponges — one that looked like a giant lily. Masses
of quillback rockfish, large lingcod and ratfish cruised beside the
current-swept bottomless wall.

Access: Grant Island is at the north end of Welcome Passage,
1½ miles south of Secret Cove or 3 miles northwest of Halfmoon
Bay.
   Launch at Secret Cove or Halfmoon Bay and go to Grant
Island. Anchor north of the lighthouse around the corner out of
Welcome Passage. Dive towards the light.

Bottom and Depths: Bull kelp and bottom kelp on the 50 to 60
foot rocky bottom north of the lighthouse, close to shore. South
towards the point, the rock wall drops almost straight down.
Over 80 fathoms on the chart.

Hazards: Current, boats and bull kelp. Dive on the slack. Fly
your diver's flag, listen for boats and ascend up the wall, well out
of the way of those boats. Carry a knife and surface with a
reserve of air; if caught in kelp you will have time to cut your way
free.

Telephones: 1. Merry Island Lighthouse radiotelephone.
                2. B and J Store, near Halfmoon Bay Wharf, inside.
                3. First Aid Station, Sechelt Highway, ½ mile
                   south of Halfmoon Bay, inside.

Facilities: Launching ramp at Secret Cove and Halfmoon Bay. A
beautiful wilderness provincial campsite is ¼ mile away at
Smuggler Cove. No drinking water, no restrooms or other
facilities at Smuggler Cove — just a place to pitch your tent.

Comments: Worth diving here just to see the unusual pink
hydrocoral and red gorgonian coral. They start at about 80 feet.
But because they're only four or five inches tall, you must look
closely to find them in this vast seascape.

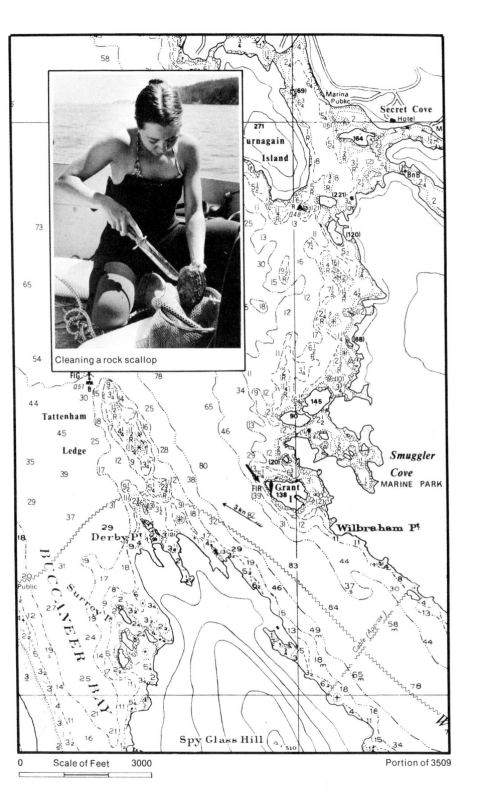

Cleaning a rock scallop

Portion of 3509

Skill: All Divers

Why go: If you want a plain old-fashioned reef — no frills, nothing special, just a good reef — Oles Cove is it. From the surface little indicates a reef. Some bull kelp, but it's difficult to see, especially at high tide. You have to go on trust. The easiest way to find the reef is to set your compass and swim under water straight out from shore. You'll see moon jellyfish and sea stars in the eelgrass. Shrimp, miniature sea pens and burrowing anemones feathering the sandy shallows. At the rocky reef, 200 or 300 feet offshore, we saw crabs in the bottom kelp, boulders covered with red anemones, white encrusting sponge, transparent sea squirts, and small orange sponges. Striped seaperch and pile perch school around the rocks. You'll see rockfish, kelp greenlings, painted greenlings, lingcod and dogfish. A typical reef and a satisfying dive.

Access: From Langdale Ferry Terminal go 31 miles to Oles Cove. Drive northwest on Sechelt Highway 101. Fourteen miles past the town of Sechelt and 4½ miles past Halfmoon Bay you comes to Oles Cove Road which forks immediately. The left fork goes to Lord Jim's Lodge. You take the right fork and wind 3/10 mile to a point where the road comes close to the water. Two or three cars can park at the side of the road. Walk down a rough 50-foot trail to a rocky entry. Follow your compass straight out from shore to the reef.

Bottom and Depths: Sand and eelgrass slope gradually from shore to 25 feet deep. Rocky reef starts 200 or 300 feet offshore and undulates easily down. Some boulders, bottom kelp and bull kelp. The reef bottoms out to sand at 50 or 60 feet.

Hazards: Boats and bull kelp, especially in summer. Fly your diver's flag, and ascend with a reserve of air; if you hear a boat you can stay down until it passes. Or better yet — follow your compass back to shore under water.

Telephone: Lord Jim's Lodge, inside.

Facilities: None.

Comments: A good afternoon's dive when the sun has warmed the rocks.

From Oles Cove, looking south towards Thormanby Island

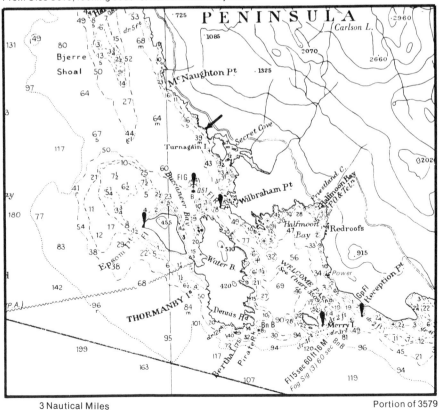

3 Nautical Miles

Portion of 3579

Skill: All Divers

Why go: Woods Bay is quick and easy — a popular place where many stop for a second dive on their way home from Pender Harbour. Current is no concern at this quiet, innocuous little bay. You can drop into the water anytime. And it's protected from the southeast wind which brings bad weather in winter. We saw moon snails, flounders and blood stars in the eelgrass. Rock-rimmed shores shelter the usual life: purple stars, seaperch, kelp greenlings, sea cucumbers and the occasional small lingcod.
For the energetic, there's a reef much farther out. But the bay is the most popular simple place to dive.

Access: From Langdale Ferry Terminal go 33 miles to Woods Bay which is right at the side of the main road. Drive northwest on Sechelt Highway 101. Fifteen miles past the town of Sechelt and 1 mile past Oles Cove Road you come to a place where you can see the water from the road. Just past here, on your left, is room for one car to park. Walk 150 yards down the old overgrown road and rocky path to the log-strewn beach.
If heading home from Pender Harbour, 5⅓ miles past Francis Peninsula Road look for a sign that says "Slow to 25". Pull off and park on your right where there is room for one car. This is Woods Bay.

Bottom and Depths: The bay is rimmed with rocky shore undulating down to 20- or 30-foot sandy bottom which slopes slowly out to deeper water.

Hazards: Fairly long walk from your car to the water.

Telephone: Lord Jim's Lodge, 1 mile south, inside.

Facilities: None at this quiet uninhabited beach.

Comments: Blackberry bushes crowd the path to the water — September's harvest time.

Blackberries crowding path at Woods Bay

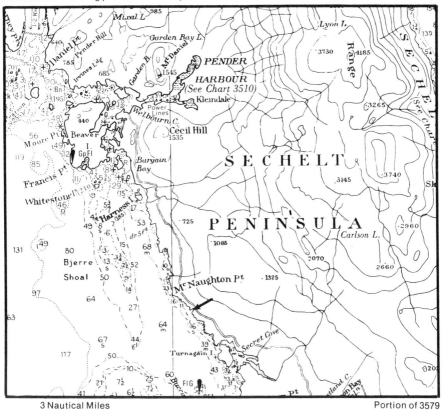

3 Nautical Miles

Portion of 3579

Skill: All Divers

Why go: If you want a quick uncomplicated dive with a wilderness feeling about it, try this quiet little bay south of Pender Harbour.
    You'll see flounders, Oregon tritons and sea stars on the sandy floor. Look for moon snails as well. Along rocky walls rimming both sides of the bay we found beautiful small green anemones contrasting with very red rocks in the shallows; purple crabs scurrying about; and purple stars sticking on the rocks. Millions of almost-transparent orange gobies dart all about. Pipefish, pile perch and striped seaperch glint in the sun. Rockfish hang along the wall. Deeper we saw sea peaches, dahlia anemones and lingcod.
    Chimney sponges at 60 feet — and you're in the wilderness.

Access: This little bay on Francis Peninsula is 43 miles northwest of Langdale Ferry Terminal. From Langdale drive 39 miles north on Sechelt Highway 101. Eight miles past Secret Cove you come to Francis Peninsula Road, the first of three access roads to the Pender Harbour area. Turn left down Francis Peninsula Road, cross Bargain Narrows to the peninsula, or Beaver Island as it used to be called, and go 4 miles. The road winds all over the place. A quarter mile past Martin Road it curves south, high above the water. Below is the bay. Park at the side of the road and walk down a steep 100-foot trail to the beach. This walk is the hard part of the dive. Entry is easy. So is the dive.

Bottom and Depths: The bay is rimmed with rock walls dropping to sand bottom which slopes to deep water. Some boulders along the wall.

Hazards: The climb down to the beach — and up.

Telephone: Francis Peninsula Road and Sechelt Highway.

Facilities: None. Air fills, camping, accommodations, boat charters, rentals, and launching at nearby Pender Harbour.

Comments: An exceptionally easy and totally pleasant little dive.

Lined chiton clinging to rock

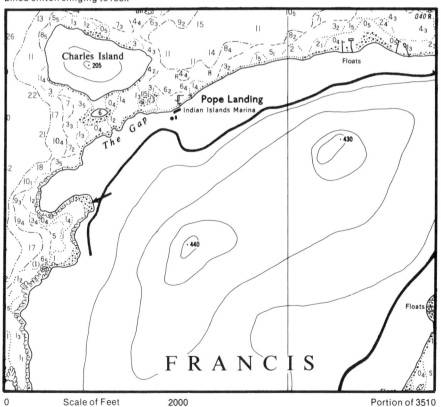

Charles Island · 205

Pope Landing
Indian Islands Marina

The Gap

· 430

· 440

Floats

Floats

F R A N C I S

0   Scale of Feet   2000   Portion of 3510

CAPE COCKBURN   **Tide Table:** Add 10 minutes
Boat Dive   onto Point Atkinson

Skill: Intermediate and Advanced Divers and Snorkelers

Why go: Tumbling in terraces, the clean-swept rocks and gravel of Cape Cockburn sheer off into deep waters like something at the end of an ancient glacier. A different dive.
At first you look around, but see little life. We saw simply smooth-carved rock ledges stairstepping down, clean undercut overhangs, and not much else. Look again. Shine your light. Stark, dark grooves slicing vertically down the smooth rock are full of pastel life. They are brimming with pink and pale green anemones so thick you can't see the rock. Under a ledge at only 25 feet we saw a sunburst of yellow cloud sponge. Small orange cloud sponges nearby. Alabaster nudibranchs gleaming white on white and petal-like pale orange nudibranchs with white tips — both only a couple of inches long — are isolated islands of delicate beauty on the vast rock fall.
Deeper, velvety-red snakelock anemones hang from the clean rock wall like exquisite flowers reaching velvet fingers into the current. Deeper still, large chimney sponges. Then darkness.
At this extreme western tip of Cape Cockburn alternate sweeps of smooth rock and sand slides slope and slice down into the dramatic dark of Malaspina Inlet.

Access: Cape Cockburn is the westernmost extreme of Nelson Island, 10 miles northwest of Pender Harbour.
Charter, rent or launch at Pender Harbour, go 10 miles north to Cape Cockburn, anchor or tie up on the shore, and go down.

Bottom and Depths: Smooth rocks, ledges and overhangs slope rapidly to 42 fathoms. South of the cape the rocks drop in ledges and terraces, as well. These are the really different dives.
For a more usual shallow reef with boulders, bull kelp, rockfish, lingcod and more life altogether, dive immediately below the light.

Hazards: Current. Dive on the slack.

Telephone: Irvines Landing, Pender Harbour.

Facilities: None at uninhabited Cape Cockburn. Air fills, boat charters, rentals, and launching, camping and accommodations at Pender Harbour.

Comments: Magnificent spot to sit and sun on the rocks.

Cape Cockburn

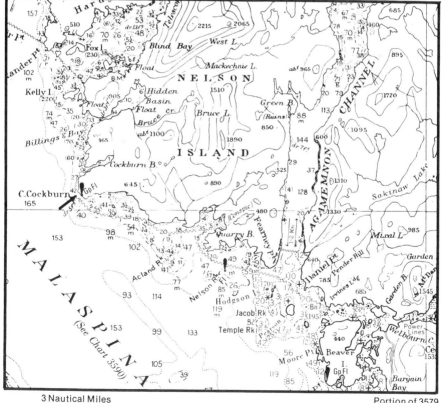

3 Nautical Miles

Portion of 3579

CALDWELL ISLAND
Boat Dive

Skill: Intermediate and Advanced Divers

Why go: Agamemnon Channel is a favourite of deep divers because of its precipitous cliffs and because it's usually protected from wind. Submarines are tested right around the corner from Agamemnon Channel north of Nelson Island where the protected inland sea plummets 369 fathoms. The whole area is exciting for those who "think deep".
Caldwell Island, ⅔ of the way up the Agamemnon Channel, combines the best of both worlds. It's a sheer drop-off — but not a bottomless one. The elevator ride stops at 100 to 120 feet.
When diving here you can see an intriguing cross-section of marine life as you slice the sea down and up. At 20 to 30 feet lots of lingcod, chitons and rock scallops. Thickets of bottom kelp and bull kelp. Greenlings so tame you can almost touch them. Red-and-black striped tiger rockfish hiding under narrow ledges. I saw a shrimp inside the deep cup of one vase sponge. A crab in another. Beautiful snakelock anemones on the wall. Pale pink fingers of hydrocoral, sea peaches, lemon nudibranchs, a rose star and puffs of nicely shaped cloud sponges. And a feather star, looking more like a fern than an animal, surprised me as it left the chimney sponge to which it clung and swam sinuously away. Then we were on the sandy bottom surrounded by millions of burrowing anemones and sea pens.
Ride over.

Access: Caldwell Island is ⅔ of the way up Agamemnon Channel and can be reached by boat from Egmont or Pender Harbour, 8 miles from Egmont, 11 miles from the entrance to Pender Harbour.
Charter, rent or launch at Egmont or Pender Harbour. Anchor at the point just south of the bay near the house and descend.

Bottom and Depths: Rocky bottom undulates quickly to 20 or 30 feet where you find lots of bull kelp and bottom kelp. Rock walls, steep tiers and ledges drop to sandy bottom at 110 or 120 feet. Some silt over all.

Hazards: Current and depth. Dive on the slack.

Telephones: 1. Egmont Marina.
2. Irvines Landing, Pender Harbour.

Facilities: None at Caldwell Island. Air fills, charters, rentals and launching, and accommodations at Egmont and Pender Harbour. Camping at Pender Harbour.

Comments: Because we knew we could safely ascend the steep sides of the cliff at this site, we did not bother to put out our diver's flag. When down, we heard a boat. When we surfaced, a man in a tug was examining our empty boat, worrying about reporting the missing persons. In deserted areas as well as populated areas, fly your diver's flag.

Brittle stars snaking through hydrocoral

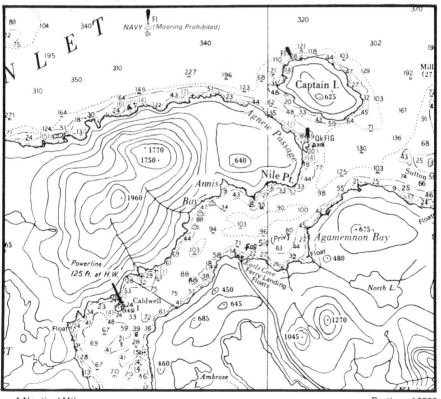

Skill: Intermediate and Advanced Divers

Why go: Popular with divers for years — and for good reason — Earls Cove has just about everything. Good diving both shallow and deep. All the animals are well-fed by the current which sweeps through Agamemnon Channel.

When diving here we saw some beautiful sea stars I'd never seen before, skinny-legged white stars with orange centres. There are chitons, giant barnacles, enormous lemon nudibranchs, lacy white burrowing cucumbers, hydroids and greenlings in bull kelp in the shallows. Lovely sea pens on the sand between small broken rocks.

Going down over the edge of the steep slope we saw lots of rockfish, pink snakelock anemones, cloud sponges and a shrimp in a chimney sponge. Coming up, several bright red-and-black striped tiger rockfish around the rocks. And a lingcod almost swam into my buddy's arms.

There's a lot at Earls Cove. You can't possibly see it all in one or two dives. It's the kind of place photographers come back to again and again and again.

Access: From Langdale Ferry Terminal go 52 miles to Earls Cove. Allow 1½ hours to drive there. Go north on Sechelt Highway 101 to the other end of the highway at Earls Cove Ferry Terminal. Park somewhere at the left. Immediately west of the terminal there is a small peninsula signposted as private property. Ask permission to walk the few steps across this peninsula, then enter the water and swim 50 to 100 yards to the rock wall at the first point and go down. Or, you can swim around the peninsula to the point.

Bottom and Depths: A wall drops to rocky bottom and broadleaf bottom kelp at 20 or 30 feet. Boulders and bull kelp are scattered over this ledge. A few sandy patches between the rocks. From here the wall angles steeply down to 90 feet. Then a sheer drop straight into Agamemnon Channel.

Hazards: Current, boats, depth and bull kelp. Dive on the slack and listen for boats. Many speedboats come in very quickly to the private dock on the peninsula, particularly early and late in the day. Fly your diver's flag and ascend close to the wall all the way to the surface. Carry a knife and surface with a reserve of air; if caught in the kelp you will have time to cut your way free.

Telephone: Earls Cove Ferry Terminal.

Facilities: Restrooms at ferry terminal and café nearby. Air fills, accommodations, boat charters, rentals, and launching at Egmont.

Comments: Earls Cove is on the shady side of the channel. Take a light!

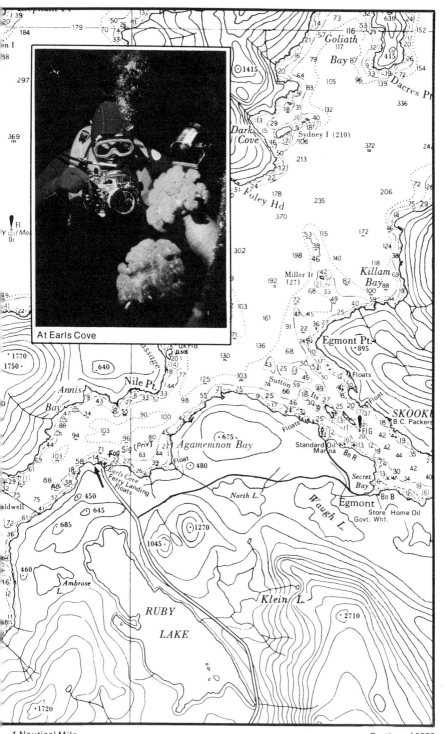

At Earls Cove

1 Nautical Mile

Portion of 3589

Skill: Intermediate and Advanced Divers

Why go: Only a few sites where you can dive from shore and see swimming scallops. Egmont is one of them. That's what lured me here — millions of swimming scallops.
A circuit of the islet reveals many other things, as well Beautiful red tube worms in the shallows. Gum boot chitons alabaster nudibranchs, lemon nudibranchs, shrimp and brigh orange branches of dead man's finger sponges. Deeper in th kelp, greenlings are all over the place. Sea peaches and trans parent sea squirts cling to the wall. Brilliant red-and-blac striped tiger rockfish hide under ledges. Swimming scallops do the bottom everywhere, raining up around you when you shadow passes over them. A real treat.
Once abundant octopuses, lingcod and rock scallops are nov seen only occasionally around the islet.

Access: From Langdale Ferry Terminal go 54 miles to Egmont Allow 1½ hours for the drive. Go north on Sechelt Highway 10 continuing 9½ miles past Garden Bay Road turnoff to Pende Harbour. At Egmont Road turn right and go east 4 miles to th government dock. Three or four cars can park at the left of th dock. You need about 15 minutes to swim from the dock to th islet.

Bottom and Depths: Rocky bottom undulates down quickly a around the islet. Bull kelp and lots of bottom kelp from 20 to 4 feet. Some big rocks, crevices and overhangs. Then the wal drops abruptly, levelling off to silty sand at 75 or 85 feet. Swim ming scallops all over the bottom on the channel side of th island.

Hazards: Current, boats and bull kelp. Dive near the slack Listen for boats and stay close to the side of the islet all the wa to the surface. Carry a knife and ascend with a reserve of air, s that if caught in the kelp you will have time to cut your way free

Telephones: 1. Bathgate's Store and Marina, inside.
                  2. Egmont Marina, 1 mile north.

Facilities: Air fills, charters, rentals and launching.

Comments: For years divers have not been welcomed at Eg mont. Residents said divers slaughtered the fish, both in and ou of season. This may be true because lingcod and rock scallop are rare around the island. Now that charters and boat rentals ar available, divers can easily spread out for spearfishing and col lecting shellfish. Let's keep the islet at Egmont for sightseeing
A sightseeing side trip on land for non-divers and divers, too is a hike to Skookumchuck Narrows to see the spectacle c Sechelt Rapids. All the water going into Sechelt Inlet pours pas here at every change of the tide. The path branches off sout from Egmont Road. Allow an hour to walk the trail to Th Narrows. Another hour to return.

Egmont

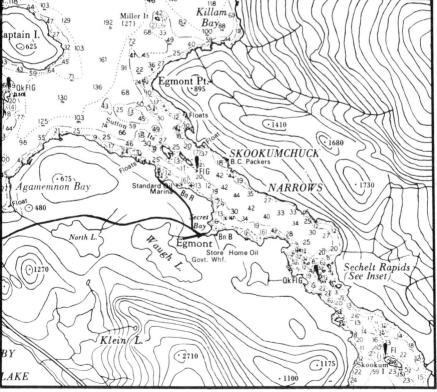

Portion of 3589

CHAPTER 3
Powell River and North

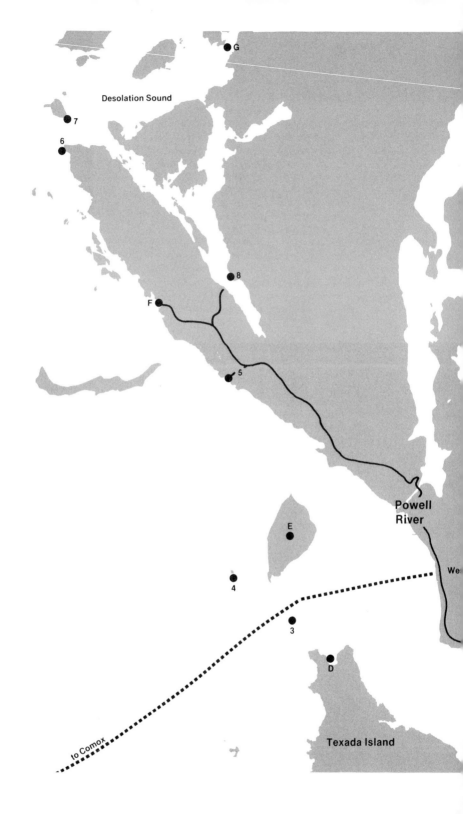

POWELL RIVER AND NORTH

Dives

1. Saltery Bay Campsite
2. Ball Point
3. Rebecca Rocks
4. Vivian Island
5. Emmonds Beach
6. Sarah Point
7. Kinghorn Island
8. Okeover Inlet

Places

A. Saltery Bay
B. Saltery Bay Picnic Site
C. Hardy Island
D. Blubber Bay
E. Harwood Island
F. Lund
G. Desolation Sound Marine Park

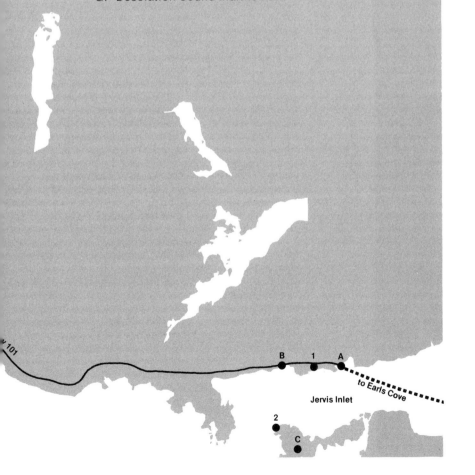

SERVICE INFORMATION*
Powell River and North

Charts: Canadian Hydrographic Service
- 3562 Redonda Islands
- 3589 Jervis Inlet and Approaches
- 3591 Cape Lazo to Discovery Passage

Tide and Current Tables: Canadian Hydrographic Service
Tide and Current Table, Volume 5

Emergency Telephone Numbers
R.C.M.P. Dial "0". Ask for Zenith 50,000

Powell River General Hospital 483-3211

●Air Station
Powell River Divers
6890 Gerrard Street, Westview
Powell River, B.C.
V8A 2T7
(604) 485-4526
*(Air station at 4307 Marine
Avenue, Westview. Telephone
Bob Briggs person-to-person
to arrange for air fills.)*

Beach Garden Resort Hotel
7074 Westminster Avenue
Westview
Powell River, B.C.
V8A 1C5
(604) 485-6267

●Boat Charters and Rentals
Beach Garden Resort Hotel
7074 Westminster Avenue
Westview
Powell River, B.C.
V8A 1C5
(604) 485-6267
or in Vancouver 669-7822
(Charters and rentals.)

Jasper
Powell River Divers
6890 Gerrard Street, Westview
Powell River, B.C.
V8A 2T7
(604) 485-4526
(Charters only.)

*All of this service information
is subject to change.

●Boat Launching
Saltery Bay Picnic Site
Highway 101, 2 miles west of
Saltery Bay Ferry Terminal

Westview
Foot of Courtenay Street
1 block north of Wharf Street

Lund
North end of Highway 101

Okeover Inlet
Foot of Malaspina Road

●Ferry Information
B.C. Ferry Information Centre
1045 Howe Street
Vancouver, B.C.
V6Z 1P6
(604) 669-1211
From Powell River: 487-9333
*(Ferries from Saltery Bay to
Earls Cove.)*

Ministry of Highways Ferries
950 Cumberland Road
Courtenay, B.C.
V9N 2E4
(604) 334-4432
*(Ferries from Westview,
to Comox.)*

●Tourist Information
Visitor's Information Bureau
6807 Wharf Street, Westview
Powell River, B.C.
V8A 1T9
(604) 485-4701

SALTERY BAY CAMPSITE
Shore Dive

Skill: All Divers and Snorkelers

Why go: If you're in the Powell River area you must dive Saltery Bay either coming or going. It's a beautiful wilderness site less than a mile from the ferry. And you're sure to see ratfish and big chimney sponges.
Common sights in the shallows at Saltery Bay are dozens of small blackeye gobies slipping about in the bottom kelp. We saw kelp crabs, orange dead man's finger sponges, sculpins, rockfish and lingcod. Move down the wall at your left into a garden of anemones — dahlia, snakelock and plumose. Or roll over the edge of the drop-off on your right covered with thousands of prickly green urchins and you're into the never-neverland of big chimney sponges curving down the steep slope like huge pipes. Ratfish, shimmering blue and silver, soar slowly beneath you, lazily rippling their pectoral fins. A red-and-black flash as a tiger rockfish dashes into a crevice. Decorator crabs. And white puffs of cloud sponges below. Deeper, yelloweye rockfish.
Saltery Bay is a beautiful dive. And accessible.

Access: From Powell River centre go 22 miles south on Highway 101 to Saltery Bay Provincial Campsite. If you reach the ferry you have gone ½ mile too far. Drive into Saltery Bay Campsite and park by a sign pointing to Beach Trail. Walk 300 yards along the wide trail through the woods to a rocky cove. Easy entry over a rocky beach. Swim straight out and down over the wall. Dive the right face to see sponges. The left face to see anemones.

Bottom and Depths: Rocky bottom covered with lettuce kelp undulates to 30 or 40 feet deep. Smooth rock rolls over into a drop-off 150 feet offshore. Crevices along the wall.

Hazards: Boats and poor visibility in summer. Listen for boats and ascend with a reserve of air staying close to the bottom all the way to shore, well out of the way of those boats. A compass is useful to guide you straight out and back over the undulating bottom.

Telephone: Saltery Bay Ferry Terminal.

Facilities: Camping, picnic tables and pit toilets at Saltery Bay Campsite. Lots of big trees around each campsite clearing. Boat launching less than 1 mile west of the campsite at Saltery Bay Picnic Site.

Comments: A family of five river otters sat on the rocks at the right of the cove, eating fish, the last time I dived at Saltery Bay. As we entered the water they slipped away. One more touch of wilderness that adds up to a good total experience. It's the sort of thing that happens at Saltery Bay.

Ratfish

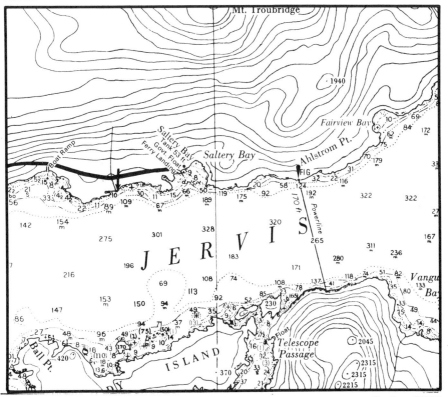

Skill: All Divers

Why go: Cloud sponges — the most fabulous I've seen anywhere — burgeon orange and yellow and white down the steep slopes of Ball Point at Hardy Island.
Pale green and golden bottom kelp decorates the shallows in gossamer folds veiling tube worms, seaperch, alabaster nudibranchs, sea lemons, painted greenlings, sea cucumbers, blackeye gobies and kelp greenlings. We saw seals and rock scallops.
Lots of lingcod, juvenile yelloweye rockfish, dahlia anemones, tiger rockfish, some chimney sponges and great puffs of cloud sponges like huge rainless clouds in a prairie sunset sky.
Life is in zones. Lots of animals in the kelp down to 40 feet. From 40 to 60 feet, not much except red-and-pink striped dahlia anemones. And then sponge, sponge, sponge. . . .
If you like cloud sponges — you'll love Ball Point!

Access: Ball Point is on the Jervis Inlet side of Hardy Island. From Saltery Bay go 2 miles south to Hardy Island. A small cove just south of Ball Point is convenient for anchoring or beaching your boat.

Bottom and Depths: Rocky bottom covered with kelp falls away in irregular ledges to 30 or 40 feet. Then a steep rock wall slopes down.

Hazards: Some current, small boats, broken fishing line and depth. Dive near the slack. Listen for boats and ascend close to the bottom all the way to shore, well out of the way of those boats. Carry a knife.

Telephone: Saltery Bay Ferry Terminal.

Facilities: Beautiful place for a wilderness picnic on the rocks at Ball Point. Picnic tables, pit toilets and launching ramp at Saltery Bay Picnic Site. Camping at Saltery Bay Provincial Park.

Comments: I went there because of the exclamations of another diver: "Fantastic! It would take three big barrels to hold one sponge!"

Giant cloud sponge

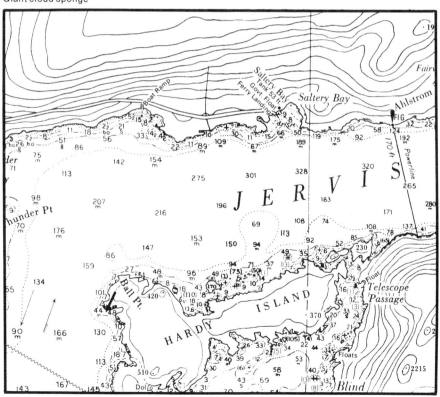

1 Nautical Mile

Portion of 3589

REBECCA ROCKS   **Tide Table:** Add 10 minutes
Boat Dive   onto Point Atkinson

Skill: Intermediate and Advanced Divers

Why go: Even a dark stormy day feels sunny and bright under water at the beautiful reef undulating around Rebecca Rocks. It's full of all the life a reef should have: lacy white nudibranchs, bright pink limpets, lemon nudibranchs, blue and orange sea stars and alabaster nudibranchs. We saw sea cucumbers and rock scallops. Lots of fish, too. Kelp greenlings everywhere. Lingcod, rock greenlings and millions of very small rockfish. A dogfish in the distance.
  At the south edge of the reef you can drop into sponge country — but to me Rebecca Rocks is most beautiful for the large area of shallow reef swarming with life.

Access: Rebecca Rocks is 1½ miles northwest of Texada Island in Algerine Passage, and 8 miles west of Westview and Powell River. Charter or launch in Westview and go to Rebecca Rocks. Anchor, do not tie onto marker. It is a federal offense to make fast to a marker or tamper with any aid to navigation. Dive anywhere around Rebecca Rocks, depending upon current direction.

Bottom and Depths: Rocky reef undulates from 30 to 50 feet deep. Ledges, overhangs and some bull kelp. Deep on the south side.

Hazards: Wind, current, boats, broken fishing line and deceptively undulating bottom. Rebecca Rocks is very exposed to wind from all directions. Pick a calm day. Dive on the slack. Listen for boats and ascend with a reserve of air; if you hear a boat you can stay down until it passes. Carry a knife. Use a compass and watch the current to determine your position, so that you do not stray too far from your boat.

Telephone: Blubber Bay Ferry Landing, Texada Island.

Facilities: None.

Comments: A satisfying dive for sightseers, hunters and photographers.

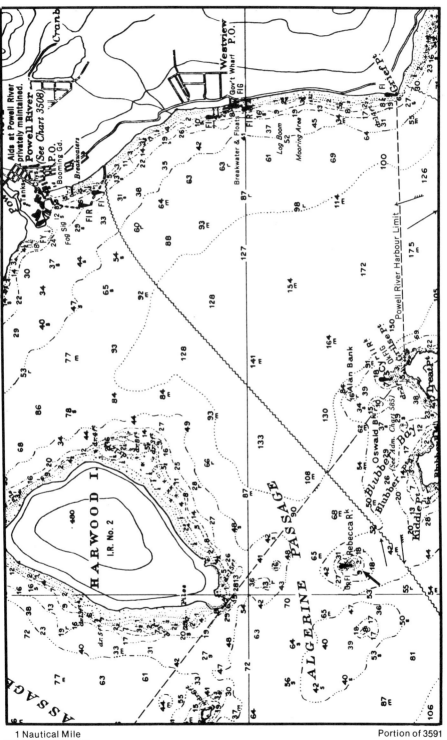

Aids at Powell River
privately maintained.
Powell River
(See Chart 3508)

Westview P.O.

Gov't Wharf

HARWOOD I.
I.R. No. 2

ALGERINE PASSAGE

1 Nautical Mile

Portion of 3591

VIVIAN ISLAND   **Tide Table:** Add 10 minutes
Boat Dive   onto Point Atkinson

Skill: Intermediate and Advanced Divers

Why go: Vivian Island is an exceptional three-in-one dive, including the remains of a wreck in 40 or 50 feet, a sheer sponge-covered wall dropping off to 115 or 125 feet, and abalones, rock scallops and huge limpets in the 20- or 30-foot shallows.
The wreck of the *Shamrock*, a 61-ton tug which ran aground and sank, is scattered down the southeast wall. The shape of a ship is gone — but bricks from the boilers lie in 40 or 50 feet of water for all divers to see. Who last fired those boilers? Did those people have to swim to the cactus-covered island? What happened to the anchor and the chain winch machinery that have not been recovered? Are they hidden at the bottom of the wall?
Drifting down the wall the gorgeous variety of sponges pushed away all thoughts of the *Shamrock*. Lots of lemon yellow cloud sponges. Some orange. Many fluffy white ones. Vase sponges, too. Snakelock anemones flow from the wall. I saw the orange-and-white stripes of one juvenile yelloweye rockfish hiding in a sponge. Another hanging near the wall. Lots of quillback rockfish.
It's a richly decorated wall — fabulous both going down and coming up. So much to see in the shallows — in the land of urchins, rock scallops, and abalones. You could easily use two tanks of air.

Access: Vivian Island is at the southern end of Shearwater Passage, 10 miles west of Westview and Powell River and 1½ miles west of the southern tip of Harwood Island. Charter or launch in Westview. Anchor near the southeast corner of the island in 40 or 50 feet of water and go down.

Bottom and Depths: Rocky bottom with some boulders at 20 or 30 feet slopes off quickly to 40 or 50 feet and the edge of the creviced wall. Sheer wall drops straight down to 115 or 125 feet. Clean white sand at the base of the wall.

Hazards: Wind, current, boats, depth and broken fishing line. Vivian Island is very exposed to winds from all directions. Pick a calm day. Dive near the slack. Listen for boats and ascend with a reserve of air; if you hear a boat you can stay down until it passes. Carry a knife.

Telephone: Blubber Bay Ferry Landing, Texada Island.

Facilities: None at this uninhabited island.

Comments: Before moving on, row ashore and explore cactus-covered Vivian Island, but be careful not to disturb nesting gulls.

Out of Westview to Vivian Island

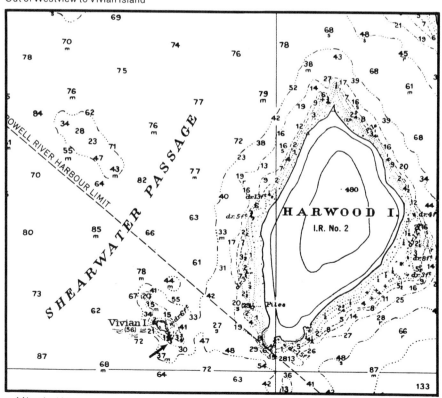

1 Nautical Mile

Portion of 3591

EMMONDS BEACH
Shore Dive

Skill: All Divers

Why go: Emmonds Beach is good for a quick dive anytime day or night, and you can see life typically found both on sand and on rock walls.
Emmonds Beach presents few complications. Access is easy over a narrow pebble beach. The swim is a moderate one to the place where the bottom drops off quickly. At low tide it is particularly easy. A large rock that dries on eight-foot tides is 100 yards offshore. The drop-off is just the other side of this rock. When I dived at Emmonds Beach, because the rock was not visible, we set our compasses, swam out over slowly sloping sand till we reached the rock, then up and over and down the other side where we dropped onto narrow ledges stairstepping steeply down.
Swimming over the sand we saw fuzzy burrowing anemones, sculpins, hermit crabs, flounders and shiners. Masses of rockfish hang all around the rock. Over the rock and down the wall we saw sunflower stars, mustard-yellow trumpet sponges, tiger rockfish, lacy white burrowing cucumbers and several lingcod. Small cloud sponges start at 70 or 80 feet. And the inevitable emerald-eyed ratfish hover by the wall.
Ratfish and cloud sponges — almost always part of the Powell River area underwater scene.

Access: From Powell River centre go 10½ miles to Emmonds Beach. Head north on Highway 101 for 9½ miles until you see a small sign at an unpaved road saying Emmonds Road. Turn left and go towards the sea, keeping left at two forks. Go just over 1 mile to the end of the road. Walk 50 feet to the pebbly beach and swim straight out. If the solitary rock is not visible, set your compass on a 150-degree heading towards Vivian Island which is 6 miles away or towards the right of the tip of Harwood Island. Swim straight out 100 yards before going down. Descend and continue on a straight line under water. Go over the rock and down the wall.

Bottom and Depths: Smooth sand slopes to 30 or 40 feet at the base of the solitary round rock. The top of the rock dries on 8-foot tides. Beyond the rock, the creviced wall drops away in steep, narrow ledges.

Hazards: Boats and poor visibility, in summer. Small boats are moored immediately over the dive site. Listen for boats and ascend with a reserve of air; if you hear a boat you can stay down until it passes. If the tide is low, ascend up the side of the rock and swim to shore on the surface.

Telephone: Lund Breakwater Inn, 4½ miles north.

Facilities: None.

Comments: Emmonds Beach is a pleasant place for picnics and a popular site for local divers. A very civilized feeling on this pebbly crescent of beach encircled by summer homes.

Beyond the boat, the rock; Harwood Island in distance

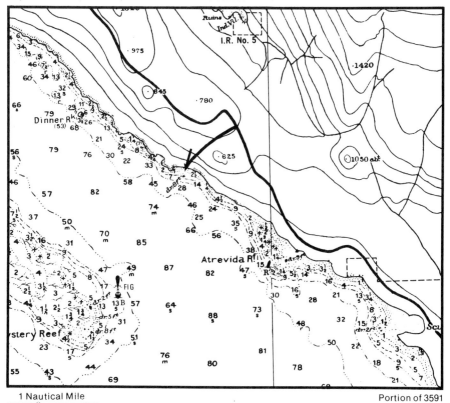

1 Nautical Mile

Portion of 3591

SARAH POINT
Boat Dive

Tide Table: Add 10 minutes
onto Point Atkinson

Skill: Intermediate and Advanced Divers

Why go: Sarah Point is at the top of Malaspina Peninsula, the northernmost inhabited mainland coast connected by road and ferry to southwestern British Columbia. It's wilderness. It drops quickly. And I like that.
  Stark is the word to describe Sarah Point. Angular rocks drop away quickly. Large and beautiful dahlia anemones reach sticky red fingers into the current flowing past the dark rock wall. Big chimney sponges start at 60 feet. Cloud sponges, just over the lip of the narrow ledge at 80 feet. At 100 feet, cloud sponges are magnificent.
  When I dived at Sarah Point large fish were noticeably absent. Perhaps because it was summer, the surface waters were warm and the fish had gone deep. But we did see numerous small rockfish, some kelp greenlings, sea pens in the sand on the narrow ledges, and nudibranchs in the kelp.

Access: Sarah Point is at the top of Malaspina Peninsula, 21 miles north of Powell River and 6 miles beyond Lund, the end of the road going north. Charter out of Westview or launch at Lund and follow the coast 6 miles northwest through Thulin Passage. Anchor or land in a small cove just south of Sarah Point and go down.

Bottom and Depths: Angular broken rock covered with bottom kelp slopes quickly to 30 feet. Some boulders. Narrow ledges drop in steep stairsteps down, down and down. And silt over all.

Hazards: Boats, current and broken fishing line. Small boat traffic is extremely heavy in late summer at this popular salmon-fishing site. Fly your diver's flag, listen for boats and ascend close to the bottom all the way to shore, well out of the way of those boats. Dive near the slack. Carry a knife and ascend with a reserve of air; if caught in transparent fishing line you will have time to cut your way free.

Telephone: Lund Breakwater Inn.

Facilities: None at this wilderness point. Government dock, launching ramp, café and grocery store at Lund.

Comments: Bring along your salmon rod for after the dive.

Sarah Point with Kinghorn Island behind

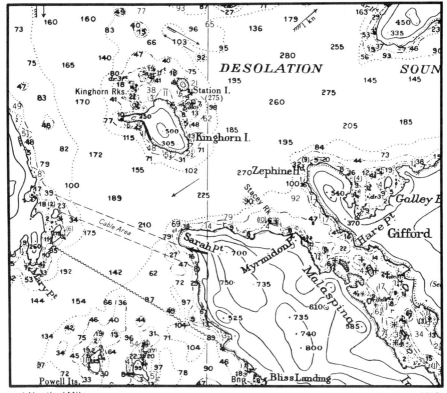

1 Nautical Mile

Portion of 3591

KINGHORN ISLAND   **Tide Table:** Add 10 minutes
         Boat Dive   onto Point Atkinson

Skill: All Divers

Why go: Kinghorn Island sits in the entry to Desolation Sound at the doorway to wilderness waters.
Desolation Sound — the name alone was enough to lure me north. I looked at the chart, saw the drop-off and knew I had to dive at Kinghorn Island. Large broken rock falls away rapidly through several zones of wilderness waters. Surface water barely covers the profusion of swirly pink tube worms by the rocky shore. Slightly deeper, large golden-brown and filmy green bottom kelp hides nudibranchs, painted greenlings or convict fish, and gum boot chitons, the largest chitons in the world. We saw masses of cucumbers, an occasional abalone, brittle stars, rock scallops, kelp greenlings and seaperch. One perfect rose star. Then we slid through thousands of silvery fish flashing in unison at the 25-foot thermocline, the point where the water changes from surface warm to year-round cold.
Below the thermocline, clusters of pink dahlia anemones. Some white ones with pink and purple tentacles. Others with red spots on white stalks. Their colours stand out against the stark, dark rocks. Chimney sponges begin at 60 feet. Looking inside we saw a small decorator crab. Cloud sponges start at 100 feet. And big lingcod lurk in the cold, dark depths.
If you like wilderness — both under water and above — you'll like Kinghorn Island.

Access: Kinghorn Island is in Desolation Sound just above the tip of Malaspina Peninsula, 22 miles north of Powell River and 7 miles beyond Lund, the end of the road going north. Charter out of Westview or launch at Lund and follow the coast 7 miles northwest through Thulin Passage, past Sarah Point to the southeast corner of Kinghorn Island. Anchor or beach your boat and go down.

Bottom and Depths: Large broken rocks covered with bottom kelp down to 30 or 40 feet. From here the fall away is rapid, and as deep as you want to go.

Hazards: Some current. Dive near the slack.

Telephone: Lund Breakwater Inn.

Facilities: None at uninhabited Kinghorn Island. Government dock, launching ramp, café and grocery store at Lund.

Comments: Wilderness camping at nearby Desolation Sound Marine Park, but absolutely no facilities — not even drinking water. Just a place to pitch your tent.

Brittle star

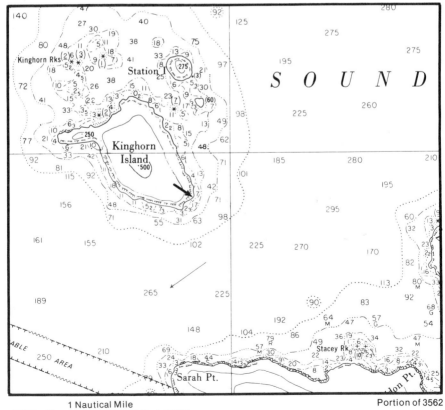

1 Nautical Mile

Portion of 3562

OKEOVER INLET
Boat Dive

Skill: All Divers

Why go: You want to see a feather star swim. You're looking for a protected inlet because the wind is blowing outside. Or maybe you just love drop-offs. Any one of these is good enough reason to go to Okeover Inlet.

When I dived at Okeover Inlet we tumbled through the incredibly still waters, slipping over large smooth boulders falling like gentle giant steps. Slow somersaults through space. The motion was enough to make the dive. At 80 feet lacy pink-beige feather stars reach out from the smooth rock wall. I pulled one off to see it swim, and wished I had a movie camera to keep the exerience of this delicate feather duster come-to-life. On our way up I wished for a still camera to photograph the brilliant orange and red long-stemmed hydroids that look like tulips clustering under the overhangs. Sea peaches, tube worms, moon jellyfish, orange encrusting sponges and strange mussels all live at Okeover Inlet.

This wall has been well-known by both line and spear fishermen for years. Huge lingcod and yelloweye rockfish used to live here, but I did not see even one. Because these fish are territorial, an area can be overfished. Millions of fish must be hiding up and down the long, deep rock-walled inlet, but not at this wall. Spear fishermen will find good hunting by fanning out all over Okeover Inlet.

Access: The wall is on the east side near the southern tip of Okeover Inlet. From Powell River go 12 miles to Okeover Inlet. Heading north on Highway 101, go 10 miles to Malaspina Road. Turn right and drive 2 miles to the government dock and launching ramp at the end of the road. Launch and go 1 mile to the high rock bluff on the opposite shore. Tie up by the rocks and go down.

Bottom and Depths: Big boulders drop off steeply in huge giant steps. Dive as shallow or as deep as you want.

Hazards: Boats and poor visibility, in summer. Listen for boats and ascend close to the rock wall all the way to the surface, well out of the way of those boats.

Telephone: Okeover Inlet, by the restaurant at the top of the hill above the government wharf.

Facilities: Government dock and launching ramp.

Comments: Good winter dive.

Rock bluff at Okeover Inlet

CHAPTER 4
Campbell River to Kelsey Bay

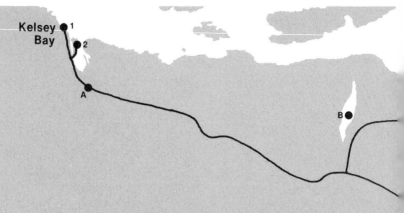

CAMPBELL RIVER TO KELSEY BAY

Dives

1. Kelsey Bay Breakwater
2. Ship Breakwater
3. Rock Bay
4. Chatham Point
5. Menzies Bay
6. Tyee Spit
7. Big Rock
8. Willow Point
9. Whiskey Point
10. Copper Cliffs
11. Rebecca Spit
12. Wa-Wa-Ki Beach
13. Viner Point
14. Mitlenatch Island

Places

A. Sayward
B. McCreight (Bear) Lake
C. Seymour Narrows
D. Seymour Lookout
E. Tyee Plaza
F. Quathiaski Cove
G. April Point
H. Heriot Bay
I. Drew Harbour
J. Black Creek
K. Miracle Beach

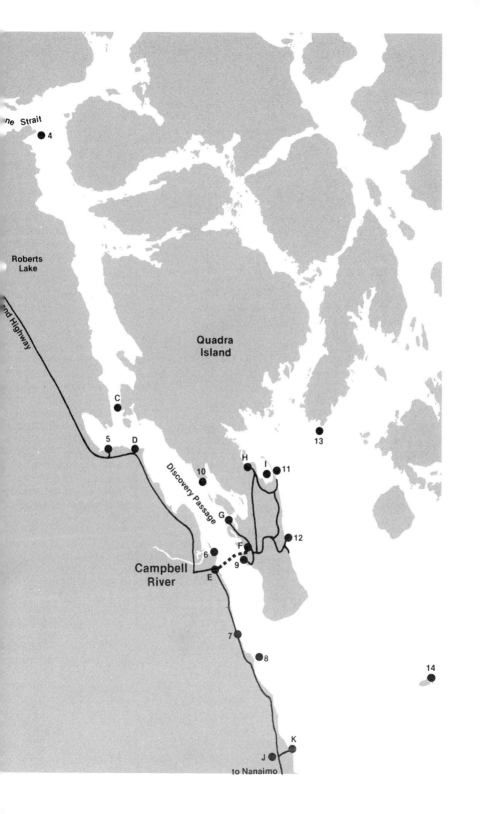

SERVICE INFORMATION*
Campbell River to Kelsey Bay

Charts: Canadian Hydrographic Service
- 3556 Plans in the Vicinity of Discovery Passage
- 3565 Discovery Passage
- 3566 Johnstone Strait (Eastern Portion)
- 3567 Johnstone Strait (Central Portion)
- 3591 Cape Lazo to Discovery Passage
- 3594 Discovery Passage, Toba Inlet and connecting channels

Tide and Current Tables: Canadian Hydrographic Service *Tide and Current Table, Volume 6.*

Emergency Telephone Numbers
R.C.M.P. Dial "0". Ask for Zenith 50,000

R.C.M.P. (Campbell River) 286-6221
Ask for *staff* member immediately.

•Air Stations
Seafun Divers
1761 Island Highway
Campbell River, B.C.
V9W 2A8
(604) 287-3622

Tyee Marine and Fishing
Supplies
880 Island Highway
Campbell River, B.C.
V9W 2C3
(604) 287-2641

**•Boat Charters, Rentals
and Launching
Quadra Island**
April Point Lodge
West side Quadra Island
Box 1
Campbell River, B.C.
V9W 4Z9
(604) 285-3329
(*Rentals only.*)

Rebecca Spit Marine Park Ramp
East side Quadra Island
(*Launching only.*)

Taku Resort Ramp
East side Quadra Island
(*Launching only*)

Campbell River
Campbell River Lodge
1760 Island Highway
Campbell River, B.C.
V9W 2E7
(604) 287-7446
(*Charters and rentals.*)

Campbell River Sportfishing
Tyee Plaza
Box 321
Campbell River, B.C.
V9W 5B1
(604) 287-3032
(*Charters and rentals.*)

The Dolphins Resort
4125 Discovery Drive
Campbell River, B.C.
V9W 4X6
(604) 287-3066
(*Rentals only.*)

Foot of Larwood Road
Willow Point
(*Launching only.*)

Haida Inn
1342 Island Highway
Campbell River, B.C.
V9W 2E1
(604) 287-7402
(*Charters only.*)

Painter's Lodge
1625 McDonald Road
Box 460
Campbell River, B.C.
V9W 5C1
(604) 286-6201
(*Charters and rentals.*)

A.J. Parkyn Boat Charter
Small boat harbour, ¼ mile
south of Tyee Plaza
Box 331
Campbell River, B.C.
V9W 5B6
(604) 287-7775 or 285-3578
(*Charters only.*)

Safari Queen Charters
Box 65
Campbell River, B.C.
V9W 4Z9
(604) 287-8501
(*Charters only.*)

Seaside Motel
87 South Island Highway
Campbell River, B.C.
V9W 1A2
(604) 287-3343
(*Rentals and launching.*)

Tyee Spit Ramp
Campbell River, B.C.
(*Launching only.*)

South of Campbell River
Miracle Beach Resort
R.R. 1
Black Creek, B.C.
V0R 1C0
(604) 337-5171
(*Charters, summer only.*)

Pacific Playgrounds Ltd.
R.R. 1
Saratoga Beach
Campbell River, B.C.
V9W 3S4
(604) 337-5600
(*Rentals and launching.*)

Shelter Bay Resort
R.R. 2
Campbell River, B.C.
V9W 5T7
(604) 923-5338
(*Rentals and launching.*)

•**Ferry Information**
Ministry of Highways Ferries
950 Cumberland Road
Courtenay, B.C.
V9N 2E4
(604) 334-4432
(*Ferries from Campbell River
to Quadra Island.*)

•**Tourist Information**
Visitor's Information Centre
Tyee Plaza
1235 Island Highway
Campbell River, B.C.
V9W 2C5
(604) 286-6261

Campbell River Museum
Tyee Plaza
P.O. Box 101
Campbell River, B.C.
V9W 4Z9
(604) 287-3103

*All of this service information is
subject to change.

KELSEY BAY BREAKWATER
Shore Dive

Tide Table: Add 30 minutes onto Alert Bay

Skill: All Divers and Snorkelers

Why go: Popular for good reasons — several different diving activities and safe, current-free diving are available anytime day or night at the Kelsey Bay Breakwater.
Old bottles and fishing lures lie around the frothy white anemone-covered piers of the government dock. Rockfish shelter under the riprap of the breakwater. Others swim free-wheeling through the nearby bull kelp. When diving here my buddy found a prawn at 30 feet. I'm not sure whether that means there's prawning here at night. But I do know there are lots of other different things to see and photograph. Painted greenlings, often called convict fish, dahlia anemones, quillback rockfish, copper rockfish, and urchins are some of the animals we saw during a quick dive at Kelsey Bay Breakwater. Both the breakwater and dock are protected and out of the main sweep of current through Johnstone Strait.

Access: From Campbell River go 49 miles to Kelsey Bay. Head north on Island Highway. Kelsey Bay Breakwater is at the very end of the road going north. You can't miss it. Jump off the dock and dive along the outside of the breakwater.

Bottom and Depths: Small rocks, with bull kelp attached and overlaid with silt, lie around the dock pilings and along the base of the breakwater made of angular broken rocks. It's 10 or 20 feet deep down to 40 or 50.

Hazards: Small boats, bull kelp and broken fishing line. Fly your diver's flag. I flew mine from the corner of the dock and this is the only place I have ever come up from a dive and had a boater come to say she had noticed my flag. Apparently everyone in Kelsey Bay recognizes the diver's flag. Listen for boats, as well, and ascend close to the breakwater or a piling. Carry a knife and surface with a reserve of air; if caught in kelp or line you will have time to cut your way free.

Telephone: Kelsey Bay Store.

Facilities: Government dock and store.

Comments: Advanced divers may want to go to the second point west beyond the dock to beautiful wilderness water where you'll see small cloud sponges under overhangs at only 25 feet. Large sponges at 40 feet. And lingcod. Because it is current-swept, dive on the slack.

Kelsey Bay Breakwater

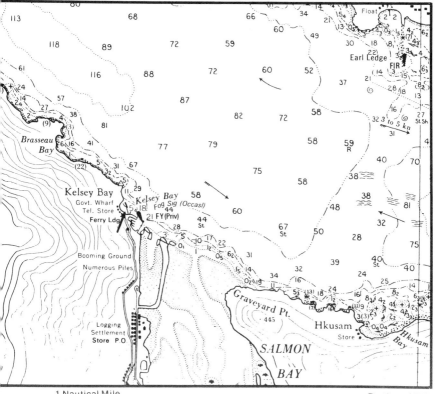

113   68   66 34 14 Float 2 1 2

118 89   72   59 60 49   30 18 62

61 116 88 72 60 52   Earl Ledge 4

24 57 102 87   37 FIR

27 38   82 72 58 28 18 13

2 (9) 81   32 3 to 5 kn St Sh

Brasseau 16 41 77 79 58 59 R 31

Bay (22) 5 31 67 75 58 40 70

32 29   58   38

Kelsey Bay 11 Kelsey Bay 58   48 38 81
Govt. Wharf Fog Sig (Occasl) 60   32
Tel. Store 18 44   67 St 50 28 75
Ferry Ldg 21 FY(Priv) 44 St   39 40 St 40
   28   24

Booming Ground 31 32 24 25
Numerous Piles 34 16   8

Graveyard Pt. Hkusam Hkusam
Logging 445 Store Bay
Settlement
Store P.O   SALMON

    BAY

1 Nautical Mile

Skill: All Divers and Snorkelers

Why go: Under the shadow of the breakwater of ships there is a
amazing amount of colourful life and the site is so shallow an
accessible.
     Masses of colourful dahlia anemones cluster on the rock
bottom under the first ship. They look like a delicious heap of pal
green and pink bonbons. Other anemones encrust the hull. W
saw small golden-dotted shrimp. A pair of grass-green slim ee
like gunnels, 18 inches long. Then another. And another. Almo
completely hidden in the kelp by their colour and shape, the
looked like diminutive moray eels.
     While swimming to the next ship, we saw thousands of sma
silvery fish flying up out of the smooth white sand like a glitterin
silver lamé curtain. Heady stuff. So unexpected and beautifu
     If lucky you may see giant skates. They're found on this kind c
bottom — and you often hear stories of giant skates at Kelse
Bay.

Access: From Campbell River go 49 miles to Kelsey Bay. Headin
north on Island Highway as you come into Sayward you will se
houses rising on the hill on your left. Only 2/10 mile farther tur
right onto a paved road which becomes a narrow gravel dyke. Thi
curves ½ mile through the water to the ship breakwater. Park b
the side of the road and pick a ship. We started with the first on
on our right. The entry is easy over the sand.

Bottom and Depths: Smooth sand from 10 to 30 feet deep. Muc
of the area dries on very low tides. Small rocks and lettuce kel
under the ships.

Hazards: Shallow depths make staying down difficult. Wear extr
weight.

Telephone: Kelsey Bay Store, by the government dock.

Facilities: None.

Comments: A surprisingly different and pleasant dive. I must g
there again.

Ship Breakwater

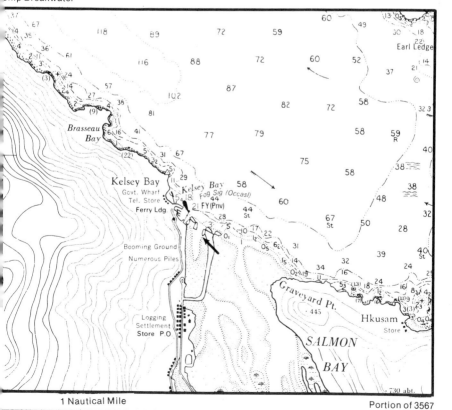

1 Nautical Mile

Portion of 3567

ROCK BAY
Shore Dive

Skill: All Divers and Snorkelers

Why go: Both shallow diving in the kelp and deep diving to sponge land are available at this current-free site where you can dive at any time of day. It is excellent for photography with water that's usually clear and with a good mixture of marine life. Entry is easy. Plus there's the chance of a valuable bottle find.
Back in the late 1800's there was a large logging community at Rock Bay. A big hospital was built there in 1906 or 1907. Though the hospital was abandoned some years ago when the logging operation closed down, right up until the mid-1950's the hospital plumbing was still connected and you could still take a cold shower. It was made for divers! Today not much remains of the large community at Rock Bay: the hospital ruins, a government dock, and old bottles hidden under the sea.
When diving here I saw lots of marine life. Kelp greenlings delicate nudibranchs, a bright red blenny with blue markings, lingcod, a huge octopus sprawled across a rock as though sunning himself, and a cloud sponge so orange it was almost red. One blue swimming scallop clapped right up to my buddy's mask and almost lost my regulator from laughing.

Access: From Campbell River go 34 miles to Rock Bay. Head north on Island Highway. Five miles past Roberts Lake Resort is a small road signposted to Rock Bay. The sign is small and easy to miss. If you cross Amor de Cosmos Creek you have gone 200 yards too far. Turn right down Rock Bay Road and drive over its potholes for 12 miles to Rock Bay, where you can drive almost to the water's edge.

Bottom and Depths: It's easy to make either a shallow or a deep dive at this site. Rocky bottom scattered with boulders and bull kelp slopes gently to 30 or 40 feet. Some sand between the boulders. Then a rapid drop to as deep as you want to go.

Hazards: Boats, current and bull kelp. Listen for boats and ascend close to the bottom all the way to shore. Stay away from the point and you will have no trouble with current. Carry a knife and ascend with a reserve of air, so that if caught in the kelp you will have time to cut your way free.

Telephone: Roberts Lake Resort, on Island Highway 5 miles south of Rock Bay Road turnoff.

Facilities: Government dock and room to pitch your tent, but no fresh water or other facilities. Parking space for eight or ten cars.

Comments: This popular checkout site is still unspoilt and has much to offer all divers.

Rock Bay

1 Nautical Mile

Portion of 3594

CHATHAM POINT   **Tide Table:** Subtract 30 minute:
Boat Dive   from Owen Bay

Skill: Intermediate and Advanced Divers

Why go: Lingcod — large and small — live at this current-swep
rounded reef. Giant red urchins and a scattering of swimming
scallops.
   You may meet "Minkie", a 40-foot long pike whale who lives
near Chatham Point.

Access: Chatham Point is at the top of Discovery Passage, 2¾
miles east of Rock Bay.
   Charter out of Campbell River or hand launch an inflatable o
other small boat over the beach at Rock Bay, 34 miles northeas
of Campbell River. Head north on Island Highway. Five miles
past Roberts Lake Resort is a small gravel road signposted to
Rock Bay. The sign is small and easy to miss. If you cross Amo
de Cosmos Creek you have gone 200 yards too far. Turn righ
down Rock Bay Road. Drive 12 miles along this rough gravel roac
filled with potholes to Rock Bay, where you can drive almost to
the water's edge and launch an inflatable or other hand-launch
able boat. Then go east to Chatham Point and land on the rocks
halfway between the shore and the lighthouse marking Beave
Rock. Descend and dive towards Beaver Rock.

Bottom and Depths: The reef between the rocks and lighthouse
rounds down quickly to a sandy bottom at 50 or 60 feet. Much
deeper beyond the light. In summer thick bull kelp grows on the
reef.

Hazards: Current and bull kelp. Dive on the slack. At this site the
current is *always* running in one direction or the other and you
must dive on the slack when the current at least slows down. Do
not rely on the tables alone. Sit by the water and watch for the
current to slacken, then go in. On large tidal exchanges a pickup
boat is advisable. Current combined with kelp can be really
hazardous. Carry a knife and ascend with a reserve of air; if
caught in the kelp you will have time to cut your way free.

Telephone: At Roberts Lake Resort, on Island Highway 5 miles
south of Rock Bay Road turnoff.

Facilities: None at Chatham Point. Charters out of Campbell
River.

Comments: Chatham Point, where Discovery Passage turns
northwest into Johnstone Strait, is an unspoilt wilderness of big
fish and worth every ounce of effort required to dive.

Male lingcod on guard

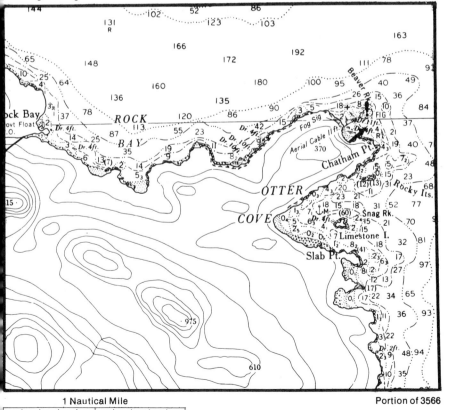

1 Nautical Mile

Portion of 3566

Skill: All Divers and Snorkelers

Why go: Menzies Bay is the closest place to Campbell River where you can dive anytime of day without considering the current.

Right next to Seymour Narrows and some of the wildest currents on our coast, Menzies Bay is a marked contrast to the usual Campbell River area site. Here you find easy access to an easy, current-free dive. It's a pleasant place to snorkel over the sand and eelgrass to look for Dungeness crabs, especially in winter.

Maybe giant skates, flounders, hermit crabs, and moon snails, too.

Access: From Campbell River centre go 10 miles to Menzies Bay. Heading north on Island Highway 1½ miles past Seymour Narrows Viewpoint, just before a wooden bridge, you come to a small unpaved road turning off to the right. If you reach Bloedel, you've gone too far. Turn right down the small road, then angle left a short way to the water. Park at the side of the road. Very easy entry over level sand beach.

Bottom and Depths: Shallow sand bottom with lots of eelgrass and silt. When I dived here it was only 7 to 12 feet deep for a long way out. We swam about ⅓ mile offshore before the sand sloped sharply to 40 feet.

Hazards: Small boats, in summer, and shallow depths make for difficulty in staying down. Listen for boats and ascend with a reserve of air. Wear extra weight.

Telephone: Duncan Bay Store, 6½ miles south.

Facilities: None. Lots of parking space at the side of the road. Air fills, accommodations, charters, rentals, and launching in Campbell River.

Comments: A nice spot for a picnic among old pilings on the beach.

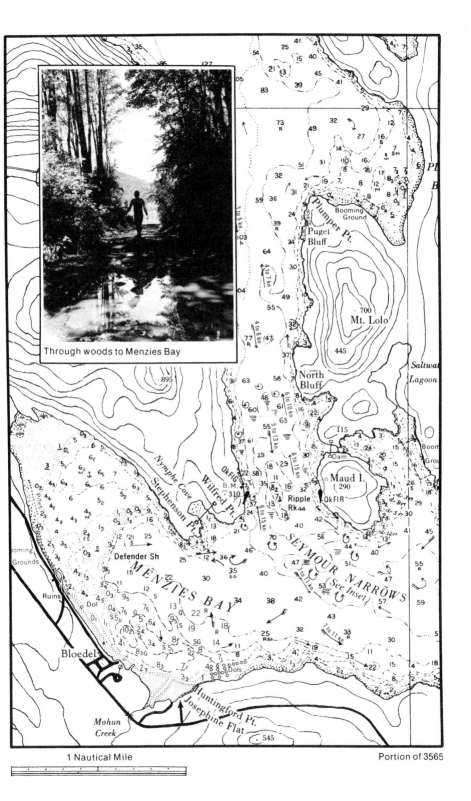

Through woods to Menzies Bay

1 Nautical Mile

Portion of 3565

Skill: All Divers

Why go: Night diving under the wharf at Western Mines — or Argonaut Wharf as it is still called by most — is a favourite of local divers. When seeing the spot I realized why night diving here is a favourite. It would be unsafe to dive at Tyee Spit by day, because of so many small salmon-fishing boats going past, and so many people fishing from the wharf. At night, too, the resident octopuses come out — I saw four on one night dive here. Fishing lures are more easily seen in the flash of your light at night. These can be profitable salvage. Lots of animal life, too. Decorator crabs, red and pink dahlia anemones and white plumose anemones on the pilings. Flatfish all over the bottom. Some red Irish lords and a cabezon. And masses of gray cod on the sand beyond the pilings.

Enormous skates used to live here. I've heard of 125-pound giant skates with a seven-foot wingspan at Tyee Spit, but haven't seen any. They must have been hunted out. Today all that's left of them is the legend.

Access: From Campbell River centre go 2 miles to the site on Tyee Spit. Heading north on Island Highway, 1 mile past the ferry and Tyee Plaza turn right at Spit Road. Go 1 more mile onto the spit. Just past the large buildings and wharf on your right is a beach with a very easy entry over the sand. Swim to the wharf and go down.

Bottom and Depths: Twenty- to 30-foot sandy bottom gradually deepens as you move into the channel. Rocks around the pilings where octopuses hide.

Hazards: Small boats, current, and broken fishing line. Use a compass or stay close to the pilings. Listen for boats and ascend with a reserve of air up a piling, well out of the way of those boats. Dive near the slack. Carry a knife.

Telephone: 1300 block Island Highway, between Spit Road and Tyee Plaza.

Facilities: Sandy beach, launching and roadside parking at Tyee Spit. Air fills, accommodations, charters, and rentals in Campbell River.

Comments: Tyee Spit is a good place to see an octopus — but just look. Love 'em and leave 'em so they don't disappear like the giant skates. Octopuses can be killed by rough handling.

Entry point at Tyee Spit

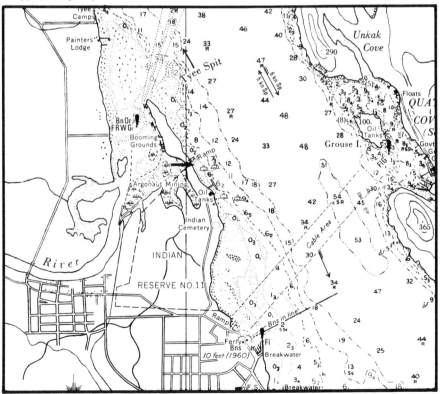

1 Nautical Mile

Portion of 3565

Skill: Intermediate and Advanced Divers

Why go: A good mix of fish live on the reef in front of Big Rock and because of the back eddies Big Rock is quite a safe place to dive. Since the bottom is varied the fish are varied, too, but visibility is usually poor. We could see only five to eight feet. The water was murky with silt stirred up by the current and back eddies. Through the silt we saw a great variety of fish. Red Irish lords, small lingcod, flounders and rockfish. An octopus, too. Urchins, giant barnacles and pale orange sponges, nourished by the current, cling tight to the rocks. And lots of purply-red geoduck (pronounced gooey-duck) clams poke up through the silt, with a strand of bull kelp attached to each one. I watched, fascinated, as we drifted slowly down current touching first one then another siphon. As we touched them each geoduck retracted into the sand, pulling the kelp down with it.

Access: From Tyee Plaza in Campbell River centre, go 3 miles south on Island Highway to Big Rock. Three or four cars can park about 100 feet south of Big Rock. Enter the water, swim out and drift to a point opposite Big Rock Motel. The most interesting part of the reef is from here on south. Swim to the kelp and go down.

Bottom and Depths: The reef at Big Rock parallels the shore and is about 20 or 30 feet deep. Gently sloping sandy bottom scattered with rocks and some boulders forms the reef. Bull kelp attached to the rocks and geoducks.

Hazards: Current, boats and bull kelp. Current is not as vicious at Big Rock as at many other Campbell River sites because of that back eddy. However, plan to dive on or near the slack. Salmon fishing boats are a consideration at Big Rock as at most Campbell River sites. Listen for boats and ascend with a reserve of air; if you hear a boat you can stay down until it passes. Carry a knife so that if caught in the kelp you can cut yourself free.

Telephone: Big Rock Store.

Facilities: Rentals, launching, and accommodations. Air fills and charters in Campbell River.

Comments: A good quick dive!

Red Irish lord

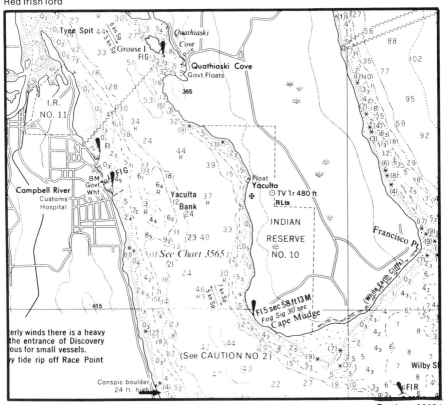

erly winds there is a heavy
the entrance of Discovery
ous for small vessels.
y tide rip off Race Point

1 Nautical Mile

Portion of 3594

Skill: Advanced Divers and Snorkelers

Why go: Willow Point Reef is a favourite of spear fishermen —
particularly free divers. One look at this large horseshoe-shaped
reef tells you why. It is filled with fish. And it is only 12 feet deep.
When diving here I saw lots and lots of small lingcod and kelp greenlings. The big
ones are probably here, too, but I missed them. You may see
an octopus, as well. White smooth rocks are covered with green
urchins, giant red urchins and red algae crusting over them. Bright
yellow sponges the size of bricks, a yellow nudibranch feeding on
the sponge and large tennis ball sponges.
In addition to lots of life there is lots of current. Willow Point is
very dangerous. Though the reef is close to shore and looks easy
to dive, it is very treacherous. The current sweeps past Willow
Point laterally out into the middle of Discovery Passage. For that
reason Willow Point is a boat dive.
But all this current also feeds the fish.

Access: From Campbell River go 4½ miles south to Willow
Point. Campbell River is a boat-oriented place. Launching ramps
line the coast for all the salmon fishing boats. When here we
launched very close to Willow Point. Heading south on Island
Highway one block past Willow Point Shopping Centre at Adams
Road, you reach Larwood Road on your right and a road with no
name on your left. We launched at this road end and went north to
Willow Point. The horseshoe-shaped reef is 100 yards offshore
and can be spotted by the bull kelp growing on it. Dive from a
"live" boat with a pickup person who will follow you if the current
sweeps you away.

Bottom and Depths: Rocky bottom with bull kelp from 10 or 20
feet deep.

Hazards: Current, bull kelp and boats. Dive on the slack with a
pickup boat. Carry a knife. Listen for boats and ascend with a
reserve of air; if you hear a boat you can stay down until it passes.

Telephone: Island Highway and Adams Road, 1 block north of
Larwood Road.

Facilities: Launching at foot of Larwood Road, just south of
Willow Point. Air fills, accommodations, charters, and rentals in
Campbell River.

Comments: For dedicated spear fishermen only!

Pickup boat at foot of Larwood Road

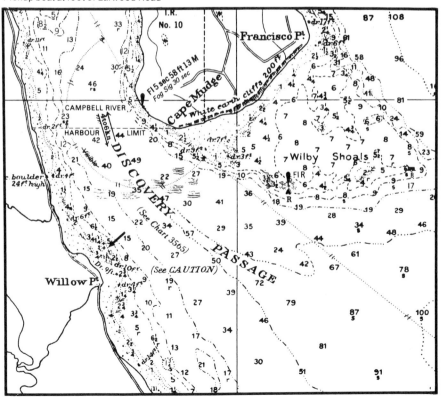

1 Nautical Mile

Portion of 3591

Skill: Advanced Divers

Why go: The most accessible burst of colour and life in the Strait of Georgia is splashed across the bottom at Whiskey Point. As though created by a painter gone deliriously wild, tiers of rock covered with colour cascade in gradual folds from the shores of Quadra Island down into Discovery Passage. Swimming under water close to the side each rock I put my hand on is yet another colour — red, yellow or purple. Strawberry anemones so close together that you can write your name in them. I touched some and they closed. Changed from fuzzy multi-tentacled flowers to small bright red berries in a basket. Purple algae are splashed on the rocks. Bright blue starfish. And sunny yellow encrusting sponges over all the rest.

Masses of life — some different from any I have seen elsewhere — covers the clean-swept rocky bottom. Strange sponges that look like tennis balls. Others like orange bath sponges. Purple-spotted Puget Sound king crabs. Snakelock anemones. Barnacles the size of baseballs, some abalones and some rock scallops. Fish hide under every ledge. Lingcod, red Irish lords and kelp greenlings so tame they'll eat from your hand.

A fantastic dive.

Access: From Campbell River it is a 15-minute ferry ride and 5-minute drive to Whiskey Point. Take the ferry from downtown Campbell River to Quathiaski Cove on Quadra Island. From the ferry Whiskey Point is on your right. Driving off the ferry, go up the hill. Take the first right, following signs towards Cape Mudge Village. Go ½ mile and turn right again. Continue 1 more mile to the end of the road. Two or three cars can park. You are now looking back at Quathiaski Cove. Enter the water and snorkel south towards Whiskey Point. Work your way south under water to a most beautiful wall at 50 feet.

Bottom and Depths: Clean-swept rocks tier down from 30 to 60 to 90 feet. A lot of bull kelp.

Hazards: Current, up-currents, down-currents, whirlpools, small boats and bull kelp. Though you can reach this dive by road, the spot is so dangerous that on most days you should have a "live" boat ready in case you are swept away. Strong swimmers can dive here without a pickup boat on slight tidal exchanges. One rule of thumb suggested as safe by a local diver is a change of two feet, or less. Be geared up and ready one hour before slack tide, watching and waiting for the current to slow down. Best on an ebbing tide when there is less of a rip at Whiskey Point. Ascend along the bottom all the way to shore, well out of the way of the many salmon fishing boats. Carry a knife and ascend with a reserve of air so that if caught in a down-current or kelp you will have time to free yourself.

Telephones: 1. Quathiaski Cove Ferry Landing.
                2. "Q" Cove Store, up the hill from the ferry.

Facilities: None at Whiskey Point. Boat rentals and accommodations on the west side of Quadra Island. Air fills, charters, and launching in Campbell River.

Comments: A gorgeous dive. Well worth waiting for the right moment!

Whiskey Point from above Quathiaski Cove, Quadra Island

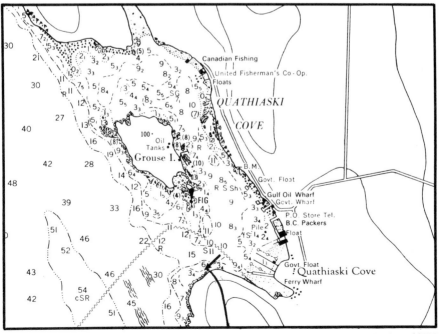

0   Scale of Feet   2000

Portion of 3556

Skill: Intermediate and Advanced Divers

Why go: Copper Cliffs, an immense rock wall rising over 300 feet straight up out of Discovery Passage, is almost too big to be true. Under water everything is equally big. Everything from boulders to cloud sponges to lingcod. Enormous white plumose anemones cluster on the steep rock wall that falls away before you. A school of huge black rockfish swims past. Excellent visibility makes everything seem even more oversized. Giant boulders, dotted with thousands of tiny orange cup corals are scattered on a large ledge below. In only 60 feet of water big clumps of cloud sponges with small skinny brittle stars oozing out of them, billow between mammoth rocks.

During one dive here my buddy and I saw fifteen or twenty lingcod, each three or four feet long, and lots of red-and-black striped tiger rockfish. Peeping under a large boulder covered with strawberry anemones on its north face, we saw a mosshead warbonnet. Even this was large for its species, about four inches long. I looked up while swimming up-current and there was a yelloweye rockfish, commonly called red snapper, staring at me. Colourful giants fed by giant currents. Grandiose!

Access: Copper Cliffs is on the west side of Quadra Island in Discovery Passage, 3½ miles north of Campbell River.

Charter or rent on the west side of Quadra Island or in Campbell River. Or launch your own boat at Tyee Spit and go north to that immense rock wall. You cannot miss it. Good diving from the cleft in the middle of the wall to the cove at the north end of it.

Bottom and Depths: Clean-cut rock wall drops away 50 or 60 feet to a ledge with large boulders. Then the bottom drops away again to over 100 feet.

Hazards: Current and small boats. Dive precisely on the slack. Be geared up and ready one hour before slack tide, watching and waiting for the current to slow down. Very powerful currents run through here. On large tidal exchanges leave a pickup person in your boat, in case you are swept away. This is a popular salmon-fishing area: in summer, small boats come within inches of the wall. Listen for boats and ascend close to the wall all the way to the surface well out of the way of them.

Telephone: 1300 block Island Highway, between Spit Road and Tyee Plaza.

Facilities: None at Copper Cliffs. Rentals and accommodations on west side of Quadra Island. Air fills, charters, and launching in Campbell River.

Comments: Eagles in the sky and cormorants on the cliffs.

Fishing boat at Copper Cliffs

1 Nautical Mile

Portion of 3565

Skill: All Divers

Why go: If you've missed slack or just want a straightforward Quadra Island dive, Rebecca Spit is a good place to go. Access is easy. Swim out over the gently sloping rocky bottom scattered with eelgrass, bottom kelp, Japanese weed and orange and white burrowing cucumbers. You'll find a single shallow ledge dropping from about 20 feet to 40 feet. I was told an octopus lives at the ledge, but I didn't see it. They're probably easier to find at night. However, a lot of other little things are easy to find at Rebecca Spit. We saw many small rockfish, some kelp greenlings, flounders, lots of little hermit crabs, a couple of rock scallops, a spider crab and red rock crabs. Beyond the ledge legions of sea pens sprout from the sharply sloping sand.

Access: From Campbell River you are a 15-minute ferry ride and a 5-mile drive away from Rebecca Spit Provincial Park. Take the ferry from downtown Campbell River to Quathiaski Cove on Quadra Island. Coming off the ferry drive up the hill and go straight ahead for 1 mile. At the junction, turn left and go north on Heriot Bay Road 3½ miles towards Drew Harbour. Turn right and go less than 1 mile to Rebecca Spit Park. Drive as far out the spit as you can go and park on the east side. Walk a few feet from your car to the rocky beach. Then swim straight out and down to find the ledge.

Bottom and Depths: Rocky bottom with eelgrass, bottom kelp and Japanese weed slopes gently to 20 feet. Here a rock ledge drops to 40 feet. Beyond the ledge, sharply sloping sand.

Hazards: Small boats, especially in summer and fall. This is a popular salmon-fishing spot. Use a compass, listen for boats and ascend with a reserve of air, keeping close to the bottom all the way up to shore.

Telephone: We-Way-Akay Campground, just outside Rebecca Spit Park.

Facilities: Picnic tables, launching ramp and pit toilets at Rebecca Spit Park. Camping and hot showers at campground close by.

Comments: Fresh oysters on the beach at Rebecca Spit. Oysters are edible all year, but the best ones are found at very low tide in springtime.

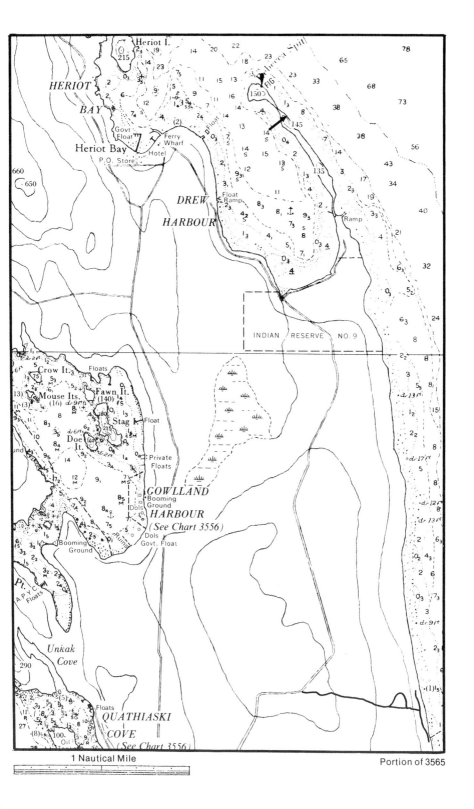

HERIOT I.

HERIOT

BAY

Heriot Bay
P.O. Store

Govt
Float

Ferry
Wharf

Hotel

DREW

HARBOUR

Float
Ramp

Ramp

INDIAN RESERVE NO. 9

Crow It.

Floats

Mouse Its.

Fawn It.

Stag I.

Doe
It.

Float

Private
Floats

GOWLLAND

Booming
Ground

HARBOUR

(See Chart 3556)

Dols

Dols

Govt. Float

Ruins

Booming
Ground

Pt. C

Floats

Unkak
Cove

Floats

QUATHIASKI

COVE

(See Chart 3556)

Oil

1 Nautical Mile

Portion of 3565

Skill: All Divers

Why go: There's a wide cross-section of life at this relatively current-free site where access is so easy — Wa-Wa-Ki Beach. Descend from shore through several zones in rapid succession. Rocky bottom with bull kelp from shore to 30 feet gives way to silty sand from 30 to 75 feet. Steep clay undercut with inconspicuous narrow slit ledges slopes off at 75 to 100 feet. This range of substrate provides homes for many different kinds of animals. Lingcod, tiger rockfish and octopuses live down the slitted slope. And yelloweye rockfish, commonly called red snapper, down deep. Moving up to the silty sand we saw a giant nudibranch, beige with blue tips, and numerous inch-long nudibranchs, white with beige tips.

But my favourite part of this dive is up in the kelp at 20 or 30 feet. Here, just hang still in the water and let the life come past. The rockfish accepted us as part of their scene and swam right up to our masks. One rockfish yawned at us, his thick yellow lips opening wide. A huge cloud of herring passed around us. I wondered which way was up and which down. We saw dozens of needlefish, stroked a red Irish lord, and saw a hermit crab living in an orange sponge which had dissolved the crab's adopted shell home.

Access: From Campbell River to Wa-Wa-Ki Beach on Quadra Island is a 15-minute ferry ride and a 3-mile drive. Take the ferry from downtown Campbell River to Quathiaski Cove. Coming off the ferry, drive up the hill and continue straight for 1 mile. At the junction turn left and go along Heriot Bay Road to Smith Road, a good gravel road. Turn right and continue along Smith Road. Go down the steep hill and take the first turn to your left. Three or four cars can park close to the 5-foot walk to the rocky beach. An easy entry over large rocks. Swim straight out and down.

Bottom and Depths: Rocky bottom to bull kelp at 20 or 30 feet. Silty from 40 to 75 feet. Narrow slit ledges down to 100 feet.

Hazards: Small fishing boats. Listen for boats, use your compass and ascend along the bottom all the way to shore well out of the way of those boats.

Telephones: 1. "Q" Cove Store, up hill from ferry.
2. Quathiaski Cove Ferry.

Facilities: None at Wa-Wa-Ki Beach. Camping, hot showers, accommodations, and launching at Drew Harbour, east side of Quadra.

Comments: Beautiful wild rocky beach strewn with logs bleached silver by the sun and sea.

Wa-Wa-Ki Beach

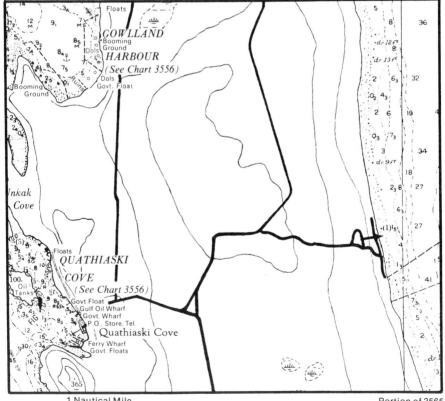

1 Nautical Mile   Portion of 3565

Skill: All Divers

Why go: A stark, dark wall lush with red snakelock anemones drops off to nowhere. Really different from other Campbell River area sites. Deeper, there are sponges and juvenile yelloweye rockfish. A ratfish followed us around like a pet. The wall dropped off cleanly and deep and we felt as though we were in a huge room. Up in the shallows we saw large sea peaches, bright orange tube sponges, large dead man's finger sponges, lots and lots of nudibranch eggs and orange solitary cup corals in only five feet of water.
We had gone to Viner Point expecting to find rock scallops and abalones. But we found something else that was good. The drop-off.

Access: Viner Point is at the southernmost tip of Read Island, 3½ miles east of Quadra Island. Launch at Heriot Bay or Drew Harbour on the east side of Quadra Island and go northeast to Viner Point. A small cove on the southeast tip of Read Island is convenient for anchoring. Dive on the wall north of this cove.

Bottom and Depths: Rocky bottom covered with bottom kelp down to 30 or 40 feet. Then a smooth wall sheers off down to deep water over 100 feet.

Hazards: Small fishing boats. Viner Point, like many other good dive sites in the Campbell River area, is popular with salmon fishermen. Listen for boats and ascend close to the wall and rocks right up to the surface.

Telephone: Heriot Bay Inn.

Facilities: None at wild and untamed Viner Point. Launching ramps at Drew Harbour on the east side of Quadra Island. Picnic tables and pit toilets at Rebecca Spit Park. Camping and hot showers at campground next to park. Trailer hookups, nearby. Accommodations and store at Heriot Bay.

Comments: In late summer and fall, take your fishing rod to catch a salmon on your way home.

Snakelock anemone

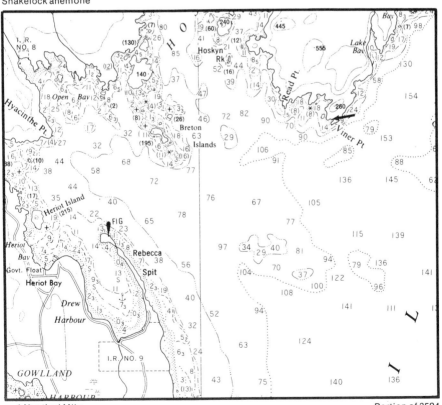

1 Nautical Mile

Portion of 3594

Skill: All Divers

Why go: Mitlenatch Island is a showcase for abalones, the best place to see them in the Strait of Georgia. Abalones are protected. It is illegal to take any within 1000 feet of Mitlenatch Island; consequently, their future is guaranteed. Abalones are difficult to see. Look on the rocks for a black fuzzy mantle surrounding a mottled shell. A ring of small holes rims one side of the shell. Abalones emit puffs of blue "smoke" from these holes when frightened. They're fascinating animals as they glide over beautiful kelp-covered shallows around Mitlenatch Island. Big seaperch glisten blue and yellow around the spring-green bottom kelp. We saw schools of black and silver fish. Large red-and-maroon striped painted greenlings guard their territories. Rockfish crowd the crevices. Small orange cup corals, dahlia anemones and huge rock scallops dot the rocks. Big orange sea peaches are bulbous under narrow ledges. Furry white anemones fuzz the space under other overhangs. Orange encrusting sponges spread across the rocks. Abalones glide over any rocks that are left.

A couple of dogfish were cruising around the base of this island where abalone is king.

Access: Mitlenatch Island stands alone in the middle of the Strait of Georgia. It is 7¾ miles east of Miracle Beach Provincial Park where Nature House is headquarters for visitors to Mitlenatch.

The island can be reached from Miracle Beach, from Campbell River, or even from the other side of the Strait of Georgia. But pick a calm day. Wind, current and fog are all potential hazards which can make crossing to Mitlenatch difficult. Charter or launch at Miracle Beach Resort and go east 7¾ miles to Mitlenatch. Or charter out of Campbell River and go to Mitlenatch. Anchor in Northwest Bay, Southwest Bay or Harlequin Cove. Excellent shallow diving below the "hide" on the north side of the island and all along the reef going north.

Bottom and Depths: Rocky reef extends ¾ mile northwest. The 25- to 35-foot deep reef covers a large area.

Hazards: Current. Dive on the slack.

Telephone: Black Point Store, Island Highway.

Facilities: Picnic tables and pit toilets. No overnight camping at Mitlenatch. Camping, hot showers, trailer hookups, accommodations, charters, rentals and launching at Shelter Bay, Saratoga Beach or Miracle Beach.

Comments: Thousands of sea birds breed at Mitlenatch: glaucous-winged gulls are most numerous; pelagic cormorants are on the high southern bluffs; and pigeon guillemots fly under water. During summer, park naturalists take guided tours around Mitlenatch Nature Park.

The "hide"

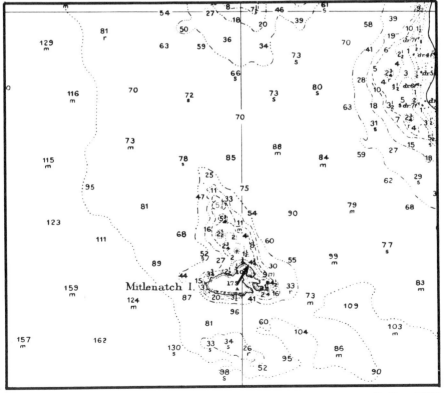

1 Nautical Mile

Portion of 3591

CHAPTER 5
Nanaimo, Hornby Island, and South to Sansum Narrows

NANAIMO, HORNBY ISLAND, AND SOUTH TO SANSUM NARROWS

Dives

1. Heron Rocks
2. Norris Rocks
3. Ford Cove Reef
4. Madrona Point
5. Cottam Point
6. Dolphin Beach
7. Nankivell Point
8. Amelia Island
9. Yeo Islands
10. Sunrise Beach
11. Jesse Island
12. Snake Island
13. Round Island
14. Evening Cove
15. Coffin Island
16. Maple Bay Reef
17. Octopus Point

Places

A. Fanny Bay
B. Buckley Bay
C. Denman Island
D. Qualicum Beach
E. Nanoose Bay
F. Schooner Cove
G. Northbrook Mall
H. Departure Bay
I. Gabriola Island
J. Dodd Narrows
K. Yellow Point
L. Ivy Green Park
M. Ladysmith
N. Saltair
O. Duncan
P. Cowichan Bay

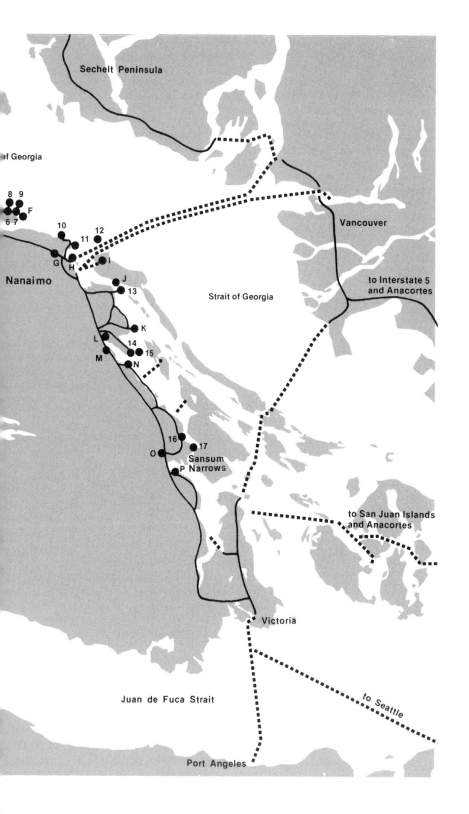

Sechelt Peninsula

of Georgia

8 9
F
6 7

10   12
  11
G H   i

Nanaimo

J
13

Strait of Georgia

K

L
   14
M   15
   N

Vancouver

to Interstate 5
and Anacortes

16
O   17
   Sansum
P Narrows

to San Juan Islands
and Anacortes

Victoria

to Seattle

Juan de Fuca Strait

Port Angeles

SERVICE INFORMATION*
Nanaimo, Hornby Island,
and South to Sansum Narrows

Charts: Canadian Hydrographic Service
- 3452 Haro Strait to Stuart Channel
- 3456 Approaches to Nanaimo Harbour
- 3470 Plans in the Vicinity of Saltspring Island
- 3471 Plans in Stuart Channel
- 3579 Burrard Inlet to Discovery Passage
- 3585 Nanoose Harbour and Approaches
- 3590 Ballenas Islands to Cape Lazo

Tide and Current Tables: Canadian Hydrographic Service
Tide and Current Table, Volume 5

Emergency Telephone Numbers
R.C.M.P. Dial "0". Ask for Zenith 50,000

Rescue Coordination Centre (Victoria) 388-1543

R.C.M.P. (Nanaimo) 754-2345

R.C.M.P. (Duncan) 746-4125

●Air Stations
Hornby Island
Bob Zielinski
R.R. 1, Ford Cove
Hornby Island, B.C.
V0R 1Z0
(604) 335-2807

North of Nanaimo
Seafun Divers
4740 Roger Street
Port Alberni, B.C.
V9Y 3Z2
(604) 723-5511

Nanaimo
Seafun Divers
300 Terminal Avenue
Nanaimo, B.C.
V9R 5C8
(604) 754-4813

South of Nanaimo
Duncan Scuba Sea
2682 James Street
Duncan, B.C.
V9L 2X6
(604) 748-3931 or 748-8690

●Boat Charters, Rentals
and Launching
For Hornby Island
East side of Denman Island
Beside ferry landing

Fanny Bay Fishing Resort
R.R. 1
Fanny Bay, B.C.
V0R 1W0
(604) 335-2439
(Rentals in summer only. No charters. Launching nearby.)

Pacific Village Motel Resort
R.R. 1
Fanny Bay, B.C.
V0R 1W0
(604) 335-2333
(Charters, rentals and launching.)

North of Nanaimo
Beachcomber Marina
Claudet Road, off North West
Bay Road
Box 21, R.R. 1
Nanoose Bay, B.C.
V0R 2R0
(604) 468-7222
(*Charters and launching only.*)

Clayton's Fishing Resort
Off North West Bay Road
R.R. 1
Nanoose Bay, B.C.
V0R 2R0
(604) 468-7111
(*Charters, rentals and launching.*)

Schooner Cove Marina
Dolphin Drive
Box 9, R.R. 1
Nanoose Bay, B.C.
V0R 2R0
(604) 468-7044
(*Launching only.*)

Wright Mate Charters
Box 10, Marina Way
R.R. 1
Nanoose Bay, B.C.
V0R 2R0
(604) 468-7602
(*Charters only.*)

Nanaimo
Bell Buoy Marina
1340 Stewart Avenue
Nanaimo, B.C.
V9S 4E1
(604) 753-2514

Brechin Point Civic Ramp
Foot of Brechin Road
Departure Bay
(*Launching only.*)

Leeshore Resorts Ltd.
Box 285
Nanaimo, B.C.
V9R 5K9
(604) 754-2879
(*Charters only.*)

Seafun Divers
300 Terminal Avenue
Nanaimo, B.C.
V9R 5C8
(604) 754-4813
(*Charters only.*)

South of Nanaimo
Anchor Marina Ltd.
Cowichan Bay, B.C.
V0R 1N0
(604) 746-5424
(*Rentals only.
Launching nearby.*)

End of Barnes-Murdock Road
Off Cedar Road
(*High tide only.*)

Coho Marina
Cowichan Bay, B.C.
V0R 1N0
(604) 746-7909
(*Rentals and charters.
Launching nearby.*)

Cove Yachts Ltd. (1976)
Birds Eye Cove
6261 Genoa Bay Road
R.R. 1
Duncan, B.C.
V9L 1M3
(604) 748-8136
(*Rental sailboats only.*)

Government Wharf
Ladysmith
(*Launching only.*)

Government Wharf
Maple Bay
(*Launching only.*)

Genoa Bay Marina
R.R. 1
Duncan, B.C.
V9L 1M3
(604) 746-7621
(*Rentals and launching.*)

Inn of the Sea
R.R. 1
Yellow Point Road
Ladysmith, B.C.
V0R 2E0
(604) 245-4257
(*Rentals only.*)

Kumalockasun Campsite
Coffin Point
R.R. 1
Ladysmith, B.C.
V0R 2E0
(604) 245-3397
(*Gravel launching.*)

Pier 66
Cowichan Bay, B.C.
V0R 1N0
(604) 748-8444
(*Rentals only.
Launching nearby.*)

Seaview Marina and Motel
R.R. 2
Ladysmith, B.C.
V0R 2E0
(604) 245-3768
(*4 miles south of Ladysmith at
Saltair. Rentals in summer
only. No charters.*)

Wilcuma Lodge and Resort
R.R. 2
Cobble Hill, B.C.
V0R 1L0
(604) 748-8737
(*Rentals. Charters in summer
only. No launching.*)

●Ferry Information
B.C. Ferry Information Centre
1045 Howe Street
Vancouver, B.C.
V6Z 1P6
(604) 669-1211
From Nanaimo: 753-1261
(*Ferries from Departure Bay to
Horseshoe Bay.*)

C.P. Rail Ferries
Nanaimo Terminal
Front Street
Nanaimo, B.C.
V9R 5J3
(604) 754-2331
(*Ferries from Nanaimo to
Vancouver.*)

Ministry of Highways Ferries
301 - 190 Wallace Street
Nanaimo, B.C.
V9R 5B1
(604) 754-2111
(*Ferries from Nanaimo to
Gabriola Island.*)

Leeshore Resorts Ltd.
Box 285
Nanaimo, B.C.
V9R 5K9
(604) 754-2879
(*Pedestrian ferries from
Nanaimo to Newcastle Island.*)

●Tourist Information
Nanaimo Tourist Bureau
100 Cameron Road
Nanaimo, B.C.
V9R 2X1
(604) 753-1191

*All of this service information is subject to change.

Skill: All Divers

Why go: Heron Rocks is one of the most magnificent of shore dives. The fish life is fantastic. And masses of invertebrates, too. Have you ever, on one dive, seen a pair of wolf eels, lots of little rockfish, ten large lingcod, numerous yelloweye rockfish, ratfish, tiger rockfish, pink-and-white giant nudibranchs, red dahlia anemones, orange cup corals, staghorn bryozoans, rock scallops, gum boot chitons, blood stars, rose stars and giant red urchins? That's Heron Rocks at Hornby Island.

The bottom is interesting too — even if there were no life. At the tide line, wave-carved rocks drop in shallow ledges making smooth scooped out places where you can sit to put on your gear. Under water, beautiful corridors through the rocks give an almost lacy feeling to the slope.

Access: Going to Hornby Island is complex. Arranging to stay at Heron Rocks is complex, too. The campsite is a cooperative campsite and tent camping is available only if the site is not filled with members. After May 15th reservations open to non-members. Apply to
Mrs. Joan Breece, Reservations
The Heron Rocks Camping Cooperative Association
141 Woodward Avenue
Sausalito, California
94965
(415) 332-2453
Heron Rocks is 66 miles and two 15-minute ferry rides from Nanaimo. Heading north on Island Highway, go 51 miles beyond Northbrook Mall in Nanaimo and 23 miles past Qualicum Beach to the Denman Island Ferry at Buckley Bay. Cross to Denman Island in 15 minutes and drive 7 miles across Denman following signs to the Hornby Island Ferry. Then cross to Hornby, another 15-minute ferry ride.

At Hornby Island drive off the ferry and head up the hill to your left. Continue 5½ miles along the main road to the Co-Op Store. Turn right onto St. Johns Road. Almost 2½ miles past the Co-Op Store you will come up and over and down a big hill to a small sign saying "Harrison Brown, Heron Rocks". Turn left and go to The Heron Rocks Camping Cooperative. Walk from the parking area south on a path to the water. There is an obvious point sticking out on your left. Enter just to the right of it and work your way under water around left to the point.

Bottom and Depths: Smooth rocky shore scattered with small round rocks graduates to sand. At 15 or 25 feet deep, eelgrass. Then a steep sand slope to the wall and huge boulders. Ledges and overhangs down to the base of the wall at 65 or 75 feet. Some bottom kelp.

Hazards: Wind from the southeast in winter can make entry difficult.

Telephone: The Co-Op Store.

Facilities: Tent camping only. Air fills available at Ford Cove, ½ mile west of Heron Rocks.

Comments: Both camping and diving are worth the advance planning required to dive at this beautiful conservation area.

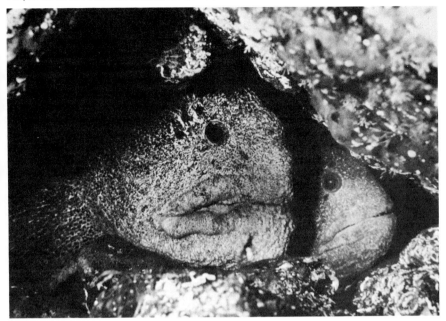

Pair of wolf eels

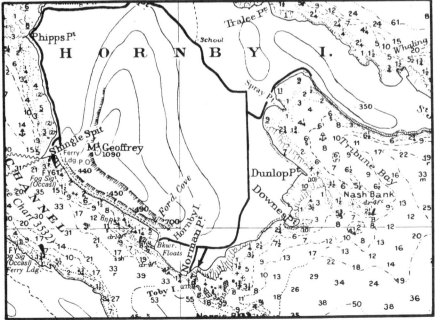

1 Nautical Mile

Portion of 3590

Skill: Intermediate and Advanced Divers

Why go: A circuit of Norris Rocks is sure to produce supper or a mass of photographs — whichever you want. Norris Rocks swarms with lingcod. On one dive here we saw at least fifty, the first one in twenty feet of water while we were starting down. Sightseeing is excellent, as well. In addition to the usual pretty white, brown and beige plumose anemones under the overhangs, sea cucumbers, rockfish and kelp greenlings, there are gorgeous orange and white sea stars, dahlia anemones, sea pens, orange cup corals, rock scallops and brittle stars. But the dive is most memorable for lingcod.

Access: Norris Rocks site is 1½ miles southeast of Norman Point at the southern tip of Hornby Island. Launch at the ramp by the ferry landing on the east side of Denman Island and go southeast a couple of miles to Norris Rocks. Or rent a boat or launch on Vancouver Island at Deep Bay or Fanny Bay and go 3 to 6 miles past the southern end of Denman Island and past Norman Point at the southern tip of Hornby Island to Norris Rocks.
From Nanaimo go 51 miles by road and take a 15-minute ferry ride to Denman Island. Heading north on Island Highway, 14 miles past Qualicum Beach you are at the Deep Bay turnoff, then Fanny Bay, where you can rent or launch. Or take the 15-minute ferry ride to Denman Island then drive 7 miles to another launching ramp at the ferry landing on the east side of Denman. From here, only 2 miles southeast to Norris Rocks.

Bottom and Depths: Shallow rocky bottom covered with lettuce kelp. Some bull kelp undulates around the rocks down to 40 or 50 feet. Some big boulders and sand between.

Hazards: Current. Dive near the slack.

Telephone: Grocery store, Hornby Island Ferry Landing.

Facilities: None at Norris Rocks. Air fills nearby.

Comments: Excellent hunting, but before spearfishing be sure to check the season. Based on 1977 regulations, lingcod season is closed from December 1st through the last day of March. This date might be extended. See current regulations.

Norris Rocks off snowy shores of Norman Point, Hornby Island

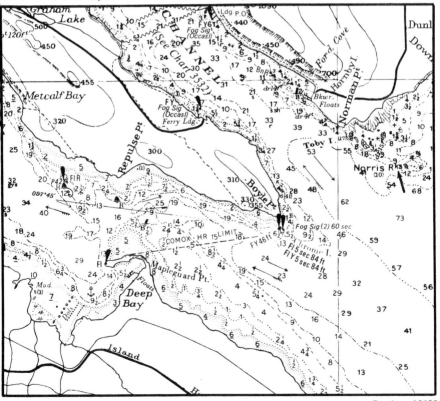

1 Nautical Mile

FORD COVE REEF　　　　**Tide Table:** Point Atkinson
Boat Dive

Skill: Intermediate and Advanced Divers

Why go: An underwater garden opens before you on the channel side of the reef at Ford Cove.
When diving here I had the sensation of everything being pretty, pretty! And the fish! There seem to be big fish everywhere. Lingcod and large cabezons. Rockfish and kelp greenlings all over the place. Schools of black rockfish. Dogfish mixed in with the rest. And we even saw a little grunt sculpin.
Gorgeous forests of sea pens tilt out of pools of sand between the rocks. We saw sea peaches. Giant red urchins. Decorator crabs. And a couple of swimming scallops. A jungle of bull kelp, white and orange burrowing cucumbers and lettuce kelp so fine it's like nylon stockings.
Flounders and eelgrass flourish in the sand between the reef and Hornby Island.

Access: Ford Cove Reef is ½ mile northwest of Ford Cove at the southwest end of Hornby Island, in Lambert Channel between Denman and Hornby Islands, and has a marker on it. If you have a paddleboard, an inflatable or other small boat that you can lift over the bushes, launch at Ford Cove.
Ford Cove is 67 miles and two 15-minute ferry rides from Nanaimo. Heading north on Island Highway, 51 miles beyond Northbrook Mall and 23 miles past Qualicum Beach, you reach the Denman Island Ferry at Buckley Bay. Cross to Denman Island in 15 minutes and drive 7 miles across Denman Island following signs to Hornby Island Ferry. Then cross to Hornby, another 15-minute ferry ride. At Hornby Island drive off the ferry and head up the hill to your left. Continue 5½ miles along the main road to the Co-Op Store. Turn right onto St. Johns Road and go 3 more miles to Ford Cove. Launch by the dock and go north 200 yards to the marker on the reef. Do not tie onto marker. It is a federal offense to make fast to a marker or tamper with any aid to navigation.
If you have a larger boat, launch at the ramp next to the ferry landing on the east side of Denman Island and go 1½ miles northeast across the water to Ford Cove. Or launch or rent a boat on Vancouver Island at Deep Bay or Fanny Bay and go 3 to 6 miles to the southern end of Denman Island and north to Ford Cove.

Bottom and Depths: Rocky reef bottoming out to sand at 30 or 40 feet parallels the shore of Hornby Island. The reef dries on 14-foot tides.

Hazards: Current, boats and bull kelp. Dive on the slack. Listen for boats and ascend close to the reef and marker all the way to the surface. Carry a knife and ascend with a reserve of air so that if caught in the kelp you will have time to cut your way free.

Telephone: Grocery store, Hornby Island Ferry Landing north of Ford Cove.

Facilities: Small store at Ford Cove. Air fills nearby.

Comments: An excellent "mixed bag" at Ford Cove.

Ford Cove

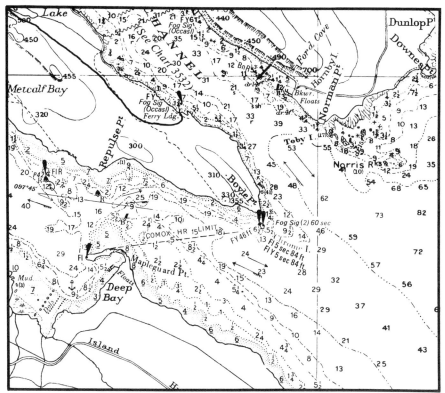

1 Nautical Mile

Portion of 3590

Skill: All Divers and Snorkelers

Why go: An octopus every five minutes — that's what I saw here! And they are shallow. There are wolf eels, too, out deeper. But you have to look hard for both. Madrona Point, commonly called Arbutus Point, is rimmed with beautiful rocky ledges and overhangs making all kinds of places for octopuses to hide. Crabs — a ready meal for octopuses — scurry over the sand which comes up to the rock wall rimming the point. You will see a good mixture of anemones, sea stars, some nudibranchs and rockfish as well. In winter, perhaps sea lions. A vast plain of ghostly white sea whips stretches north in deep water offshore from the rocky overhangs to the ledge which drops into wolf-eel country and sponge land.

Access: From Nanaimo go 20 miles to Madrona Point. Heading north on Island Highway, go 13 miles beyond Northbrook Mall. Past Nanoose, just across Bonell Creek Bridge and before a gas station, turn right into North West Bay Road. Follow this road 4½ miles as it winds around and heads north. Do not turn right at Stewart Road. Keep going on North West Bay Road to Arbutus Drive. Turn right and go to Madrona Drive. Turn left and go 1 more mile to the turnaround at the end of the road. Lots of room to park. Walk down a short, flat path between tall trees to the layered rock ledges of Madrona Point. Enter and swim around the rocky shores to look for an octopus or snorkel north and go down to look for wolf eels.

Bottom and Depths: Rock wall filled with nooks and crannies where octopuses hide. It drops to flat sandy bottom at 25 or 35 feet. This slopes gradually out for a long way. The sea whips are on muddy bottom at 80 or 90 feet. Set your compass and head north across the plain of sea whips. After 100 yards you will come to a ledge that drops off to deeper water where the wolf eels live.

Hazards: Boats. Listen for boats and ascend with a reserve of air; if you hear a boat you can stay down until it passes.

Telephone: Island Highway and North West Bay Road.

Facilities: None.

Comments: Beautiful rock ledges for a picnic.

Octopus jetting away

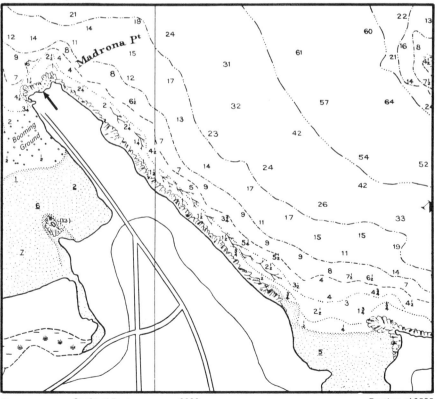

Scale of Feet 0 — 3000 Portion of 3585

Skill: All Divers and Snorkelers

Why go: Beautiful for sightseeing and photography. Good for dinner-sized lingcod. Variety. Variety. Diving here is like jumping into an aquarium. Cottam Point teems with life. Millions of little rockfish, nudibranchs, sea stars, kelp greenlings and red rock crabs. Lingcod lie on the rocks. Painted greenlings pose for their pictures. Large white fluffy anemones tilt their heads between the crevices. Huge boulders, covered with so many small orange fuzzy anemones that you can't see any rock at all, stand immoveable between olive-coloured bull kelp banners flying in the current. If you look, you may see an octopus or a wolf eel. And sea lions, in winter.

When I dived here my buddy didn't know whether to use his speargun or camera; therefore he took both. I held one while he used the other. So much to see: a dive at Cottam Point always seems too short.

Access: From Nanaimo go 20 miles to Cottam Point. Heading north on Island Highway go 13 miles beyond Northbrook Mall. Past Nanoose, just across Bonell Creek Bridge and before a gas station, turn right into North West Bay Road. Go almost 2½ miles to Claudet Road and turn right. After 1 mile you turn left, and Dorcas Point Road goes off to the right. Keep going just over 1 mile more to Sea Dog Road. Turn left to the water. Follow the steep path by the cable 5 or 10 feet down to the rocks. On your left is a house. In front of it is Cottam Point. The reef goes straight out from the point towards Mistaken Island. An easy entry over smooth rocks.

Bottom and Depths: Smooth rocks roll gently down into the water where Japanese weed, lettuce kelp and bull kelp grow luxuriantly over the ledges and rocky reef. Scattered boulders and some sand between. The reef is 50 or 60 feet deep.

Hazards: Small boats, current, bull kelp and wind. Very heavy boat traffic close to shore. Fly your diver's flag, listen for boats, use a compass and ascend along the bottom all the way to shore, well out of the way of those boats. Current can run up to 2 knots and more. Dive near the slack when there are large tidal exchanges. Carry a knife and ascend with a reserve of air; if caught in the kelp you will have time to cut your way free. Do not dive at Cottam Point if wind from the northwest makes entry difficult.

Telephone: Island Highway and North West Bay Road.

Facilities: None. Even parking space is very limited. Room for one or two cars.

Comments: Good visibility year-round, ranging from 30 feet in summer to 100 and more in winter.

From Cottam Point, looking towards Mistaken Island

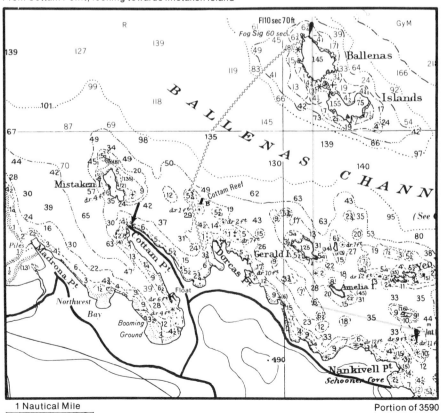

1 Nautical Mile

Portion of 3590

DOLPHIN BEACH   **Tide Table:** Point Atkinson
Shore Dive

Skill: All Divers and Snorkelers

Why go: Sponge land is right at hand. I know of no other dive from shore where sponges are so easily accessible with such an easy entry and such a short swim as at Dolphin Beach. Dolphin Beach is good for the deep diver. Good for shallow divers and snorkelers, too. We saw seaperch and rockfish swimming in the bull kelp and hiding in crevices. White-petalled alabaster nudibranchs and an assortment of others. Moon snails in the eelgrass. Deeper were ratfish, some lingcod and round orange sponges clinging to the wall. Big chimney sponges start at 80 feet.

Because this site has been popular for years, food fish have been nearly hunted out in the shallows. Over the wall there are still some lingcod left for the hunter — down in "The Basement".

Access: From Nanaimo go 20 miles to Dolphin Beach. Heading north on Island Highway go 13 miles beyond Northbrook Mall. Past Nanoose, just across Bonell Creek Bridge and before a gas station, turn right into North West Bay Road. Go almost 2 miles to Stewart Road. Turn right following signs towards Schooner Cove and go 2½ miles to Blueback Drive and Dolphin Drive. Continue 3/10 mile down Blueback Drive. As you go around a corner and down into a little dip, the road comes very close to the water. There are houses close by on either side. This is Dolphin Beach. Park by the road, walk 4 or 5 feet through the brush to the rocky beach. Swim straight out and down.

Bottom and Depths: Rocky beach gives way to eelgrass and sand in the shallows, then Japanese weed, rocks and bull kelp. Some deep cracks in the rocks. Beyond the kelp steeply sloping sand falls away quickly to 80 feet where a stark rock wall drops off to 110 or 120 feet in "The Basement".

Hazards: Bull kelp, especially in summer, and wind in winter. Carry a knife and ascend with a reserve of air, so that if caught in the kelp you will have time to cut your way free. Wind can make entry difficult.

Telephone: Schooner Cove Marina, ½ mile east.

Facilities: None at Dolphin Beach.

Comments: The rocky beach is good for winter bonfires. Despite the surrounding homes Dolphin Beach feels wild and secluded.

From April 15th through October 15th telephone Parksville Forest Ranger, 248-5715, and ask if beach bonfire permit required.

At Dolphin Beach

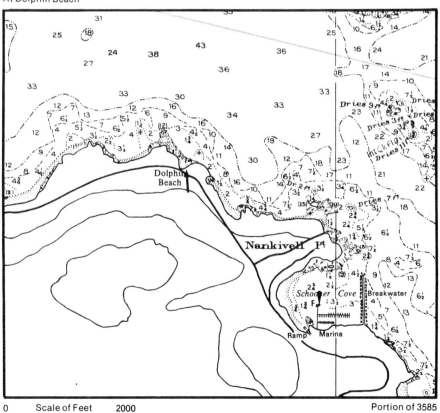

0   Scale of Feet   2000   Portion of 3585

Skill: All Divers and Snorkelers

Why go: Nankivell Point, commonly called Schooner Cove, is a colourful, shallow rocky reef with a little bit of everything. In spite of a lot of diving here there are still some shellfish left. A few abalones and some scallops hide in the rocks. Giant red urchins, small green urchins, sea stars, rockfish, shrimp and hermit crabs are plentiful. During one dive at this site, I saw a couple of 1½-foot long lingcod, a brown Irish lord, alabaster nudibranchs and one large octopus. River otters, sea lions and harbour seals are here sometimes too. The bottom is covered with life.

Access: From Nanaimo go 20 miles to Nankivell Point. Heading north on Island Highway go 13 miles beyond Northbrook Mall. Past Nanoose, just across Bonell Creek Bridge and before a gas station, turn right into North West Bay Road. Go almost 2 miles to Stewart Road. Turn right following signs towards Schooner Cove and go 2½ miles to Blueback Drive and Dolphin Drive. Continue down Blueback Drive ½ mile. Shortly past Tyee Crescent as you come up over the hill and can see a marina, turn left and go to the end of Grilse Road. Two or three cars can park at the road end. An easy entry over rocky beach. Go down and work your way left towards the obvious rocky area.

Bottom and Depths: Rocky bottom 30 or 40 feet deep with lettuce kelp and bull kelp. Crusted over with life.

Hazards: Wind in winter and bull kelp in summer. Exposed to northwest wind, big surf can make entry difficult. Carry a knife and ascend with a reserve of air, so that if caught in the kelp you will have time to cut your way free.

Telephone: Schooner Cove Marina, ½ mile southeast.

Facilities: None at Nankivell Point. A small crescent of beach with a few homes around. Launching ramp nearby at Schooner Cove.

Comments: Although Nankivell Point is great for beginners, it's a good dive in anybody's books.

Rocky shores, rocky reef

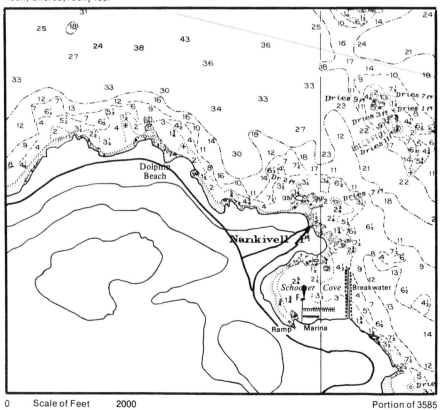

Dolphin Beach

Nankivell Pt

Schooner Cove

Breakwater

Ramp   Marina

0   Scale of Feet   2000

Portion of 3585

Skill: All Divers

Why go: Gorgeous shallow and deep — Amelia Island is a beautiful dive. My favourite kind of place. I love to go over an immediate cliff, like this, that drops off to infinity. Or seems to. Below you it's dark and black and there is no bottom. Big chimney sponges — some hiding decorator crabs inside — sweep down the wall. Small swimming scallops look infinitesimal against the dark abyss. Yellow cloud sponges and bright orange sponges that appear to have come from the bathtub are scattered down the wall. A dogfish swims out of the dark and circles. You see a yelloweye rockfish.

It's time to go up, but not too fast. There's a lot to see on the way. Stop at the shallow shelf at 10 feet. Glimmering white nudibranch eggs, like a perfect coil of apple peel, hang from the rocks. Painted greenlings, kelp greenlings, decorator crabs, abalones and rock scallops hide in the kelp. Bull kelp, bright green lettuce kelp, red kelp and blue purply kelp that's almost transparent. An extravaganza of kelp. A heap of Christmas tissue paper.

Access: Amelia Island is on the south side of Ballenas Channel, 10 miles northwest of Nanaimo, just over 1 mile northwest of Schooner Cove where there is a launching ramp.

From Nanaimo go 20 miles to Schooner Cove. Heading north on Island Highway go 13 miles beyond Northbrook Mall. Past Nanoose, just across Bonell Creek Bridge and before a gas station, turn right into North West Bay Road. Go almost 2 miles to Stewart Road. Turn right following signs towards Schooner Cove. Launch, go 1 mile northwest to Amelia Island and anchor. The drop-off is in the middle of the south side of Amelia Island.

Bottom and Depths: Rocky shores go to a shallow shelf at 10 or 20 feet where there is bull kelp and other kinds of bottom kelp. From here the drop is right off to 40 fathoms.

Hazards: Current, depth and bull kelp. Dive near the slack. Carry a knife and ascend with a reserve of air, so that if caught in the kelp you will have time to cut your way free.

Telephone: Schooner Cove Marina.

Facilities: None at uninhabited Amelia Island. Launching at Schooner Cove. Charters, rentals and launching at Northwest Bay.

Comments: Amelia Island is only one of the beautiful dives in the Ada, Winchelsea and Ballenas Islands area so famed for sponges.

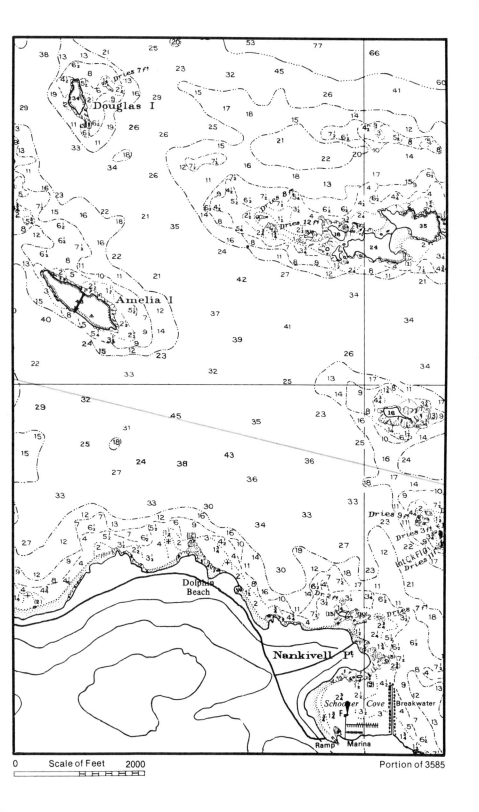

Douglas I

Amelia I

Dolphin
Beach

Nankivell Pt

Schooner Cove

Breakwater

Ramp   Marina

0   Scale of Feet   2000

Portion of 3585

Skill: All Divers

Why go: The Yeo Islands are only one mile offshore. Because several islands make up this group, someplace is almost always sheltered from the wind. And it's beautiful shallow diving on all sides. A very diveable site for all. We revelled in the other-worldly moon snails and big graceful orange sea pens. Lots of clams and rock scallops. Giant red urchins, huge orange peel and lemon nudibranchs hide in the very thick kelp. Small perfect-petalled alabaster nudibranchs, too. Enormous gum boot chitons stick to the rocks. My buddy found a small gorgeous aqua-coloured chiton that looked like a turquoise.

Diving at the Yeo Islands on a sunny day is like dipping into a bright box of jewels.

Access: The Yeo Islands are on the south side of Ballenas Channel, 10 miles northwest of Nanaimo, just 1 mile north of Schooner Cove where there is a launching ramp.

From Nanaimo go 20 miles to Schooner Cove. Heading north on Island Highway go 13 miles beyond Northbrook Mall. Past Nanoose, just across Bonell Creek Bridge and before a gas station, turn right into North West Bay Road. Go almost 2 miles to Stewart Road. Turn right following signs towards Schooner Cove. Launch and go 1 mile north to the Yeo Islands. Anchor wherever there is shelter. The southeast corner is a good spot.

Bottom and Depths: White sand bottom scattered with small broken rock provides enough attachment area for lots of bull kelp which is very thick in summer. A huge shallow area, from 25 to 35 feet deep, lies all around the Yeo Islands.

Hazards: Bull kelp. Carry a knife and ascend with a reserve of air, so that if caught in the kelp you will have time to cut your way free.

Telephone: Schooner Cove Marina.

Facilities: None at the Yeo Islands. Launching at Schooner Cove. Charters, rentals and launching at Northwest Bay.

Comments: When collecting shellfish remember that an abalone or a rock scallop takes three or four years to mature so that it can reproduce. Undisturbed, both of these shellfish may live up to fifteen years.

Schooner Cove, Ada and Winchelsea Islands beyond

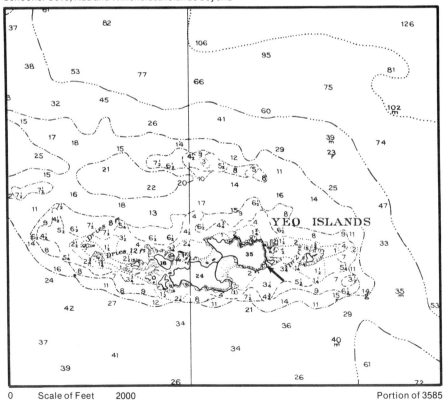

SUNRISE BEACH   **Tide Table:** Point Atkinson
       Shore Dive

Skill: All Divers and Snorkelers

Why go: Quick and easy, Sunrise Beach is a good place to drop into the water if you're in Nanaimo and have only a couple of hours for a dive.
Entry is exceptionally easy over a small rocky beach at a road end. Then swim out and to the left a very short way over shallow rocks covered with bottom kelp to a shallow ledge that parallels the shore. You'll see all the animals that go with this kind of bottom: lots of decorator crabs, nudibranchs, hairy crabs and maybe an octopus. During one quick dive here I saw a dozen small colourful painted greenlings.
An agreeable little dive.

Access: From Nanaimo go 6 miles to Sunrise Beach. Heading north on Island Highway turn northeast onto Departure Bay Road at Northbrook Mall. Go along Departure Bay Road for 1 mile to Hammond Bay Road. Turn right and go 4 miles to Entwhistle Drive. Turn right and go ½ mile to Fillinger Crescent and continue 2/10 mile to a road which turns left and ends at the sea. Room for a couple of cars to park. An easy entry over rocky beach.

Bottom and Depths: A shallow shelf parallels the shore and drops to 30 or 40 feet. Bottom kelp on the rocks and some sand between.

Hazards: Wind from the southeast can cause surf which makes entry difficult.

Telephone: Departure Bay Store, 5½ miles back where Departure Bay Road dips down by the water.

Facilities: None at Sunrise Beach. Picnic tables and restrooms 5½ miles back at Departure Bay Beach.

Comments: "Nanaimo", an Indian word meaning "meeting of the tribes".

Painted greenling, or convict fish

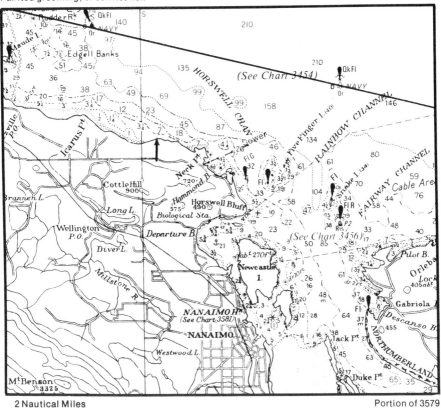

2 Nautical Miles

Portion of 3579

Skill: All Divers

Why go: Would you believe rock falls and tunnels, a wreck you can enter, walls covered with bright red colonial anemones, and old bottles from the 1800's? All at one site? Jesse Island is safe and easy to dive day or night. Less than a mile from the launching ramp, this popular checkout site is picturesque and pretty for photographers and sightseers. Locally honoured as a reserve, you would be unpopular if you took any marine life. The one lingcod I saw at Jesse Island looked mangy anyway. But there are lots of other interests for divers.
My buddy pointed out something I'd never seen before. A hermit crab had moved into a small shell, then a yellow sponge had covered the shell, dissolving the hermit crab's adopted home. A nudibranch was eating the sponge!

Access: Jesse Island is situated in Departure Bay 1 mile north of Nanaimo. Charter or rent in Nanaimo or launch at Brechin Point Public Launching Ramp and go 1 mile north to Jesse Island. Anchor in a little bay at the northwest, and dive along the north side of Jesse Island.

Bottom and Depths: The 30-foot fish boat wreck is in 80 or 90 feet of water about the middle of the north side of the island. Bottles from old Nanaimo coal ships may be found anywhere. Carved limestone arches and tunnels along the north side, even above the surface. Depths at the base of the rock wall range from 30 feet at the northwest corner to about 50 or 60 feet at the northeast end. Sandy bottom to the base of the wall.

Hazards: Small boats, especially in summer. Departure Bay is heavily populated and salmon fishing is popular just outside the bay. Listen for boats and ascend with a reserve of air right up the side of the island.

Telephone: Departure Bay Ferry Terminal.

Facilities: None on uninhabited Jesse Island. Newcastle Marine Park, an island in Nanaimo Harbour, is nearby. Drinking water, campsites, picnic tables, mooring buoys and playing fields at the park which can be reached from Nanaimo by pedestrian ferry. The ferry operates on schedule in summer only. At other times by special arrangement. It leaves from behind the Civic Arena at the foot of Bowen Road which becomes Comox Road as it nears the water.

Comments: Jesse Island is convenient and easy to dive at night, particularly if you launch at Brechin Point Civic Boat Ramp. A big bright light by the ramp makes sorting your gear easy.

Hermit crab in sponge

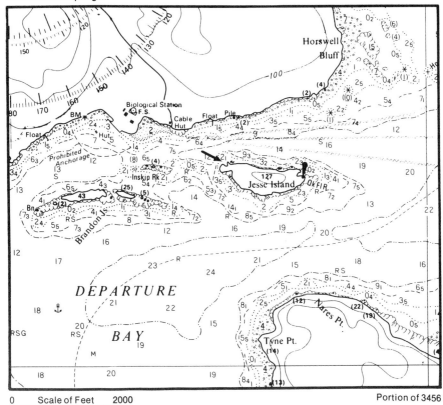

Skill: All Divers

Why go: Good sightseeing, abundant lingcod and rockfish and some yelloweye rockfish, commonly called red snapper, at Snake Island. Though close to Nanaimo, which has been a diving centre for many years, Snake Island is not overfished because it can only be reached by boat. In addition to game fish we saw many more animals: kelp crabs, sea stars and nudibranchs. Some anemones. Bright orange dead man's finger sponges poke up through the bottom kelp in the shallows. Bull kelp around 30 feet, and chimney sponges starting at 80. We saw harbour seals which frequent this area.
An all-around dive.

Access: Snake Island is 3 miles west of Departure Bay just south of the Horseshoe Bay-Departure Bay B.C. Ferry route. Charter or rent in Nanaimo or launch at Brechin Point Civic Boat Ramp and go northeast to Snake Island. Anchor in the bull kelp at the northwest corner of the island.

Bottom and Depths: Rocky bottom covered with bottom kelp and some bull kelp. Ledges and cliffs fall away fairly quickly all around the island. On the Nanaimo side, caves undercut the island at 140 feet. The chart shows a drop to 800 feet.

Hazards: Boats, bull kelp and wind. Listen for boats and ascend along the bottom all the way to shore. Carry a knife and surface with a reserve of air, so that if caught in the kelp you will have time to cut your way free. Consider the wind when planning a dive. Snake Island is very exposed to wind from all directions.

Telephone: Departure Bay Ferry Terminal.

Facilities: None.

Comments: Maybe it's myth, but local spear fishermen say that the northwest corner of each island in the Nanaimo area is the most productive for hunting.

Juvenile yelloweye rockfish, or red snapper

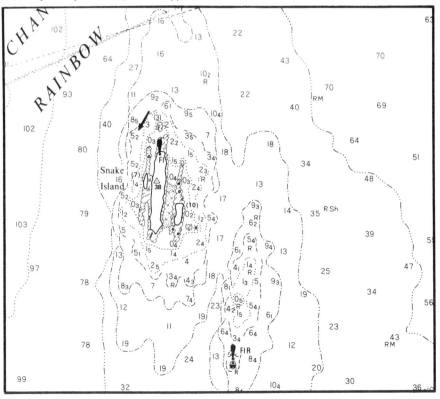

0   Scale of Feet   2000

Portion of 3456

Skill: Advanced Divers

Why go: Rockfish, lingcod, octopuses, anemones and nudibranchs abound on the current-swept ledges north of Round Island. When here we saw an enormous variety of dahlia anemones. We saw leather stars and sea pens. First one lingcod appeared, then another. During one dive we saw six lingcod — each at least fifteen pounds. Many species of rockfish — including tiger rockfish — were on the ledges. Then we saw an octopus sitting out in the open on a rock. I stroked him. His mantle reddened and he wriggled under my touch. He became nervous and slowly jetted to five feet away where he stopped and waited for us to catch up with him. We approached slowly, and stroked him again. He writhed, seeming to enjoy every minute of it, reddened more and then speckled. That octopus never tired of our company, but we were nearly out of air! As we moved towards shore we passed large sea lemons and delicate orange nudibranchs with white tips. We picked up a couple of rock scallops as we swam back through the shallows. Sea lions and killer whales have also been seen at Round Island.

Access: Round Island is 1 mile south of Dodd Narrows in Stuart Channel, only 300 yards across the water from Vancouver Island. If you think you can swim it, don't. Currents are treacherous. Launch 9 miles southeast of Nanaimo at the foot of Barnes-Murdock Road and go by boat 300 yards east to Round Island. Or charter or rent in Nanaimo, or launch at Brechin Point Civic Boat Ramp in Nanaimo and go 9 miles south through Dodd Narrows to Round Island. Anchor or land in the small horseshoe-shaped cove at the northwest tip. Follow a compass heading due north through the kelp and down.
Barnes-Murdock Road Ramp is convenient but only useable at high tides. To go there from Nanaimo drive south on Island Highway. Take Cedar turnoff and go east. After 1.8 miles, just after crossing a bridge, turn right following signs to Cedar Road and Yellow Point Road. Go ½ mile to Ming's Grocery. Turn left and go ⅓ mile to Holden Corso Road. Continue along Holden Corso Road 1⅓ miles then along Barnes Road for 1⅓ miles. At Murdock Road angle right and go ½ mile. Launch and cross 300 yards to Round Island.

Bottom and Depths: Rocky shore gives way to white sand, then kelp attached to small rocks in 20 or 30 feet of water. Northward the bottom slopes gradually to 50 feet where rocky ledges stairstep to 60 feet and more.

Hazards: Strong current and bull kelp. Dive on high slack. The current is more acute on a falling tide than on a rising tide. Carry a knife so that if caught in the kelp you will have time to cut your way free.

Telephones: 1. Ming's Grocery, Cedar Road & Yellow Point Rd.
2. Departure Bay Ferry Terminal.

Facilities: None on uninhabited Round Island.

Comments: Pleasant place for a picnic.

From foot of Barnes-Murdock Road, looking east towards Round Island

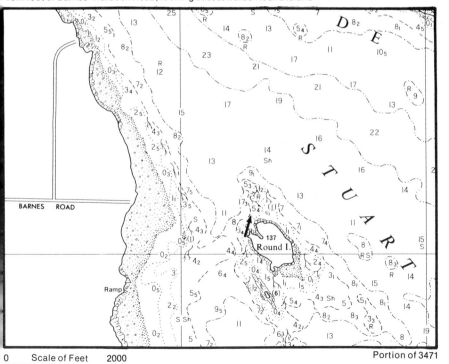

0   Scale of Feet   2000

Portion of 3471

Skill: All Divers and Snorkelers

Why go: Acres of sightseeing along this rocky reef reaching a long, thin finger out into Evening Cove. Hordes of rockfish live around the rocks. Anemones, sea stars, sea peaches, little nudibranchs, and sculpins. Octopuses on the reef if you can find them. Once on a night dive I found one too easily. I was poking along the rocks and saw one small white tentacle coiling and uncoiling. I suddenly realized that I was almost lying on the mantle of a very large, very red octopus. It must have been 25 pounds, at least, and in only 15 feet of water. The octopus was just as startled as I was. He tried to escape under a small ledge much too narrow to shelter him. I backed off and moved on.

Hermit crabs, flounders, pipefish and burrowing anemones live on the sand on either side of the reef. Box crabs in the middle of the cove. A variety of life, easy access and lack of current add up to Evening Cove being a good dive anytime — day or night.

Access: From Nanaimo go 16 miles southeast to Evening Cove. Heading south on Island Highway, 10 miles past Nanaimo you come to a road signposted to Mañana Lodge and Kumalockasun Campsite. Turn left. When you come to a "V", bear right and continue past Mañana Lodge. Go 3½ miles farther along Shell Beach Road to Elliott Road. Turn right and drive to the water's edge. Four or five cars can park.

To find the reef, face the cove. Look for four small rocky points jutting into the water between Coffin Point and Sharpe Point. The reef goes out from the second small point on your right, 75 yards west of the road end. Follow the finger of rocks straight out into the cove.

Bottom and Depths: A shallow ridge of rocks reaches out into Evening Cove. Some bottom kelp on the rocks. Sand scattered with small rocks on either side at 15 to 35 feet. A very definite reef-like reef and shallow for a very long way out, finally going to 50 feet deep. Then a break, but farther out the reef comes up to 30 feet again.

Hazards: Poor visibility, small boats and red jellyfish in the fall. Fly your diver's flag, listen for boats and ascend with a reserve of air, so that if you hear a boat you can stay down until it passes. If you have seen any red jellyfish, you and your buddy should check one another for stinging tentacles before removing your masks and gloves.

Telephone: Island Highway, 1/10 mile north of road to Evening Cove and Coffin Point.

Facilities: None at Evening Cove. Campsite with gravel launching ramp and showers at Coffin Point. Ivy Green Park Provincial Campsite nearby at the head of Ladysmith Harbour.

Comments: Evening Cove is as beautiful above water as below, particularly in spring when the old orchard is in bloom. But respect private property surrounding the site, especially the private oyster beds.

Evening Cove

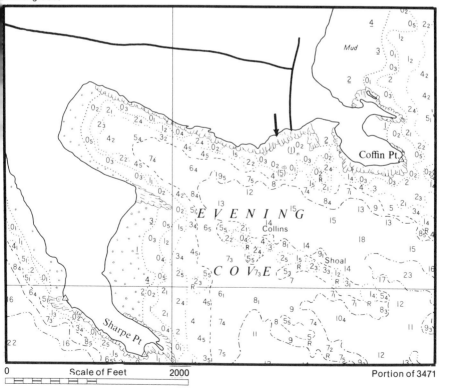

0   Scale of Feet   2000   Portion of 3471

Skill: Intermediate and Advanced Divers and Snorkelers

Why go: Coffin Island is an extravaganza ranging from minute sea pens to giant nudibranchs to thousand-pound sea lions. Wine-red giant nudibranchs tipped with mauve, and others that glitter like tinseled bows on a Christmas parcel, seem flung across the sea floor. We saw tiny alabaster nudibranchs, giant red urchins, sea squirts, large elegant orange plumose anemones, sea stars and lots of small white anemones. Feather stars on the smooth rock rolling away down deep. Burrowing anemones, minute sea pens and giant sea pens in the sand.

By mistake I put my hand on a large cabezon. We noticed rockfish in the crevices and a couple of large lingcod lying on their chins. A huge pair of playful sea lions made many passes near us, but never touched us. I couldn't decide whether to be frightened or delighted. I could not take my eyes off their eyes. Exciting to have them with us throughout the dive! You're more likely to meet them in winter.

Access: Coffin Island is 300 yards east of Coffin Point in Stuart Channel, ¾ mile south of the 49th parallel which runs through Ladysmith.

Because Coffin Island is a ½-mile swim from the closest access point at the road end at Evening Cove, use a boat. Either launch over the log-strewn beach at Evening Cove or at the gravel ramp nearby. Or in summer rent a boat at Saltair, 4 miles south of Ladysmith, and go north by water to Coffin Island. Anchor north of Coffin Island and go down.

From Nanaimo go 20 miles southeast to Evening Cove or the ramp at Coffin Point or 17 miles southeast to Saltair.

Bottom and Depths: A large area of 25- or 35-foot rocky bottom scattered with boulders and broadleaf bottom kelp all around Coffin Island. Some white sand, eelgrass and bull kelp. About 300 yards north of the island, smooth stark, dark rock rolls from 50 or 60 feet to 80 or 90 feet.

Hazards: Current, and broken fishing line. Boats, poor visibility and bull kelp in summer. Red jellyfish, in the fall. Wind in winter. Dive on the slack. Carry a knife. Fly your diver's flag, use a compass and listen for boats, ascending with a reserve of air; if you hear a boat you can stay down until it passes. If you have seen any red jellyfish, you and your buddy should check one another for stinging tentacles before removing your masks and gloves. Coffin Island is exposed to winds from all directions.

Telephone: Island Highway, 1/10 mile north of road to Coffin Point.

Facilities: None at Coffin Island. Campsite with showers and gravel launching ramp at Coffin Point. Ivy Green Park Provincial Campsite nearby at the head of Ladysmith Harbour.

Comments: Winter is the best time to dive Coffin Island.

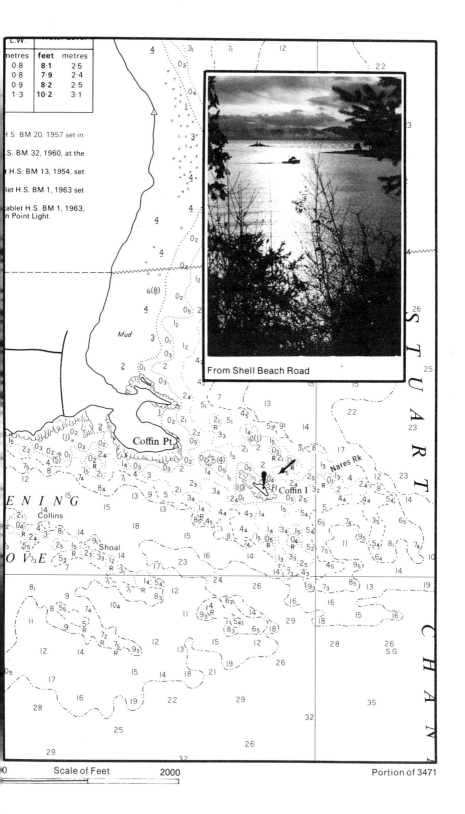

L.W.			
metres	feet	metres	
0·8	8·1	2·5	
0·8	7·9	2·4	
0·9	8·2	2·5	
1·3	10·2	3·1	

H.S. BM 20, 1957 set in

S. BM 32, 1960, at the

H.S. BM 13, 1954, set

let H.S. BM 1, 1963 set

ablet H.S. BM 1, 1963,
n Point Light.

From Shell Beach Road

Mud

Coffin Pt.

Nares Rk

Coffin I

ENING

Collins

Shoal

O V E

S T U A R T

C H A N

Scale of Feet   2000

Portion of 3471

MAPLE BAY REEF   **Tide Table:** Fulford Harbou
      UNDERWATER SANCTUARY
      Shore Dive

Skill: All Divers

Why go: An underwater sanctuary, Maple Bay Reef offers a very
pleasant afternoon of sightseeing and photography. One of the
beauties of Maple Bay Reef is that it is shallow, and therefore
usually bright enough for available light photography. And there
are fish, octopuses and a variety of invertebrates along the three
arms of the reef.
      When diving here we saw masses of nudibranchs. My buddy
was kept very busy taking pictures. We saw some giant silver
nudibranchs — grey with white tips. Several leopard nudibranchs
and lemon nudibranchs sitting on the edge of broadleaf kelp
Large orange plumose anemones, small white anemones, shrimp
all over the place. And pipefish moving along jerkily through the
shallows. Seaperch hovering around the reef. Some little gold fish
that I haven't seen before. Rockfish hide in the crevices of the wall
at the end of the left arm of the reef. Lingcod, too.
      A satisfying dive.

Access: From Nanaimo go 35 miles to Maple Bay. Heading south
on Island Highway, go to Duncan. Turn left at Trunk Road
following signs the 5 miles to Maple Bay. Trunk Road becomes
Tzouhalem Road which then conveniently becomes Maple Bay
Road and goes to the government dock at Maple Bay. Room for
ten cars by the government wharf.

Bottom and Depths: At about 100 feet beyond the dock, the reef
starts. It has three arms and is trident shaped. The right arm
points towards Paddy Mile Stone. The middle arm is a rocky back
bone pointing directly out into Maple Bay. The left arm juts
towards Arbutus Point and ends as a rock wall dropping from 20 o
30 feet to 50 or 60 feet. Bottom kelp all over the reef which is 20 o
30 feet deep on top and drops a few feet on either side.
      To find the reef set your compass towards Paddy Mile Stone
the point on your right, jump off the dock and swim out 100 fee
under water.

Hazards: Small boats and poor visibility in summer. Red jellyfish, in the fall. Many, many small boats coming and going. Use a
compass. When ascending listen for boats and surface with a
reserve of air; if you hear a boat you can stay down until it passes
If you have seen any red jellyfish, you and your buddy should
check one another for stinging tentacles before removing your
masks and gloves.

Telephone: Maple Bay Trading Post.

Facilities: Government dock and small store. Launching 100
yards north of government dock.

Comments: Maple Bay is popular for night dives. By municipal
by-law the bay is a marine sanctuary and as a consequence spearfishing and specimen collecting are prohibited.

Paddy Mile Stone beyond the boat

1 Nautical Mile

Portion of 3452

Skill: Advanced Divers

Why go: Octopus Point drops off more cleanly than any drop-off I've seen. It is such a clean sweep that my buddy and I didn't try to anchor on the bottom. We anchored around a tree. Rolling over the side of our inflatable we fell straight into the abyss. Castles and turrets of staghorn bryozoans encrust the palisades in pale lemon yellow. Dream-like underwater skyscraper castles look like something from a picture book. Huge, huge lingcod swim out from the bottomless dark and slowly swim back, again. Large black rockfish cruise past in schools. Painted greenlings, tiger rockfish and an incredible number of the more-common quillback rockfish hang close to the wall.

Little space for a foothold, but many animals have toeholds on the wall. Gigantic rock scallops stud the straight-up-and-down wall like almonds down the side of a richly-decorated almond cake. Giant red urchins, pink tube worms, giant barnacles, small crabs peeping from empty barnacle shells, alabaster nudi-branchs, mustard-yellow trumpet sponges and gigantic orange peel nudibranchs cling to the sheer bluff. Tiny orange solitary cup corals and filmy white encrusting sponges dot the rocks. Red and pink dahlia anemones, fluffy white plumose anemones, and pale pink-beige sea lilies feather from the wall.

A magnificent drop-off.

Access: Octopus Point is on the west side of Sansum Narrows, 2 miles east of Maple Bay and 4 miles north of Cowichan Bay. Go by boat to the second small point south of Octopus Point. Some bull kelp on the very narrow ledge by the drop-off, but not enough room for a boat to anchor and swing. We threw our anchor around a tree and went down.

Launch or rent a boat at Maple Bay or at Cowichan Bay. From Nanaimo it is 35 miles to Maple Bay. Heading south on Island Highway, go to Duncan. Turn left at Trunk Road and follow signs 5 miles to Maple Bay. Trunk Road becomes Tzouhalem Road which then conveniently becomes Maple Bay Road and goes to the government dock and launching ramp at Maple Bay. Sailboat rentals are available at Birds Eye Cove at the south end of Maple Bay. Or continue beyond Duncan to Cowichan Bay where there are more boat rentals and launching.

Bottom and Depths: Sheer rock wall falls cleanly away to 48 fathoms, according to the chart. Some bull kelp on the very narrow broken rock ledge immediately next to the shore.

Hazards: Current, bull kelp and depth. Dive on the slack. Carry a knife and ascend with a reserve of air, so that if caught in the kelp you will have time to cut your way free.

Telephone: Maple Bay Trading Post.

Facilities: None at Octopus Point.

Comments: Best in the late morning when sun lights the water.

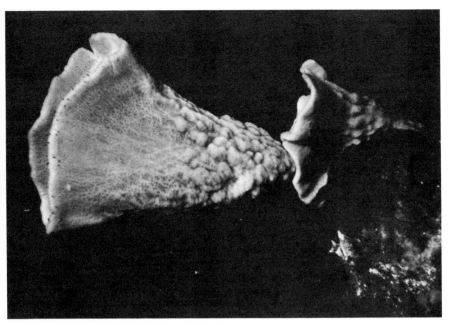

Trumpet sponges

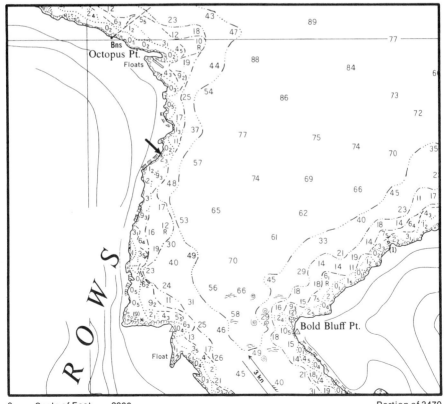

CHAPTER 6
Victoria and Saanich Inlet

Dives

1. Misery Bay
2. The White Lady
3. McKenzie Bight
4. Tod Inlet
5. Henderson Point
6. Arbutus Island
7. Forrest Island
8. Halibut Island
9. Ten-Mile Point
10. Ogden Point Breakwater
11. Brotchie Ledge
12. Wreck of the *Major Tompkins*
13. Saxe Point Park
14. Fisgard Island
15. Bentinck Island
16. Race Rocks

Places

A. Brentwood Bay
B. Mill Bay
C. Deep Cove
D. Swartz Bay
E. McDonald Park
F. Tsehum (Shoal) Harbour
G. Roberts Bay
H. Sidney
I. Sidney Spit Park
J. Island View Beach
K. Dominion Astrophysical Observatory
L. Royal Oak
M. Bay Street Bridge
N. Johnson Street Bridge
O. Parliament Buildings
P. The Inner Harbour
Q. Fort Rodd Hill
R. Colwood
S. Pedder Bay

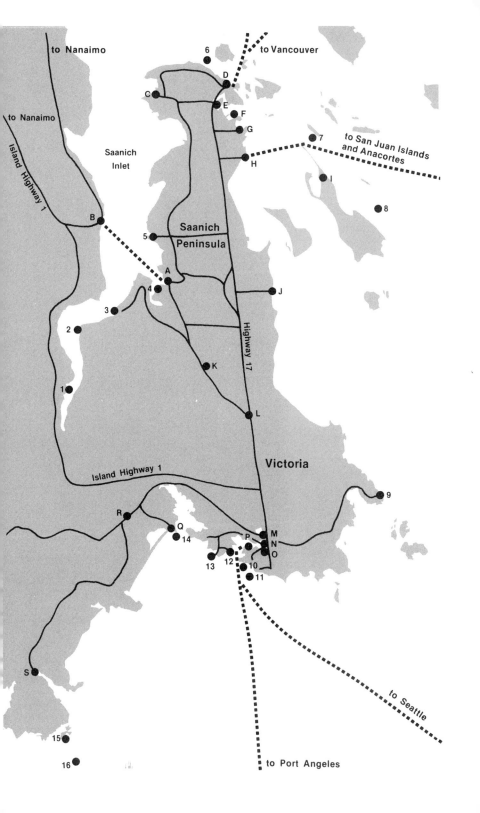

Charts: Canadian Hydrographic Service
- 3413 Esquimalt and Victoria Harbour and Approaches
- 3415 Victoria Harbour
- 3416 Esquimalt Harbour
- 3422 Race Rocks to Discovery Island
- 3423 Trial Islands to Cadboro Bay
- 3449 Race Rocks to East Point
- 3451 Discovery Island to Saltspring Island

Tide and Current Table: Canadian Hydrographic Service
Tide and Current Table, Volume 5

Emergency Telephone Number
Rescue Coordination Centre (Victoria) 388-1543

Other Numbers
Victoria Area Weather Forecast 656-3978
Victoria Marine Radio (for Race Rocks weather) 642-3431

●Air Stations

Brentwood Bay
Brentwood Inn
7172 Brentwood Drive
Box 396
Brentwood Bay, B.C.
V0S 1A0
(604) 652-2413

Sidney
Rimpac Divers Ltd.
9818 - 5th Street
Sidney, B.C.
V8L 2X3
(604) 656-6313
(Compressor rentals also.)

Victoria
Frank White's Scuba Shop
832 Fisgard Street
Victoria, B.C.
V8W 1S1
(604) 385-4713

Sea Trek Dive Centre
629 Dunedin Street
Victoria, B.C.
V8T 2L7
(604) 386-7528

●Boat Charters, Rentals and Launching

Brentwood Bay
Anglers Anchorage Marina
R.R. 1
Brentwood Bay, B.C.
V0S 1A0
(604) 652-3531
(Charters and rentals only.)

Brentwood Inn
7172 Brentwood Drive
Box 396
Brentwood Bay, B.C.
V0S 1A0
(604) 652-2413
(Charters, rentals, inflatable rentals and launching.)

Brentwood Boat Rentals Ltd.
7212 Peden Lane
P.O. Box 88
Brentwood Bay, B.C.
V0S 1A0
(604) 652-1014
(Charters and rentals only.)

Gilbert's Marine and
Guide Service Ltd.
789 Saunders Lane R.R. 1
Brentwood Bay, B.C.
V0S 1A0
(604) 652-2211
(Charters, rentals and launching.)

Rhodes' Sport Fishing
7054 Brentwood Drive
Brentwood Bay, B.C.
V0S 1A0
(604) 652-1512 or 592-2221
(*Charters only.*)

Tsartlip Campsite
800 Stelley's Cross Road
Box 70
Brentwood Bay, B.C.
V0S 1A0
(604) 652-3988
(*Launching only.*)

Sidney
Foot of Beacon Avenue Ramp
Sidney, B.C.
(*Launching only.*)

Bosun's Charters
10775 McDonald Park Road
Box 2464
Sidney, B.C.
V8L 3Y3
(604) 656-6644
(*Charters and launching only.*)

Deep Cove Marina
10992 Madrona Drive
R.R. 1, Deep Cove
Sidney, B.C.
V8L 3R9
(604) 656-2810
(*Rentals and launching only.*)

Island View Beach Ramp
Telegraph Road
Sidney, B.C.
(*Launching only.*)

Rimpac Divers Ltd.
9818 - 5th Street
Sidney, B.C.
V8L 2X3
(604) 656-6313
(*Charters. Launching nearby.*)

Roberts Bay Public Ramp
Ardwell Avenue
Sidney, B.C.
(*Launching only.*)

Shoal Harbour Public Ramp
Griffiths Road
Sidney, B.C.
(*Launching only.*)

Victoria
Chinook
697 Lomax Road
R.R. 1
Victoria, B.C.
V8X 3W9
(604) 478-7808
(*Charters only.*)

James Bay Anglers' Assoc.
75 Dallas Road
Victoria, B.C.
V8V 1A1
(*Launching only.*)

Marabell
3180 Norfolk Road
Victoria, B.C.
V8R 6H4
(604) 592-2613
(*Charters in winter only.
Minimum of 24 hours.*)

Sea Trek Dive Centre
629 Dunedin Street
Victoria, B.C.
V8T 2L7
(604) 386-7528
(*Charters and inflatable
rentals only.*)

Snoop
Box 2182
Sidney, B.C.
V8L 3S8
(604) 656-6859
(*Charters only.*)

West of Victoria
Pedder Bay Marina
Rocky Point Road
R.R. 6
Victoria, B.C.
V8X 3X2
(604) 478-1771
(*Launching only.*)

● Ferry Information
B.C. Ferry Information Centre
1045 Howe Street
Vancouver, B.C.
V6Z 1P6
(604) 669-1211
From Victoria: 386-3431
(*Ferries between Swartz Bay,
Gulf Islands and Tsawwassen.
Ferries from Brentwood Bay
to Mill Bay.*)

● Tourist Information
Department of Travel Industry
1117 Wharf Street
Victoria, B.C.
V8W 2Z2
(604) 387-6417

B.C. Steamship Company
254 Belleville Street
Victoria, B.C.
V8V 1W9
(604) 386-6731
(*Ferries from Victoria to
Seattle. Summer only.*)

Washington State Ferries
2499 Ocean Avenue
Sidney, B.C.
V8L 1T3
(604) 656-1531
(*Ferries between Sidney, San
Juan Islands and Anacortes.*)

Black Ball Transport, Inc.
814 Wharf Street
Victoria, B.C.
V8W 1T3
(604) 386-2202
(*Ferries from Victoria to
Port Angeles.*)

*All of this service information is subject to change.

Skill: All Divers

Why go: Monstrous chimney sponges reach out from the fjord-like free fall wall at Misery Bay.
You can so easily go deep. Yet there are ledges at 50 or 60 feet, if that's where you want to stop. Large lingcod were once plentiful, but they're harder to find these days. Rockfish hang near the wall, gorgeous silver nudibranchs, octopuses, wolf eels and those monstrous chimney sponges.
This bay is popular with line fishermen, too. And therefore a fine place for divers to salvage lead fishing weights.

Access: Misery Bay is on the west side near the southernmost tip of Saanich Inlet, 6 miles south of Brentwood Bay.
Charter, rent, or launch at Brentwood Bay, 15 miles northwest of Victoria on Saanich Peninsula. From the Parliament Buildings in Victoria head north on Douglas Street, or Highway 17, towards Swartz Bay Ferry Terminal. Go 10½ miles. At Keating Cross Road, turn left and follow signs to Brentwood Bay. Then by boat south 6 miles to Misery Bay, a well-defined bay just north of Sawluctus Island on the west side of Saanich Inlet. Anchor at the southern point of the bay near a small private dock and dive south around the point.

Bottom and Depths: Dark, jagged, rocky bottom is 25 or 35 feet deep near shore and falls to a broad rocky ledge at 50 or 60 feet. From here the bottom drops away into the dark fjord. Light silt over all.

Hazards: Small boats and broken fishing line. Red jellyfish, in the fall. Listen for boats and ascend close to the wall all the way to the surface, well out of the way of those boats. Carry a knife. If you have seen any red jellyfish, you and your buddy should check one another for stinging tentacles before removing your masks and gloves.

Telephone: Brentwood Bay Ferry Landing.

Facilities: None at Misery Bay. Air fills, camping, hot showers, accommodations, charters, rentals, and launching at Brentwood Bay.

Comments: A dark dive in the afternoon. Dive Misery Bay in the morning, and take a light.

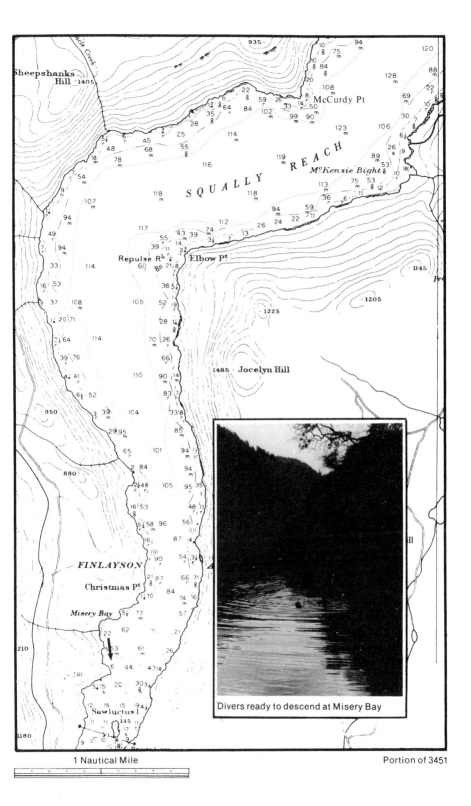

Divers ready to descend at Misery Bay

1 Nautical Mile

Portion of 3451

Skill: All Divers

Why go: "The Valley of White Sponges"... whispered in capital letters... where cloud sponges are so large a diver can jump into them. This extravagant tale helps lure one to The White Lady. Because the magical valley has thus far eluded me, I have to go back. I'm not sure if the whole thing is a dream or not, but it's a nice one.

And there's much, much more to see at this very good reef. We saw chimney sponges, tiger rockfish, lingcod, moon jellyfish, sea pens, seals, small nudibranchs and hermit crabs on the reef. Deer on the beach.

Access: The White Lady is ¾ of the way down the east side of Saanich Inlet, 3 miles south of Brentwood Bay.

Charter, rent, or launch at Brentwood Bay, 15 miles northwest of Victoria on Saanich Peninsula. From the Parliament Buildings in Victoria head north on Douglas Street, or Highway 17, towards Swartz Bay Ferry Terminal. Go 10½ miles. At Keating Cross Road, turn left and follow signs to Brentwood Bay. Then by boat south 3 miles to Repulse Rock or The White Lady, which is marked with the usual triangular "white lady" marker, 50 yards offshore from Elbow Point. Anchor, do not tie onto marker. It is a federal offense to make fast to a marker or tamper with any aid to navigation. Or land on the small rocky beach, and swim out and go down. One diver told me that The Valley of White Sponges starts at 90 or 100 feet, below the southeast corner of the marker. Another said at 105 or 115 feet, north of the marker. I have searched on the north side and did not find it. Look under a ledge on the south/southeast side and you might find "The Hidden Valley of White Sponges".

Bottom and Depths: Rocky reef covered with bottom kelp undulates in the shallows around the marker in a deceptive manner to 30 or 40 feet, then drops sharply on all sides. The reef offers good diving for beginners. Intermediate and advanced divers may want to drop deeper to explore for The Valley.

Hazards: Small boats, broken fishing line, and poor visibility. Red jellyfish, in the fall. Even when using your compass surfacing by the marker is difficult because the bottom immediately around the marker undulates in a deceptive manner. Listen for boats and ascend with a reserve of air; if you hear a boat you can stay down until it passes. Carry a knife. If you have seen any red jellyfish, you and your buddy should check one another for stinging tentacles before removing your masks and gloves.

Telephone: Brentwood Bay Ferry Landing.

Facilities: Small rocky crescent beach near the marker on Repulse Rock is pleasant for a picnic in the wilds. Air fills, camping, hot showers, accommodations, charters, rentals, and launching at Brentwood Bay.

Comments: If you find The Valley please lead me to it!

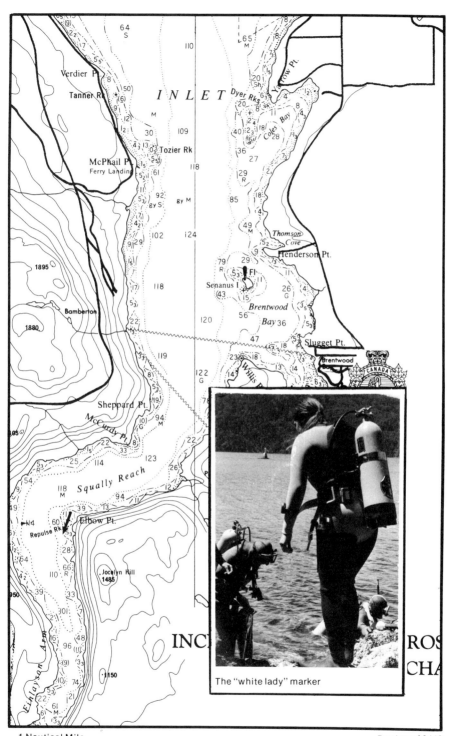

The "white lady" marker

Skill: All Divers

Why go: McKenzie Bight is an excellent protected inlet dive — a good place to go when the wind is blowing outside. An easy dive with plenty of life and no currents to consider. A variety of fish and invertebrates live here. During one dive at this site I saw small rockfish, one large lingcod, a couple of ratfish, clouds of herring and a small alabaster nudibranch laying eggs. A good spot for giant nudibranchs, especially in spring. Decorator crabs. Sea pens in the sand. Moon jellyfish billowing through the open water. Octopuses and wolf eels hiding in holes under the rocks.

Access: From the Parliament Buildings in Victoria go 20 miles to McKenzie Bight. Head north on Douglas Street or Highway 17. At Royal Oak turn off onto West Saanich Road, B.C. Highway 17A. Three miles past the Dominion Astrophysical Observatory at the 5600 block West Saanich Road, turn left into Durrance Road and go 3 miles. Just past Durrance Lake on your left, turn right down Willis Point Road, which is well-graded gravel. Go 3 miles to Mark Lane, a rough gravel road. Turn sharply left and continue 2 miles to the end of Mark Lane where there is room for one or two cars to park. Walk down a 50-foot rough path to the water.

Bottom and Depths: Dark, jagged rocks covered with bottom kelp and some silt. A fairly quick drop to coarse crushed white shell bottom at 70 or 80 feet.

Hazards: Poor visibility. Red jellyfish, in the fall. Listen for boats and ascend close to the bottom all the way to shore, well out of the way of them. If you have seen any red jellyfish, you and your buddy should check one another for stinging tentacles before removing your masks and gloves.

Telephones: 1. Prospect Lake General Store, 1 mile south of Durrance Road turnoff in 5300 block West Saanich Road.
2. Brentwood Shopping Centre, 2 miles north of Durrance Road turnoff in 7100 block West Saanich Road.

Facilities: None at McKenzie Bight. Air fills, camping, hot showers, accommodations, charters, rentals, and launching nearby at Brentwood Bay.

Comments: Because few homes are nearby, McKenzie Bight has an unspoilt feeling above water as well as below. Wild rabbits on the road and deer in the woods.

Giant nudibranch passing burrowing anemone

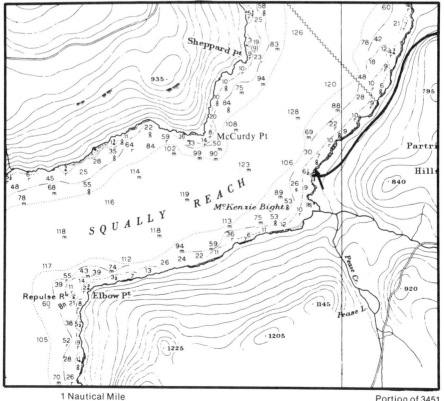

1 Nautical Mile

Portion of 3451

Skill: All Divers

Why go: Tod Inlet is well-protected from almost all winds and so close to Brentwood Bay that I cannot imagine why anything remains. But it does.
In Tod Inlet there is also a sunken barge — if you can find it. Bottles from an old Chinese settlement will make exotic "finds" for your collection. Plus the ever-present beauty of other forms of life. We saw red rock crabs and good-sized lingcod, too. I delighted in the sensation of sailing through space, pushing light and airy planets with a flick of my finger as I made my way through thousands of opalescent moon jellyfish.
Tod Inlet can provide hours of interesting diving for the treasure hunter, spear fisherman and sightseer.

Access: Tod Inlet is a long, thin finger reaching into Saanich Peninsula on the south side of Brentwood Bay in Saanich Inlet.
Charter, rent, or launch at Brentwood Bay, 15 miles northwest of Victoria on Saanich Peninsula. From the Parliament Buildings in Victoria head north on Douglas Street or Highway 17 towards Swartz Bay Ferry Terminal. Go 10½ miles. At Keating Cross Road, turn left and follow signs to Brentwood Bay. Then by boat south ¼ mile into Tod Inlet. Anchor near Butchart's Gardens and descend.

Bottom and Depths: Rocky bottom drops gradually to 30 or 40 feet, then falls away fairly quickly to 80 feet or so. Very silty.

Hazards: Small boats and poor visibility. Red jellyfish, in the fall. Listen for boats and stay close to the bottom all the way to shore, well out of the way of those boats. If you have seen any red jellyfish, you and your buddy should check one another for stinging tentacles before removing your masks and gloves.

Telephone: Brentwood Bay Ferry Landing.

Facilities: None at Tod Inlet. Air fills, camping, hot showers, accommodations, charters, rentals and launching at Brentwood Bay.

Comments: After your dive, visit Butchart Gardens overlooking the inlet.

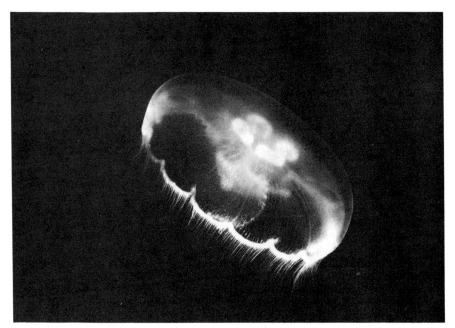

Moon jellyfish pulsing upwards

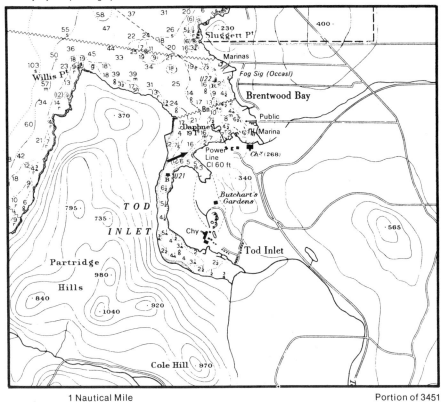

1 Nautical Mile

Portion of 3451

HENDERSON POINT
Shore Dive

Skill: All Divers and Snorkelers

Why go: Henderson Point is popular with all divers, day and night, because of easy access, few hazards and a variety of underwater life. Excellent for beginners. Nudibranchs, big and little, decorator crabs, painted greenlings, often called convict fish, kelp greenlings, seaperch, lots of little rockfish and moon jellyfish, you can expect to see them all. We saw one boulder splashed with a massive group of red anemones. Look for octopuses, rock scallops and dogfish. They are harder to find, but also present.

Access: From the Parliament Buildings in Victoria go 12 miles to Henderson Point. Heading north on Douglas Street or Highway 17 towards Swartz Bay Ferry Terminal, go 8 miles to Mount Newton Cross Road. Turn left onto Mount Newton Cross Road and go west 3½ miles crossing East Saanich Road, then West Saanich Road. Continue west on Senanus Drive for another ½ mile to the end of the road. A large gravel turnaround gives room for ten cars to park. Walk 50 yards through the woods to the easy rocky entry.

Bottom and Depths: Smooth rocks on the shore give way to small rocks scattered with bottom kelp and an occasional boulder. The slope is gentle to smooth sand at 50 or 60 feet right in front of Henderson Point. To the right, a shallow reef. South of the point, deep chasms of rock. North of Henderson Point, ⅓ mile across Thomson Cove, a wall drops straight down.

Hazards: Small boats and poor visibility, in summer. Red jellyfish, in the fall. Listen for boats and ascend along the bottom all the way to shore, well out of the way of them. If you have seen any red jellyfish, you and your buddy should check one another for stinging tentacles before removing your masks and gloves.

Telephone: Prairie Inn and Café, 3 miles back at junction of Mount Newton Cross Road and East Saanich Road.

Facilities: None at Henderson Point. Air fills, camping, hot showers, accommodations, charters, rentals, and launching at Brentwood Bay.

Comments: The rocks at Henderson Point make a good picnic spot in the afternoon sun. On your way home stop to see St. Stephen's, one of the oldest churches in British Columbia. St. Stephen's Church is down a small road which turns south off of Mount Newton Cross Road, just east of West Saanich Road. The moss-hung trees are beautiful, and the countryside around is pastoral and pretty in an English way.

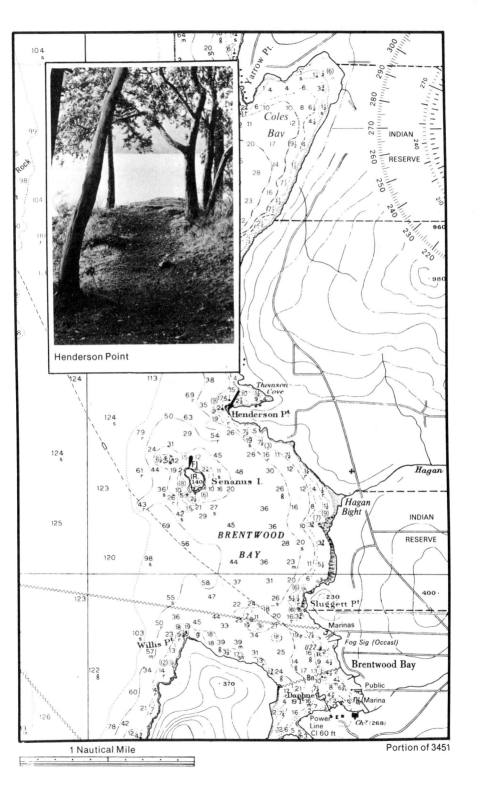

Henderson Point

1 Nautical Mile

Portion of 3451

ARBUTUS ISLAND **Tide Table:** Fulford Harbour
Boat Dive

Skill: All Divers

Why go: Arbutus Island is a perfect little gem of an island. Here you can see unusual brown cemented tube worms that form small reefs or mounds all over the bottom. And in one easy circuit you can see a cross-section of most of the life typical to the Strait of Georgia.
Sea pens, kelp greenlings, gorgeous orange spotted nudibranchs, rock scallops, octopuses, small abalones and schools of black rockfish all live at Arbutus Island. Overhangs are thick with white plumose anemones. We also saw small clumps of hard yellow staghorn bryozoans.
Arbutus Island: an easy dive with an outstanding variety of life. Beautiful by day or night.

Access: Arbutus Island is in Satellite Channel ½ mile off of the northern tip of Saanich Peninsula, ½ mile west of Piers Island.
Charter, rent or launch at Deep Cove, Brentwood Bay or Sidney. From downtown Victoria head north on Douglas Street or Highway 17 towards Swartz Bay Ferry Terminal and turn off at Sidney, Brentwood Bay or Deep Cove. Launch, go to the northern tip of Saanich Peninsula, and look for a small uninhabited island with two or three arbutus trees on it. Anchor or land, and dive all around the island. A good place to start is at the caves on the northwest corner of the island.

Bottom and Depths: A variety of substrates surrounds this one small island. Thick bull kelp in 15 or 25 feet, a vertical rock wall to 45 or 55 feet, caves and arches of rock at 30 or 40 feet, flat sand and large boulders.

Hazards: Current, small boats and, particularly in summer, bull kelp. Dive on the slack. Many small boats stop at Arbutus Island. Listen for boats and ascend close to the bottom all the way to shore, well out of the way of those boats. Wear a knife and ascend with a reserve of air, so that if caught in the kelp you will have time to cut your way free.

Telephone: Swartz Bay Ferry Terminal.

Facilities: None at Arbutus Island. Rentals and launching at Deep Cove. Air Fills, camping, hot showers, accommodations, charters, rentals, and launching at Brentwood Bay. Air fills, charters, rentals, and launching at Sidney. Camping at McDonald Provincial Park near Swartz Bay Ferry Terminal.

Comments: Arbutus Island is such a good cross-section of marine habitats and life that the Provincial Museum in Victoria is making a model of it in order to show the non-diving public a typical slice of the Strait of Georgia's underwater world. Let's treat it like a reserve and keep this perfect island intact as a permanent living display.

Arbutus Island

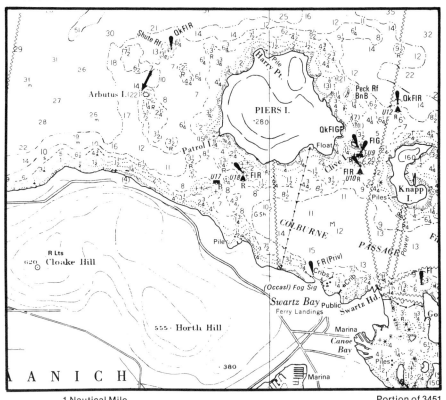

1 Nautical Mile

Portion of 3451

FORREST ISLAND **Tide Table:** Add 1 hour and 45
Boat Dive   minutes onto Fulford Harbour

Skill: All Divers

Why go: Forrest Island: excellent for beginners. Entry is easy
from the small protected bay and a rich variety of creatures inhabit
this safe, rocky site which can be dived at most times of day.
When diving here I saw a couple of small lingcod, a few rock
scallops, a wealth of urchins, white plumose anemones, red-and-
black striped tiger rockfish in a crevice, schools of small black
rockfish, a few swimming scallops, kelp greenlings, abalones and
a tiny hermit crab living inside a large bright orange sponge which
had dissolved the hermit crab's adopted shell home. In addition I
enjoyed the big rocks and rock wall drop-off coupled with the
security of having ledges on which to stop.
It would be a beautiful dive at night.

Access: Forrest Island is 2 miles east of Saanich Peninsula.
Charter, rent, or launch in Sidney. From downtown Victoria go
14 miles to Sidney. Head north on Douglas Street or Highway 17
towards Swartz Bay Ferry Terminal. Thirteen miles north you
come to Beacon Avenue and signs pointing towards Sidney. Turn
right and go to Sidney. From Sidney head east by boat to Forrest
Island. Look for a superb natural cove in the middle of the island,
with a rock standing guard 50 feet in front of it, and a scattering of
bull kelp all around. Anchor your boat or beach it in this protected
cove and enter from the beach.

Bottom and Depths: Rocky channels under water between the
shore and the rock. Around the rock the bottom drops away fairly
quickly in dark jagged shale-like ledges with big boulders tumbled
down the sides. To select the depth you want is easy at this site.
Light silt over all. Visibility best on the high slack tide.

Hazards: Current and bull kelp. Dive near the slack on large tidal
exchanges. Carry a knife and ascend with a reserve of air, so that if
caught in the kelp you will have time to cut your way free.

Telephone: Sidney Wharf.

Facilities: None on this uninhabited island. Air fills, accommodations, charters, rentals, and launching at Sidney.

Comments: Take a light for looking under rocks and into crevices.

Cove at Forrest Island

1 Nautical Mile

Portion of 3451

Skill: Intermediate and Advanced Divers and Snorkelers

Why go: Shellfish abound. Halibut Island is a beautiful shallow and colourful scenic tour complete with masses of small green urchins, giant red and purple urchins, kelp greenlings, cabezons, abalones, rock scallops and some swimming scallops. An octopus in residence, too.

Access: Halibut Island is situated in Miners Channel east of Saanich Peninsula.

Charter, rent or launch in Sidney. From the Parliament Buildings in Victoria go 14 miles to Sidney. Head north on Douglas Street or Highway 17 towards Swartz Bay Ferry Terminal. Thirteen miles north you come to Beacon Avenue and signs pointing towards Sidney. Turn right and go to Sidney. From Sidney go by boat 4 miles east and south to Halibut Island. Head past Sidney Spit, which juts into the water ¾ mile, and head around to the east side of Sidney Island. Continue south past rocky Mandarte Island which harbours a cormorant colony, to low, rounded and lightly-wooded Halibut Island. You will see a small natural cove on the northern end where you can anchor or beach your boat.

Bottom and Depths: Clean-swept white rocks splattered with mauve encrusting algae and scarlet sponge tier gently to coarse white sand bottom at 40 or 50 feet. Bull kelp at the northern tip of the island.

Hazards: Current and wind. Dive on the slack. The ever-present current never stops completely, but it affects you least near the northwest corner of the island where there is a back eddy. Wind from any direction can create difficulties in reaching this exposed site. Pick a calm day.

Telephone: Sidney Wharf.

Facilities: None at this uninhabited island. Mooring buoys, a landing float for small boats, sandy beach, campsites, picnic tables and drinking water at nearby Sidney Spit Marine Park. And plenty of crabs to catch on the sandy bottom on the west side of the spit. Air fills, accommodations, charters, rentals and launching at Sidney.

Comments: Remember rock scallops and abalones require 3 or 4 years to mature so that they can reproduce. Undisturbed, both of these shellfish may live up to 15 years. Leave some shellfish at Halibut Island for next year. . . and the next. In 1977 fisheries regulations allow you to take 12 abalones measuring at least 4 inches across the longest width of the shell. Before collecting shellfish, check current regulations.

And why "Halibut Island"? I don't know. I saw no halibut.

At north end of Halibut Island

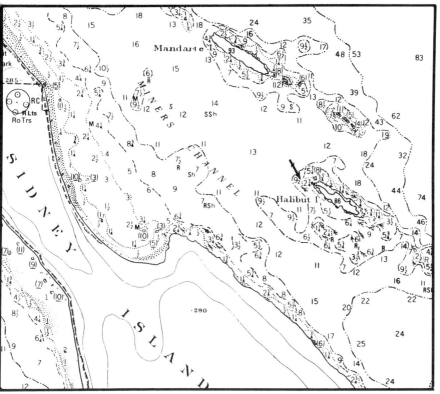

1 Nautical Mile

Skill: Intermediate and Advanced Divers

Why go: "Filter-feeder city" is the way one diver describes Ten-Mile Point where the current carries food which can be taken by marine life.
Swimming scallops would be enough to lure me to this beautiful Provincial Marine Ecological Reserve. All creatures which feed from the current flourish at this site. Particularly animals like burrowing cucumbers which put out tentacles to feed. "Suspension-feeder city" is a more accurate description. The wall is a colourful tapestry. Heaps of white burrowing cucumbers look like organ pipe cacti when their tendrils are retracted. We saw orange cucumbers. A forest of white plumose anemones, some rock scallops, quillback rockfish and other rockfish in the crevices. Small black rockfish swim past in schools. At the base of the wall, abalone shells, massive beds of giant barnacles, thousands of swimming scallops clapping up around us from the sand. You may meet a seal in the kelp.
In 1975 Ten-Mile Point was declared a Provincial Marine Ecological Reserve for scientific research. Recreational use is allowed as long as it is not damaging. Do not take any marine life. All you may take at Ten-Mile Point are photographs. In future a permit may be required to visit this area. I'm happy that this colourful site so close to the city will remain just as it is.

Access: From the Parliament Buildings in Victoria go 7½ miles to Ten-Mile Point. From downtown Victoria drive east on Fort Street which becomes Cadboro Bay Road. Continue curving along Cadboro Bay Road for 3 miles. One half mile past Cadboro Village the road becomes Telegraph Bay Road for a short way. At Seaview Road, turn right. Almost immediately turn left into Tudor Avenue. Continue on Tudor for 1 mile. Turn right at Baynes Road and go to White Rock Street. Turn left to the water. Park by the small turn-around, suit up, and climb a few feet down over the rocks to the sea.

Bottom and Depths: Rocky bottom, with some lettuce kelp and giant urchins, slopes gently to a bed of bull kelp at 30 or 40 feet. The crevice-filled rock wall drops off quickly to 80 or 90 feet and a sea floor of almost flat sand.

Hazards: Current, bull kelp and broken fishing line. Dive on the slack. Current up to 5 or 6 knots can run past this point. Be careful on large tidal exchanges. Carry a knife and ascend with a reserve of air, so that if caught in the kelp or fishing line you will have time to cut your way free.

Telephone: Cadboro Village, 2 miles back.

Facilities: None.

Comments: Under water it's a colourful site for photography. On the surface there are homes all around, but the area is not

rowded, and there's room for a picnic on the rocks at the end of the road, at
'en-Mile Point.

urrowing cucumber; sea cucumber to right

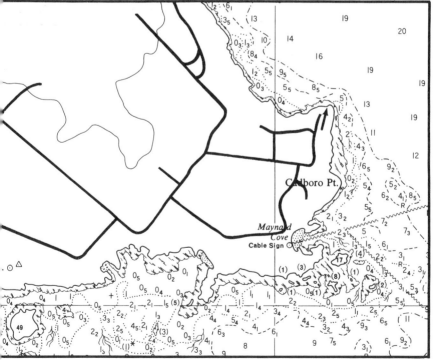

Scale of Feet 1000

Portion of 3423

Skill: All Divers

Why go: Going to Ogden Point Breakwater is a Sunday "thing to do" in Victoria — for divers and everyone else. For divers it's a popular checkout site, a favourite for sightseeing and photography.
But leave your spearguns at home. The Breakwater is a marine sanctuary — rich in marine life. We saw kelp greenlings, seaperch, tiger rockfish, lingcod and schools of black rockfish swimming through the kelp. Dahlia anemones blossom from the dark depths, urchins bristle from the rocks and clumps of white plumose anemones billow from the base of The Breakwater. You might see an octopus or a penpoint gunnel in a hole under the rocks. Look for sailfin sculpins, at night. The first half of The Breakwater is a great place for beginners to see a variety of marine life and to meet other divers.
Intermediate and advanced divers will find best diving on the last half of the outside of The Breakwater where strong currents carry more food to nourish life and fewer divers disturb the scene.

Access: From Victoria's Inner Harbour go less than 1 mile to The Breakwater. Drive south on Douglas Street bordering Beacon Hill Park to the water at Dallas Road. You are now at Mile 0 of Trans-Canada Highway. Turn right and go ¾ mile to The Breakwater. Walk along the blocks of The Breakwater just past the first bend, jump in, and dive out towards the tip.

Bottom and Depths: Broken rock is heaped along the base of The Breakwater which is 20 or 30 feet deep sloping to 80 or 90 feet deep at the end. Sand stretches out from the base. Thick beds of bull kelp rim The Breakwater which extends ½ mile into the sea.

Hazards: Bull kelp, wind and current. Carry a knife and ascend with a reserve of air, so that if caught in the kelp you can cut your way free. Southeast wind can blow up surf which makes it difficult to swim through the kelp and climb from the water. Dive the last half of The Breakwater on the slack.

Telephones: 1. James Bay Anglers' Association, 79 Dallas Road.
2. Niagara and Douglas Streets, 2 blocks north of Mile 0.

Facilities: Parking space for two dozen cars. More parking on the street.

Comments: The festive feeling on the beach is enough to make a visit to The Breakwater worthwhile. Among non-divers, you'll probably see many different kinds of action along The Breakwater. People sit along the edge with fishing poles. Mothers wheel strollers. Teenage boys lift their bikes around the gate in order to ride along the granite wall. We saw a man with a home-made anchor-like hook dragging for kelp to use as garden fertilizer. Others just sit or stand and watch. A real carnival atmosphere.

Ogden Point Breakwater

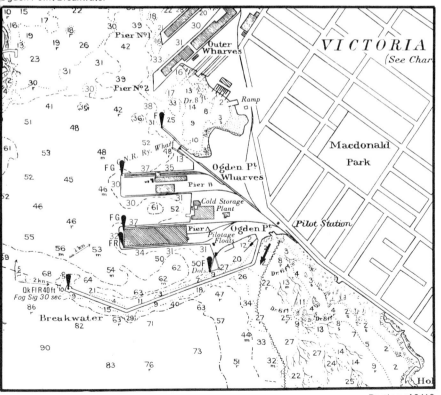

Scale of Feet 1000

Portion of 3413

Skill: Intermediate and Advanced Divers

Why go: Brotchie Ledge — part of Ogden Point area which is closed to spearfishing — is an endless source of gorgeous junk. You can't take marine life, but you can collect valuable old bottles, crockery and the other old "things" which are everywhere. Fifty to 100 years ago garbage barges regularly came from Victoria's Inner Harbour and deposited their load in this area. On one dive at Brotchie Ledge three of us found two tiger whiskey bottles, two Chinese bean pots, a large flower planter and one crockery marmalade pot. From the size of the barnacles on all of them we guessed they must be at least fifty years old. We also stumbled onto something big which might have been a boiler from a ship, probably part of the 332-foot metal-hulled *San Pedro*.
   In 1891 the *San Pedro* went down on Brotchie Ledge. Two salvage companies went bankrupt trying to salvage her before she was declared a navigational hazard and was blown up. Fragments of the *San Pedro* are flung over Brotchie Ledge. Investigate anything with giant barnacles growing on it, dig in the silty sand among the swimming scallops, and you will probably come up with some intriguing relics.

Access: Brotchie Ledge is ½ mile offshore from The Breakwater at Ogden Point just outside Victoria's Inner Harbour.
   Charter out of Victoria, launch an inflatable at The Breakwater, or launch at James Bay Anglers' Ramp, 79 Dallas Road. Go less than ½ mile offshore from The Breakwater: a marker with a small windmill indicates the ledge. The waters around the ledge itself are too deep and too current-ridden to anchor. Dive from a "live" boat. Leave someone on the boat to follow you and pick you up when you ascend.

Hazards: Wind, current, poor visibility and sailboats. Dive at Brotchie Ledge in early morning when the water is calm, on the slack, on a small tidal exchange. If you cannot coordinate all these factors, dive in the early morning when the water is calm and the pickup person can easily see your bubbles. For best visibility, try to disturb the bottom as little as possible when delving in the muck. Sailboats approach silently; spiral, look up and ascend cautiously when you have seen sailboats at Brotchie Ledge.

Telephone: James Bay Anglers' Launching Ramp, 79 Dallas Road.

Facilities: None.

Comments: Remember that Brotchie Ledge is closed to spearfishing. Do not disturb any marine life. There is so much of interest at this site. One diver collects nothing here but footwarmers, sometimes called "pigs".

Barnacled Chinese bean pot

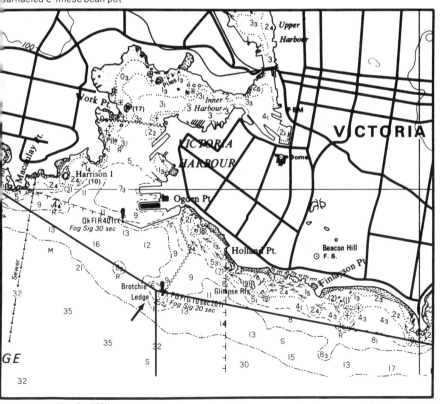

1 Nautical Mile

Portion of 3422

WRECK OF THE MAJOR TOMPKINS

Shore Dive

Skill: All Divers and Snorkelers

Why go: Superb beginner's wreck dive — or even for snorkelers — the 97-foot *Major Tompkins* was a 151-ton wooden hulled steamer which went down near Macaulay Point on February 25th 1855. "Pumpkins", as this old mail carrier was nicknamed, was built in Philadelphia in 1847 and had been in service on the Pacific for less than six months when she hit Harrison Island and went down This vessel is one of the oldest wrecks in British Columbia Though broken up quite a bit, the ghostly image of a ship is discernible in some of the wreckage. Nudibranchs and rockfish hide in the kelp. In places we saw ribs sticking up. Crusted with bottom kelp and sponges. Schools of black rockfish swim between the remaining ribs, and geoduck clams poke through the muddy sand around them.

Access: From the Parliament Buildings in Victoria go 3½ miles to the *Major Tompkins*, near Macaulay Point. Cross Johnson Street Bridge and go west on Esquimalt just over 1½ miles to Lampson Street. Turn left and go to Munro Street. Turn left into Munro, go past the ball park, and turn right down Anson Street then left into Anson Crescent. Park near the old foundation of a house overlooking Harrison Island, and follow tracks of divers 50 feet down to the water. Snorkel between Harrison Island on your right and a smaller rock on your left. When you have gone between the rocks, look to your right to the exact point where the *Major Tompkins* hit Harrison Island and went down. The spot is on a direct line between the red-roofed house on Anson Crescent and the end of the Ogden Point Breakwater. Swim to the point and go down the side of the rock through bull kelp. At the base of Harrison Island in 25 or 35 feet of water you should find yourself in the midst of the kelp-covered wreck.

Bottom and Depths: The *Major Tompkins* rests on silty sand at 25 or 35 feet at the rocky base of Harrison Island. Bull kelp attached. Shallow sand scattered with eelgrass, moon snails and urchins between the shore and Harrison Island.

Hazards: Bull kelp and wind. Carry a knife and ascend with a reserve of air, so that if caught in the kelp you will have time to cut your way free. Southeast wind can blow up surf and make entry difficult. The combination of kelp and wind can be very dangerous.

Telephone: Esquimalt Plaza, on Esquimalt 2 blocks west of Lampson.

Facilities: None.

Comments: When visibility is good you can see old "Pumpkins" from the surface on a low slack tide. Nice beach for a picnic.

Harrison Island where the *Major Tompkins* went down

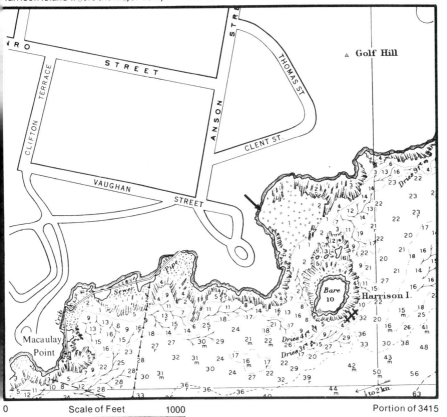

Skill: All Divers and Snorkelers

Why go: Saxe Point offers a sample of west coast underwater life without the difficulties of surf diving that usually go with it. A fabulous place to snorkel or dive, to see thick, thick shrub-like algae, big black leather stars, gooseneck barnacles, and small colourful pastel anemones. Purple plume worms flourish under rocky overhangs in only five feet of water. Immense sunflower stars, small chitons and green urchins cling to the rocks. We saw kelp greenlings, small decorator crabs and pale pink nudibranchs with brown spots. Delicate jellyfish with red eye-spots drift between the kelp. Geoduck clams, shrimp and burrowing cucumbers in the silty sand.

Because this has been a favourite picnic site of Victorians for years, you may find old bottles.

Access: From the Empress Hotel go 4 miles to Saxe Point. Cross Johnson Street Bridge and go 2 miles west on Esquimalt to Fraser Street. Turn left and follow Fraser to Saxe Point Park. Park near the plaque and walk down a short curving trail on your right to a small bay.

Bottom and Depths: Rocky bottom thick with bushy green algae and bull kelp tiers off in shallow ledges to coarse sand at 30 or 40 feet. Silty sand on the right.

Hazards: Bull kelp and wind. Thick bull kelp, especially in summer. Carry a knife and ascend with a reserve of air, so that if caught in the kelp you will have time to cut your way free. Southeast wind can blow up surf and make entry difficult.

Telephone: Esquimalt Plaza, 1 block east of Fraser and Esquimalt.

Facilities: Grassy park with beach, picnic tables, restrooms and parking lot.

Comments: The plaque by the parking lot commemorates the landing here on July 8, 1955 of Bert Owen Thomas of Tacoma, Washington, the first known person to swim the Strait of Juan de Fuca — 11 hours and 17 minutes.

Jellyfish with red eye-spots

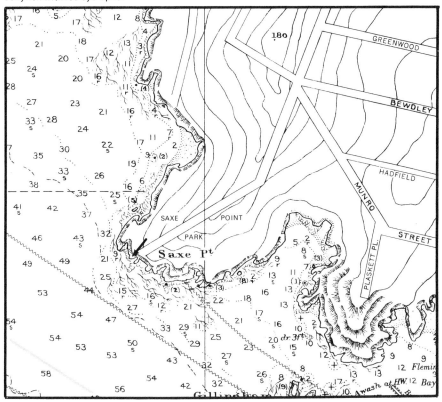

0 Scale of Feet 500

Portion of 3416

Skill: All Divers and Snorkelers

Why go: Fisgard Island is a beautiful place for beginners and snorkelers to see a colourful mixture of life in the shallows. Everything from crimson sunflower stars to purple feather duster worms, to lacy white plumose anemones, orange peel nudibranchs, prickly giant red urchins and little green urchins live here. Delicate jellyfish with red eye-spots drift through the kelp. Schools of pale green pipefish move along in small jerks. Kelp greenlings and schools of black rockfish swim past. Dungeness crabs and red rock crabs scramble along the bottom. We saw ratfish. I was even lucky enough to see the silvery flash of two salmon while ascending.

All in all, the waters around Fisgard Island have a feeling of luxuriant life.

Access: From the Parliament Buildings in Victoria go 8 miles to Fort Rodd Hill Historic Monument and Fisgard Island. Cross Bay Street Bridge and continue 5 miles along Craigflower Road, which becomes B.C. Highway 1A, towards Colwood. At Belmont Road turn left and follow signposts to Fort Rodd Hill. Park at the monument site. From here walk on a well-graded path, about 300 yards, down to the left of the old fortifications and across a causeway to the lighthouse on Fisgard Island. Dive all around Fisgard Island.

Bottom and Depths: Tumbled rocks covered with thick broadleaf bottom kelp slope to white sand scattered with small rocks at 20 or 30 feet. Some big boulders. A thicket of bull kelp in summer.

Hazards: Bull kelp and wind. Carry a knife and ascend with a reserve of air; if caught in the kelp you will have time to cut your way free. Southeast wind can blow up surf and make entry difficult.

Telephone: Colwood Plaza, 3/10 mile west of Fort Rodd turnoff.

Facilities: Grassy park, picnic tables and restrooms.

Comments: Fisgard Lighthouse was the first lighthouse on Canada's west coast and has been in continuous use since 1860. Fort Rodd Hill is a classic example of early means of defense. Maps and signs — and guides in summer — tell about the fortifications. Sixteen tame deer wander the grounds of Fort Rodd Hill Historic Monument between the well-preserved remains of three turn-of-the-century coast artillery guns. One deer will let you touch him. Nearby at Esquimalt Lagoon a beautiful stretch of log-strewn beach just invites bonfires. Obtain a fire permit from Belmont Park Fire Hall. When turning off the highway, do not turn left to Fort Rodd at the first fork in the road. Go straight ahead 400 yards to the Fire Hall which is open 24 hours a day. Telephone: 388-1826.

Fort Rodd Hill area offers something for everybody: for divers, snorkelers, and non-divers.

Fisgard Lighthouse

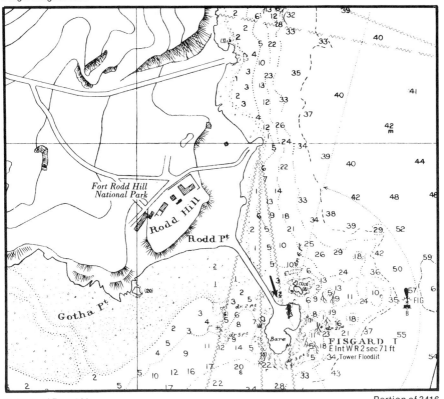

0 Scale of Feet 500

Portion of 3416

Skill: Intermediate and Advanced Divers

Why go: Finding a wreck is always fun and there's supposed to be a huge propeller still left on the *Barnard Castle*. The *Barnard Castle* hit Rosedale Reef, part of Race Rocks chain, on November 21st, 1886. She made a run for Pilot Bay at Bentinck Island, but sank just at the entry to the bay. We found great hunks of twisted metal encrusted with lots of life. And a huge three-dimensional thing that must be a boiler. Clinging to it was the biggest abalone I've ever seen in British Columbia. We saw a couple of large black rockfish, too. Apparently hordes of these fish used to live around the wreck.

Access: Bentinck Island is situated less than 1 mile off the coast south of Pedder Bay.
Charter out of Victoria or launch at Pedder Bay. From the Parliament Buildings go 18 miles southwest to Pedder Bay. Cross Bay Street Bridge and continue 7 miles along Craigflower Road, which becomes B.C. Highway 1A, towards Colwood. At Colwood, turn left and follow signs to Pedder Bay. Go 5 miles to Happy Valley Road. Turn right and go 2/10 of a mile to Rocky Point Road. Turn left and continue 3⅓ miles to Pedder Bay Marina turnoff. Launch at Pedder Bay and go around to Pilot Bay on the south side of Bentinck Island looking out towards Race Rocks.
Try to imagine where the *Barnard Castle* went down. Line yourself up between Race Rocks and a small shack on the northwest corner of the bay, and a line between the eastern point of the bay and a tall tree on the west side of the bay. Anchor in the bull kelp in 25 or 35 feet of water.
Because the ship lies north to south, search for the wreck by swimming from east to west and back again across the entrance to the bay.

Bottom and Depths: The *Barnard Castle* rests on silty sand in 25 or 35 feet of water and has bull kelp attached. Eelgrass grows in the sand around the wreck. Rock bottom at the eastern rocky point of Bentinck Island.

Hazards: Bull kelp, current, and silt causing poor visibility around the wreck. Carry a knife and ascend with a reserve of air, so that if caught in the kelp you will have time to cut your way free. On large tidal exchanges dive on the slack at the wreck. Always dive on the slack at the point.

Telephone: Pedder Bay Marina.

Facilities: None.

Comments: Do not land at Bentinck Island which is owned by the Department of National Defense. Sometimes there are explosions on the island.

Setting off from Pedder Bay for Bentinck Island

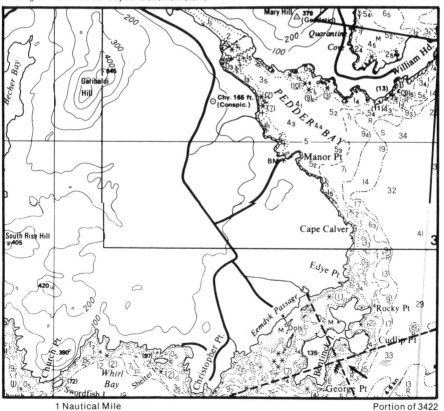

1 Nautical Mile

Portion of 3422

RACE ROCKS
Boat Dive

Current Table: Juan de Fuca Strait
1) **for Race Rocks:** at high tide, same as Juan de Fuca; at low tide, subtract 50 minutes from Juan de Fuca.

2) **For Race Passage:** at high tide, subtract 25 minutes from Juan de Fuca; at low tide, subtract 1 hour from Juan de Fuca.

Skill: Advanced Divers and Snorkelers

Why go: "Animals!" I know what that diver meant after his first dive at Race Rocks.

The most marine life I've seen anywhere lives around these infamous current-swept rocks. It's a magnificent mix of protected water sea life and outer coast wildlife — much of it in shallows. I saw big lacy basket stars in only 30 feet of water. Abalones all over the bright white rocks; jagged giant red urchins; and thick, thick bull kelp. Black serpent stars snake from hot pink hydrocoral more brilliant than tropical coral.

In The Great Race a plush carpet of brooding anemones, pink, pale green and lavender bonbons, completely covers the sea floor. Dahlia anemones, Puget Sound king crabs, pale yellow staghorn bryozoans, black rockfish, orange solitary cup corals, and harbour seals live at Race Rocks. Wintering northern sea lions and California sea lions haul out here from the end of September until May. We saw sea lions resting on the outermost rocks and scudding down the waves.

Race Rocks area also has its share of wrecks. This is probably the most densely wreck-ridden part in all of British Columbia.

Whatever your diving interest — you will love Race Rocks!

Access: Race Rocks: 3 miles offshore from Pedder Bay in the Strait of Juan de Fuca.

Charter out of Victoria or launch at Pedder Bay. From the Parliament Buildings in Victoria go 18 miles southwest to Pedder Bay. Cross Bay Street Bridge and continue 7 miles along Craigflower Road, which becomes B.C. Highway 1A, towards Colwood. At Colwood, turn left following signs to Pedder Bay. Go 5 miles to Happy Valley Road. Turn right to Rocky Point Road, then left and continue to Pedder Bay Marina turnoff. Launch at Pedder Bay and go south to Race Rocks. Tie up at the lighthouse dock at Great Race Rock. On all but the most minimal tidal exchanges, have a "live" boat follow you.

Bottom and Depths: South of Great Race Rock, bright white rocky bottom tiers gradually to 50 or 60 feet through a thicket of bull kelp. North of Great Race Rock in The Great Race, the bottom slopes gradually to 30 or 40 feet. Some bull kelp. You will find a 100 or 110 foot drop-off into Race Passage at the northwest corner of the westernmost of the Race Rocks.

Hazards: Current, wind, bull kelp and sea lions. Current can rush through The Great Race up to 6 knots and is so unpredictable that sometimes it does not turn at all, but just keeps running around Great Race Rock. Tide time varies with the size of the tide and with wind. Despite these hazards, there is always someplace to dive around Race Rocks. The south point of Great Race Rock usually has less current. Dive The Great Race and Race Passage on small tidal exchanges with a "live" boat following you in case you are swept away by the current. Wind can make reaching Race Rocks impossible. Telephone Victoria Marine Weather at 642-3431 to contact Race Rocks Light Station for an on-the-spot weather report. Carry a knife and ascend with a reserve of air, so that if caught in the kelp you will have time to cut your way free. Sea lions may approach divers and some injuries have been reported.

Telephones: 1. Race Rocks Lighthouse radiotelephone.
2. Pedder Bay Marina.

Facilities: None.

Comments: When diving here I was thrilled to find that the lighthouse keeper was a keen skin diver. Treat Race Rocks waters like a reserve and you will be welcomed warmly. Between dives we enjoyed a tour of the light station. Race Rocks is a great place both above and below the water.

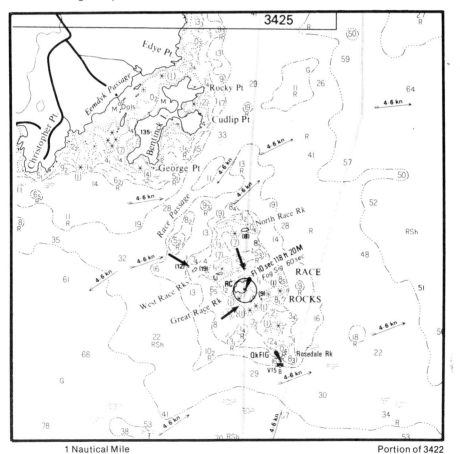

1 Nautical Mile

Portion of 3422

CHAPTER 7
Southern Gulf Islands
including Gabriola, Galiano and Saltspring

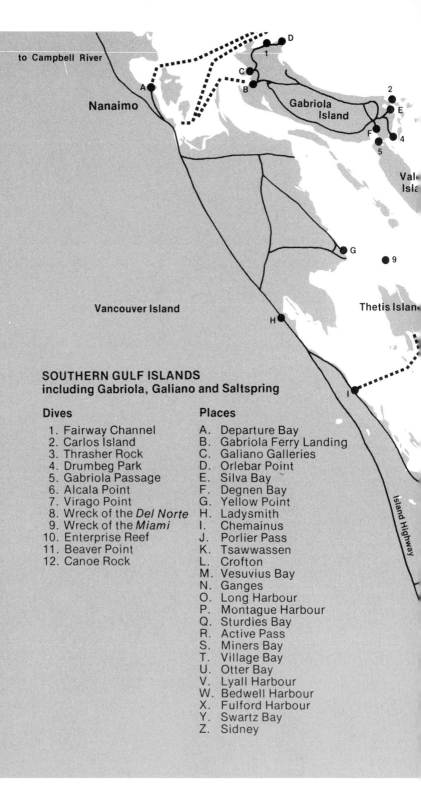

to Campbell River

Nanaimo

Gabriola
Island

A

C
B

D

1

2

E

F

4

5

Val•
Isl•

G

9

Vancouver Island

Thetis Island•

H

I

SOUTHERN GULF ISLANDS
including Gabriola, Galiano and Saltspring

Dives

1. Fairway Channel
2. Carlos Island
3. Thrasher Rock
4. Drumbeg Park
5. Gabriola Passage
6. Alcala Point
7. Virago Point
8. Wreck of the *Del Norte*
9. Wreck of the *Miami*
10. Enterprise Reef
11. Beaver Point
12. Canoe Rock

Places

A. Departure Bay
B. Gabriola Ferry Landing
C. Galiano Galleries
D. Orlebar Point
E. Silva Bay
F. Degnen Bay
G. Yellow Point
H. Ladysmith
I. Chemainus
J. Porlier Pass
K. Tsawwassen
L. Crofton
M. Vesuvius Bay
N. Ganges
O. Long Harbour
P. Montague Harbour
Q. Sturdies Bay
R. Active Pass
S. Miners Bay
T. Village Bay
U. Otter Bay
V. Lyall Harbour
W. Bedwell Harbour
X. Fulford Harbour
Y. Swartz Bay
Z. Sidney

Island Highway

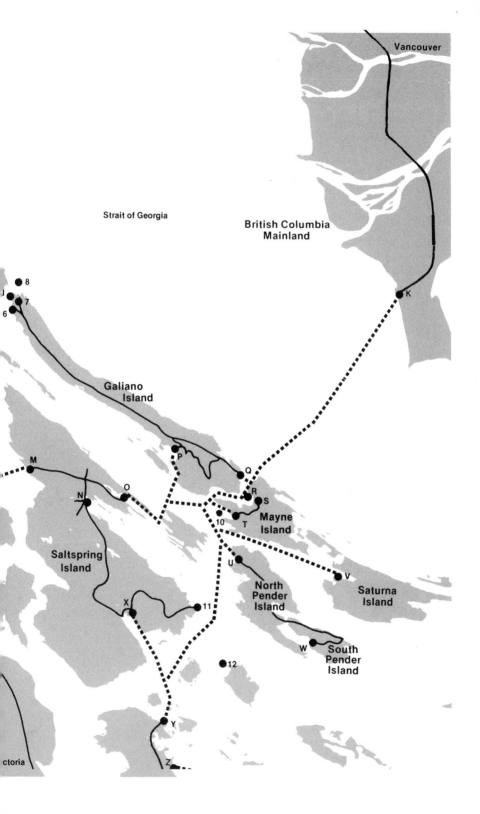

Vancouver

Strait of Georgia

British Columbia
Mainland

●8

J●
●7

6●

●K

Galiano
Island

M●

●P

Q●

●O

N●

R●
S●

●
10

T●

Mayne
Island

Saltspring
Island

U●

●V

Saturna
Island

North
Pender
Island

X●

●11

W●

South
Pender
Island

●12

ctoria

Y●

Z●

SERVICE INFORMATION*
Gulf Islands
including Gabriola, Galiano and Saltspring

Charts: Canadian Hydrographic Service
- 3450 East Point to Sand Heads
- 3452 Haro Straits to Stuart Channel
- 3453 Trincomali and Stuart Channels
- 3456 Approaches to Nanaimo Harbour
- 3473 Active Pass, Porlier Pass and Montague Harbour
- 3509 Plans in the Strait of Georgia

Tide and Current Tables: Canadian Hydrographic Service
Tide and Current Table, Volume 5

Emergency Telephone Numbers
R.C.M.P. Dial "0". Ask for Zenith 50,000.

Rescue Coordination Centre (Victoria) 388-1543

Rescue Coordination Centre (Vancouver) 732-4141

●Air Stations
Galiano Island
Alcala Resort
R.R. 2
North Galiano, B.C.
V0N 1P0
(604) 539-5720

Vancouver Island
Rimpac Divers Ltd.
9818 - 5th Street
Sidney, B.C.
V8L 2X3
(604) 656-6313
(*Compressor rentals also.*)

**●Boat Charters, Rentals
and Launching**
Gabriola Island
Degnen Bay
Gabriola Passage
(*Launching only.*)

Silva Bay Resort
Silva Bay
Gabriola Island, B.C.
V0R 1X0
(604) 247-9267
(*Charters only.*)

Surf Lodge
Berry Point
Gabriola Island, B.C.
V0R 1X0
(604) 247-9231
(*Boat rentals. Charters, out of Silva Bay.*)

Galiano Island
Alcala Resort
R.R. 2
North Galiano, B.C.
V0N 1P0
(604) 539-5720
(*Launching nearby.*)

Galiano Fishing Charters
R.R. 2
North Galiano, B.C.
V0N 1P0
(604) 539-2352 or 539-5751
(*Charters only.*)

Madrona Lodge
R.R. 2
North Galiano, B.C.
V0N 1P0
(604) 539-2926
(*Charters and rentals available
with cabin rental.*)

Montague Harbour Park
Galiano Island, B.C.
(*Launching only.*)

Salishan Resort
R.R. 2
Porlier Pass Drive
North Galiano, B.C.
V0N 1P0
(604) 539-2689
(*Rentals in spring, summer
and fall only. Launching
nearby.*)

Mayne Island
Jim Ross Charters
Miners Bay, on Active Pass
Georgina Point Road
Mayne Island, B.C.
V0N 2J0
(604) 539-2600
(*Charters only.*)

Springwater Lodge
Box 39, on Active Pass
Mayne Island, B.C.
V0N 2J0
(604) 539-5521
(*Charters only.*)

Pender Island
Otter Bay Marina
R.R. 1, Port Washington
North Pender Island, B.C.
V0N 2T0
(604) 629-3579
(*Rentals and launching.*)

Saltspring Island
Ganges Boat Basin Ramp
Head of Ganges Harbour
(*Launching only.*)

Nelson Marine
Ganges Hill
Box 556
Ganges, B.C.
V0S 1E0
(604) 537-2849
(*Rentals only.*)

Vancouver Island
Inn of the Sea
R.R. 1, Yellow Point Road
Ladysmith, B.C.
V0R 2E0
(604) 245-4257
(*Rentals only.*)

Rimpac Divers Ltd.
9818 - 5th Street
Sidney, B.C.
V8L 2X3
(604) 656-6313
(*Charters. Launching nearby.*)

● **Ferry Information**
B.C. Ferry Information Centre
1045 Howe Street
Vancouver, B.C.
V6Z 1P6
(604) 669-1211
From Saltspring Island:
537-5131
From all other Gulf Islands:
629-3222
(*Ferries between Tsawwassen,
Swartz Bay, Galiano, Mayne,
Pender and Saltspring Islands,
and from Crofton to Vesuvius
Bay.*)

Ministry of Highways Ferries
301 - 190 Wallace Street
Nanaimo, B.C.
V9R 5B1
(604) 754-2111
(*Ferries from Nanaimo to
Gabriola Island, and from
Chemainus to Thetis Island.*)

●**Tourist Information**
Ganges Crest Restaurant
Box 453
Ganges, B.C.
V0S 1E0
(604) 537-2511

Department of Travel Industry
1117 Wharf Street
Victoria, B.C.
V8W 2Z2
(604) 387-6417

How to Go — Go to Galiano, Mayne, Pender or Saltspring Island via British Columbia Ferry from mainland or Vancouver Island. On Vancouver Island go to Swartz Bay which is 20 miles north of Victoria. On the mainland go to Tsawwassen which is 20 miles south of Vancouver. Reservations are required for cars between the mainland and the Gulf Islands.

Go to Gabriola Island via Department of Highways Ferry from Nanaimo which is 69 miles north of Victoria on Vancouver Island. Nanaimo can be reached from Vancouver via British Columbia Ferry from Horseshoe Bay to Departure Bay or C.P.R. Ferry from Vancouver to Nanaimo.

*All of this service information is subject to change.

Skill: All Divers and Snorkelers

Why go: From Fairway Channel there's access to an exciting drop-off right from shore at Gabriola Island. Good shallow diving here, too. Smooth rocky beach slowly deepens to 30 or 40 feet where kelp grows. We saw all kinds of animals on the way out to the kelp: anemones, nudibranchs and sea stars. But if planning to dive deep, save your air and snorkel out well beyond the bull kelp before going down. At 75 yards past the kelp the smooth rounded rock rolls over into a drop-off. You'll see masses of quillback rockfish hanging out from the wall. Lingcod. We saw a large octopus on the edge of the smooth rock sloping down and played with him for a moment. He turned very bright red and shot off over the edge of the cliff which looks like a huge ship rolled on its side.

Over the edge of the drop-off there are ledges where you may see wolf eels. Deeper, the inevitable sponges.

Access: Fairway Channel is on the north side of Gabriola Island. It is a 20-minute ferry ride from Nanaimo to Gabriola Island and a 2-mile drive from Gabriola Ferry Landing to Fairway Channel.

From Nanaimo centre take the Department of Highways Ferry to Gabriola Island. Shortly after coming off the ferry at Gabriola Island you will see a sign pointing left up Taylor Bay Road. Follow this road, which becomes Berry Point Road, 2 miles to a place near the water where you will see an isolated public telephone booth on your right. On your left a smooth rocky beach slopes down to the water. Sometimes a boat on a pulley sits on the beach. This is the entry point. Swim straight out 75 yards past the kelp and descend.

Bottom and Depths: Smooth rocky beach slopes gradually to a large patch of bull kelp at 30 or 40 feet, 75 yards offshore. Another 75 yards beyond the kelp, in 65 or 75 feet of water, you come to the lip of the smooth rounded drop-off.

Hazards: Current, bull kelp and wind. Dive near the slack. Visibility is best on an outgoing tide. Carry a knife and ascend with a reserve of air, so that if caught in the kelp you will have time to cut your way free. Wind from the north can create surf and make swimming through the kelp difficult.

Telephone: Roadside above the beach.

Facilities: None at the site. Just a big broad rocky beach. Air fills, camping, accommodations, charters and launching nearby.

Comments: Going home, turn right on Malaspina Drive to see the intriguing weather-carved rock walls of Galiano Galleries, commonly called Malaspina Galleries. Go at low tide.

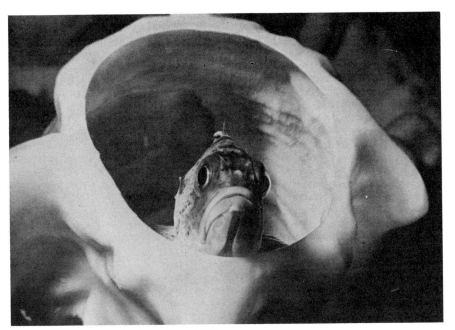

Quillback rockfish glowering from cloud sponge

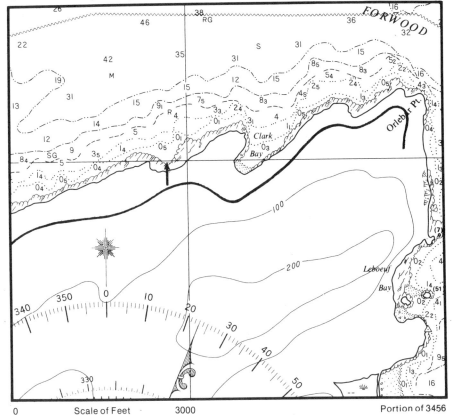

Scale of Feet

0   3000

Portion of 3456

CARLOS ISLAND   **Tide Table:** Add 5 minutes
                 Boat Dive   onto Point Atkinson

Skill: Intermediate and Advanced Divers

Why go: Grandiose broad slopes sweep down into the land of
the sponges and make Carlos Island — one of the Flat Top
Islands — popular with divers who like to dive deep.
   Often when springtime Fraser River runoff has restricted visibility in many other locations, waters are still clear around the
Flat Tops. When diving here we had a free-wheeling feeling as we
dropped from one beautiful ledge to the next — each one seeming broader and wider and more open than the one before. Stairsteps in tiers of sandstone fall to clean rocky ledges covered with
sand, then sweep down again. A tremendous sense of space.
   Sea pens live in the white, white sand. Rockfish, lingcod and
occasional swimming scallops beside the wall. Round orange
sponges. And chimney sponges, big and little, lead down to the
edge of the dark abyss where dogfish and ratfish cruise along the
edge of nothingness at Carlos.

Access: Carlos Island is in the Flat Top Islands off the northeast
end of Gabriola Island, less than 1 mile north of Silva Bay or 2½
miles north of Degnen Bay on Gabriola Island.
   Charter out of Silva Bay, Nanaimo, Vancouver or Victoria, or
launch at Degnen Bay. Go to Carlos Island, anchor north of the
island near the bull kelp and descend.

Bottom and Depths: Rocky bottom covered with bottom kelp
and bull kelp at 20 or 30 feet deep, just north of the island.
Clean-cut sandstone tiers down forming ledges which trap pools
of sand on the narrow stairsteps. This drop-off plunges to 49
fathoms.

Hazards: Some current, bull kelp and depth. Dive near the slack.
Carry a knife and ascend with a reserve of air, so that if caught in
the kelp you will have time to cut your way free.

Telephone: Silva Bay Resort.

Facilities: None at Carlos Island. Air fills, camping, accommodations, charters, and launching at Gabriola Island.

Comments: Once you've dived Carlos, why not try Gaviola,
Saturnina or Acorn Island or do a "drift" through Commodore
Passage?

Collecting for Vancouver Public Aquarium, off Carlos Island

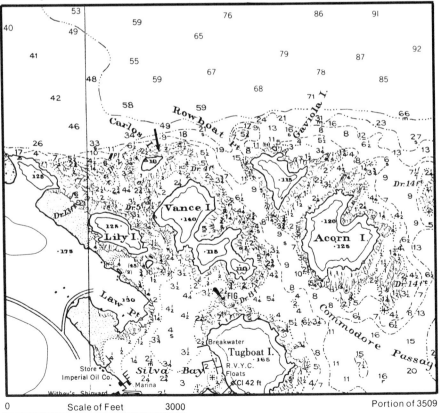

0 Scale of Feet 3000   Portion of 3509

Skill: Advanced Divers

Why go: Thrasher Rock must be one of the wildest current spots in the Strait of Georgia. Not only is the current swift, it is also capricious. When diving here I felt as though an eggbeater was working in the water. Current came from all directions. The result: some of the biggest of fish. We saw a lingcod so big that instead of admitting our presence we became as invisible as possible. We were glad when it seemed not to notice us. This is wolf-eel country, too. We saw rockfish all over the place, kelp greenlings, large seaperch, tiger rockfish and giant urchins. Plumose anemones, orange cup corals, coal and scattered bits of wreckage.

Thrasher Rock is named after the wooden sailing ship *Thrasher* stranded on the rock while under tow on the evening of July 14th, 1880. She was carrying 2,600 tons of coal loaded at Nanaimo, the old coaling centre. While diving here on May 21st, 1975, two of our divers found bits of the wreckage north/northeast of the marker at Thrasher Rock in 30 feet of water, and brought up bits of coal.

Access: Thrasher Rock, indicated by a concrete marker at the northeast tip of Gabriola Reefs in the Strait of Georgia, is just over 2 miles offshore east of Silva Bay on Gabriola Island. Charter out of Silva Bay, Nanaimo, Vancouver or Victoria, or launch at Degnen Bay and proceed to Thrasher Rock. Anchor and dive. Do not tie onto marker. It is a federal offense to make fast to a marker or tamper with any aid to navigation. The remains of the *Thrasher* are north/northeast of the marker in 25 or 35 feet of water.

Bottom and Depths: Thrasher Rock is a large round rock with some boulders and crevices. At the marker the depth is 10 feet. The reef extends 200 to 300 feet on either side. Dense bottom kelp covers the rocks. Around the rock it is 20 or 30 feet deep. North of the rock is a 50 or 60 foot ledge.

Hazards: Current and wind. Dive on the predicted slack, but use your common sense. Pull out of the dive if the current is picking up. Current is often unpredictable at Thrasher. Leave a pickup person in the boat in case you are swept away by that current. Check the wind when you plan to dive here. Winter is usually stormy. Spring is a good time to dive at Thrasher.

Telephone: Silva Bay Resort.

Facilities: None at Thrasher Rock. Air fills, camping, accommodations, charters, and launching at Gabriola Island.

Comments: To end a day of diving, warm yourself beside a fire made from the barnacled coal you found on your dive.

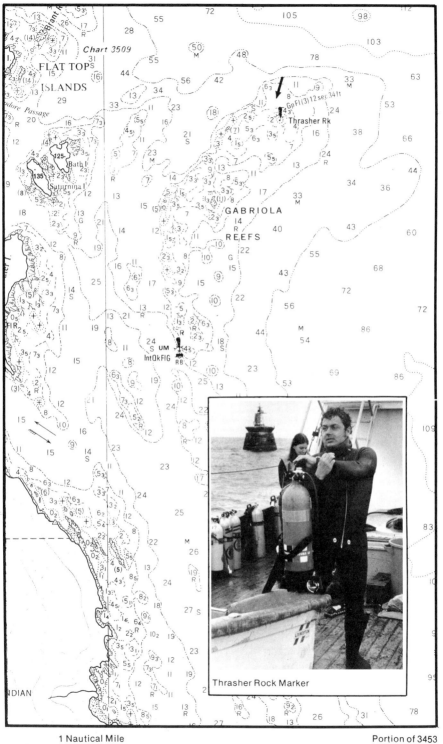

Thrasher Rock Marker

Chart 3509

1 Nautical Mile

Portion of 3453

DRUMBEG PARK   **Current Table:** Subtract 10
         Shore Dive   minutes from Porlier Pass

Skill: Intermediate and Advanced Divers and Snorkelers

Why go: At Drumbeg Park you can walk into the water from
shore near the infamous Gabriola Passage.
Drumbeg Park waters are not nearly so treacherous as at the
passage itself, but much of the same current-fed life lives there.
Swimming out along the rock-rimmed shore at your left you'll see
giant urchins, sea peaches, grunt sculpins, rockfish, giant
barnacles and burrowing cucumbers along the wall. If you stop to
watch, sometimes you will see one finger of a burrowing cucumber bend from its extended position to its mouth to lick, then move
out again to find more food. But the feeding devices of barnacles
are not so much fingers as toes. One diver described giant
barnacles feeding: "They kick the water with their feet, then lick
their toes."
When we were diving at Drumbeg Park a young dogfish came
up, observed us with curiosity, and then moved on. Strange
sponges are on the sand.

Access: Drumbeg Park is near the southeast corner of Gabriola
Island. It is a 20-minute ferry ride from Nanaimo to Gabriola
Island and a 10-mile drive from Gabriola Ferry Landing.
From Nanaimo centre take the Department of Highways Ferry
to Gabriola Island. Coming off the ferry at Gabriola Island go 9
miles along South Road and turn right onto Coast Road. Go 100
yards and turn right onto Stalker Road. Continue ½ mile to a dirt
road marked "Public Access" on a small concrete marker. Turn
left and go ½ mile to Drumbeg Park. Walk a few feet to the water
and dive along the left side of the bay towards the lights at
Rogers Reef and Breakwater Island.

Bottom and Depths: Rock-rimmed bay drops 25 or 35 feet to
current-swept sandy bottom.

Hazards: Current. Dive near the slack.

Telephone: Silva Bay Resort.

Facilities: Grassy park, beach and pit toilets. Parking for five or
six cars. Air fills, camping, accommodations, charters, and
launching nearby.

Comments: Pleasant for a day of swimming, diving and picnicing on the beach.

Drumbeg Park on Gabriola, with Rogers Reef and Breakwater Island

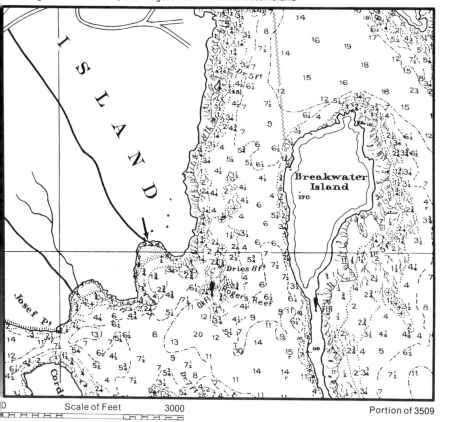

Scale of Feet 3000

Portion of 3509

GABRIOLA PASSAGE   **Current Table:** Subtract 10
Boat Dive   minutes from Porlier Pass

Skill: Advanced Divers and Snorkelers

Why go: Shallow and packed with life, as only a spot with current can be, Gabriola Pass holds excitement for everyone, for photographers, hunters and sightseers.
Gabriola Passage is where I made my first dive in a current-swept passage. I couldn't believe that the current never entirely stopped. But in retrospect, the place is not an alarming one for a first big-current-experience. Two small points stick out into Gabriola Passage, giving you someplace to swim for in case the current becomes unmanageable.
What's there? To say what isn't in Gabriola Passage is easier. We saw so much that I couldn't pick out anything at first. My buddy was also confused and couldn't decide what to do. First he pried a couple of rock scallops off the bottom. Then chased a kelp greenling. Lingcod were off-limits then, in February. Orange burrowing cucumbers poked up between giant red and small green urchins. Huge lingcod, tiger rockfish, cabezons, yelloweye rockfish and octopuses share the shallow ledges tiering down into the pass. An old anchor, too.
The shallows are also incredibly rich. Large flower-like plumose anemones flourish in five feet of water. Giant lemon nudibranchs, bright blue sea stars and little red rock crabs crowd the rocky shores. Even gorgeous sea pens in small pockets of sand. Marvelous snorkeling.

Access Gabriola Passage is the northernmost pass of the three major passages between the Gulf Islands. Porlier and Active Pass lie to the south. Gabriola Island is on the north side and Valdes Island on the south side of Gabriola Passage.
Charter out of Silva Bay on Gabriola Island, Nanaimo, Vancouver or Victoria, and go to Gabriola Passage. Or launch at Degnen Bay on Gabriola Island and go ½ mile to the south side of the passage. Have a pickup boat follow you.

Bottom and Depths: Rocky ledges tier down to 30 or 40 feet deep. One hole is 120 or 130 feet deep. Boulders and bull kelp. Some silt with the constant movement of current. The best visibility you can expect is 50 or 60 feet in winter.

Hazards: Very swift current, boats and bull kelp. Dive precisely on the slack on a small tidal exchange. Be prepared to pull out of the dive if the current starts picking up. Currents do not always run when predicted. A pickup boat is required. Listen for boats and ascend along the bottom all the way to shore, well out of the way of those boats. Use a compass and watch the current to find your direction. Carry a knife and ascend with a reserve of air, so that if caught in the kelp you will have time to cut your way free.

Telephone: Silva Bay Resort.

Facilities: None at Valdes Island. Air fills, camping, accommodations, charters, and launching nearby at Gabriola Island.

Comments: A very special dive.

Feeding an urchin to kelp greenlings

1 Nautical Mile

Portion of 3453

ALCALA POINT   **Current Table:** Porlier Pass
Shore Dive

Skill: Intermediate and Advanced Divers

Why go: Alcala Point is a fantastic shore dive. Where else can you walk a few feet to the water, drop down to 40 feet and see a basket star?
And basket stars are only a small part of the scene. As soon as you enter you're into bull kelp which streams like olive-coloured flags in the current and hides rockfish, urchins and lingcod. Clusters of white plumose anemones tumble over the rocky cliffs and overhangs like big underwater bouquets of dahlias. We saw small rock scallops among the rocks on the bottom, swimming scallops and giant barnacles the size of baseballs. Sea pens, kelp greenlings, sea stars, octopuses, tiger rockfish, wolf eels, cucumbers and lots of sea lemons. A lively painted greenling, maroon-and-grey striped and angry, may try to drive invaders away from his territory by attacking their masks with all of his four or five inches. I thought I saw a blue-eyed red brotula slip between the slits of the rocks.
A photographer could spend a lifetime in these waters.

Access: Alcala Point is the extreme northwest of Galiano Island, a 1- to 1½-hour ferry ride and 35 miles away from either Vancouver or Victoria.
To go to Galiano Island take a ferry from Swartz Bay, 20 miles north of Victoria, or from Tsawwassen, 20 miles south of Vancouver. Go to Sturdies Bay or Montague Harbour on Galiano Island. Reservations are required for cars on ferries between the mainland and the Gulf Islands. Once on Galiano Island follow Porlier Pass Road north. Go 15 miles until you see the diver's flag marking a road that curves down to your left to Alcala Resort. In front of the compressor shed at Alcala, follow a 10-foot path down the rocks to the water.

Bottom and Depths: Rock ledges and overhangs drop to a broad ledge at 50 or 60 feet. Small pockets of sand. Thick patches of bull kelp. Particularly beautiful ledges just to the north.

Hazards: Current and bull kelp. Dive precisely on the slack. Carry a knife and ascend with a reserve of air, so that if caught in the kelp you will have time to cut your way free.

Telephone: Alcala Resort, beside the compressor shed.

Facilities: Air fills, parking, camping and cabins. Launching nearby.

Comments: Alcala is ideal for night diving. It's so easy to walk into the phosphorescent night sea. So luxurious to return quickly to a hot shower and dinner after your dive.

At Alcala Point

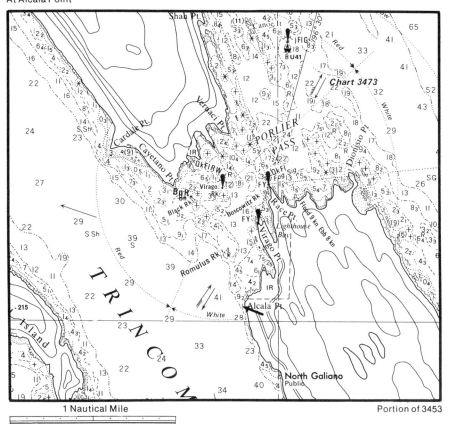

1 Nautical Mile

Portion of 3453

VIRAGO POINT   **Current Table:** Porlier Pass
        Shore Dive

Skill: Intermediate and Advanced Divers and Snorkelers

Why go: It's difficult to avoid superlatives when speaking of diving at Galiano Island. I become excited just thinking about it. You'll see almost everything at Virago Point. Because the life is shallow, this is a marvelous place for snorkeling. All kinds of anemones — snakelock, plumose and burrowing — live along this rocky shore which drops to white sand bottom. Gorgeous white plumose anemones cover the rocks. Not large, but in incredible numbers.

Swimming out, we saw large orange sea pens and little hermit crabs in the sand on our left. Crimson creeping pedal cucumbers, giant barnacles, tube worms and lots of small green urchins cling to the rocks on your right. You'll surely see an octopus if you look in all the holes. Rockfish are all over the place. Kelp greenlings, cabezons and lingcod. Schools of seaperch and huge black rockfish. There are nudibranchs in the kelp forest, rock scallops, dead man's finger sponges and basket stars. An abundance of everything.

You can't see the bottom because of the life.

Access: Virago Point, at the north end of Galiano Island and jutting into Porlier Pass, a 1- to 1½-hour ferry ride and 35 miles away from either Vancouver or Victoria.

To go to Galiano Island take a ferry from Swartz Bay, 20 miles north of Victoria, or from Tsawwassen, 20 miles south of Vancouver. Go to Sturdies Bay or Montague Harbour on Galiano Island. Reservations are required for cars on ferries between the mainland and the Gulf Islands. Once on Galiano, follow Porlier Pass Road to the north end of the island. Go 15 miles until the road bends right and comes close to the water. This is Baines Bay. Park at the side of the road. Walk down a small path through the bushes, enter, and snorkel or dive towards the lighthouse at Virago Point.

Bottom and Depths: Rocky shore with ledges, overhangs and boulders bottoms out to sand at 30 or 40 feet. It gradually deepens to 80 or 90 feet at the tip of the point by the lighthouse. A forest of bull kelp, in summer.

Hazards: Current and bull kelp. Dive precisely on the slack. On flooding tide, current becomes stronger and stronger the closer you go to Virago Point. Carry a knife and ascend with a reserve of air, so that if caught in the kelp you will have time to cut your way free.

Telephone: Alcala Resort, ½ mile back along the road.

Facilities: None immediately at Virago Point. Air fills, camping, cabins, charters, boat rentals and launching, nearby. Camping, picnic tables, mooring buoys and concrete launching ramp at the southwest end of the island at Montague Harbour Marine Park.

Comments: No other accessible snorkeling spot so exciting!

On path to Baines Bay

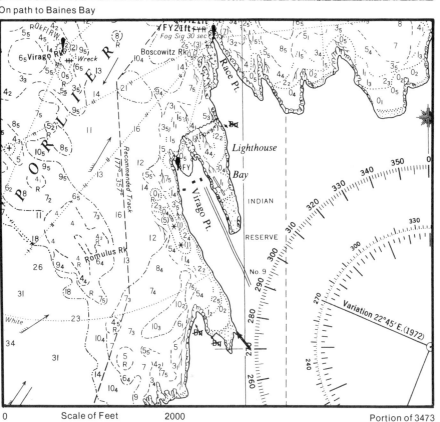

Scale of Feet

0   2000

Portion of 3473

Skill: Advanced Divers

Why go: An elegant 190-foot sidewheel passenger steamer converted to collier, the *Del Norte* went down in 1868 after hitting Canoe Islet at the northeast entrance to Porlier Pass. She lay undiscovered, a "virgin wreck", until 1972. Her location was not generally known, and she was not dived on by sport divers until 1975. Even now you have an opportunity of finding valuable old relics. Current has scattered remains over the reef. And because of the current you haven't many days in a year you can easily search for treasure here.

Copper and brass and who knows what else are lying on the bottom waiting to be found. On the first sport diving expedition on the *Del Norte* in early 1975, one diver came up with an ornate brass deck lamp. Others swam through the boilers. An anchor might yet be found on the reef.

Even without a wreck, Canoe Islet would be an exciting dive. I'll never forget drifting down through a curtain of silvery fish into a rocky field of basket stars. I touched one. It opened its intricate arms. Schools of black rockfish parted as we swam off to look for the wreck. We rounded a rock and looked straight into the face of a huge lingcod. Giant sea cucumbers all seemed to be in action. We saw kelp greenlings, orange cup corals, seaperch and feather stars.

Access: Canoe Islet is ½ mile north of Vernaci Point at the northeast end of Porlier Pass.

Charter, rent, or launch at North Galiano or charter out of Vancouver or Victoria. Anchor south of Canoe Islet. The *Del Norte* broke in two with the stern in deeper water. It is difficult to find. Bits and pieces of the *Del Norte* are scattered in 70 or 80 feet of water 200 yards south/southeast of Canoe Islet.

Bottom and Depths: Rocky bottom, 70 or 80 feet deep. Big boulders are scattered around and you may find lumps of coal.

Hazards: Very strong current. Dive on the slack on a small tidal exchange — not more than two feet. The current is most dangerous on an ebbing tide. Plan to dive on a high slack. Leave a pickup person in the boat in case you are swept away by that current.

Telephone: Alcala Resort, northwest corner of Galiano Island.

Facilities: None at Canoe Islet. Air fills, camping, cabins, charters, rentals and launching ramps nearby at Galiano Island.

Comments: A staggeringly beautiful dive. Add the excitement of a wreck, and you have a winner!

Waiting for current to slacken

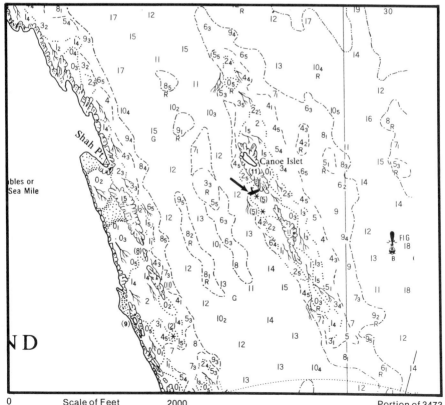

Portion of 3473

WRECK OF THE MIAMI
Boat Dive

Skill: All Divers

Why go: The *Miami* is a good safe wreck to dive and it is still recognizable as a ship. It's shallow, easy to find, and easy to dive. Even though sport divers have been diving the *Miami* since 1956 there are still things to be found at the site. A porthole was found in March 1975. Her sheer size means there's lots to explore. The *Miami* was a 320-foot, 3,020-ton steel freighter that carried coal. In 1900 she caught on White Rocks, now named Miami Islet, and went down.

In addition to the fun of swimming around and over a skeleton ship and hoping to find trophies, you'll see lots of marine life living around the wreck. Huge rockfish hide under the shadow of the hull. Huge lingcod use the wreck for shelter in spawning season. Millions of small white plumose anemones dot the dark rounded ribs. We saw giant barnacles, sea peaches and painted greenlings. Giant nudibranchs between the broadleaf bottom kelp. Millions of feathery burrowing anemones and clams in the silty sand around the *Miami*.

Fantastic on a sunny, still day for available light photographers who want to shoot a wreck.

Access: The *Miami* rests on a reef north of Miami Islet in Trincomali Channel, 1½ miles northwest of Pilkey Point on Thetis Island.

Charter, rent or launch at the north end of Galiano Island and go 7 miles northwest to the red buoy that marks the reef. Rent or launch at Yellow Point on Vancouver Island and go east 2 miles to the red buoy. Or charter out of Nanaimo, Vancouver or Victoria. Be careful not to hit the wreck. It dries on 11-foot tides. On a low tide you may spot it from your boat. If not, line up on a direct line between the red marker, Miami Islet and Pilkey Point. Anchor on that line near the bull kelp 100 feet south of the red marker and go down. Swim south under water along the west side of the reef until you see the huge hulk.

Bottom and Depths: The reef is silt-covered smooth rock and slopes gently down to 50 or 60 feet. On summer low tides a large portion of the *Miami* projects above water. The main hull rests on the bottom at 25 or 35 feet. The ship broke its back over the ledge. Some of it slipped down the western slope and some parts lie in 50 or 60 feet of water. Because of tidal effect she is very widely spread across the reef and changes all the time. One can still make good "finds".

Hazards: Current, wind, poor visibility and the wreck itself. Dive on the slack. Wind from any direction can make for difficulties in going to the *Miami* which is in an extremely exposed position. Visibility can be poor in summer, because of plankton growth, and at any time of year if too many divers stir up the silt. A still, sunny day in winter is the best time to dive. Be careful of sharp metal projections from the wreck.

Telephone: Alcala Resort, North Galiano.

Facilities: None at Miami Islet.

Comments: This reef collects wrecks. The *Robert Kerr*, a wooden vessel converted to collier which went down in 1911, lies in slightly deeper water on the reef farther south of the *Miami*. More difficult to find than the *Miami*, but if you're on a large boat and have lots of air you may want to look for it, as well. Take a light!

From Miami Marker, looking south towards Pilkey Point on Thetis Island

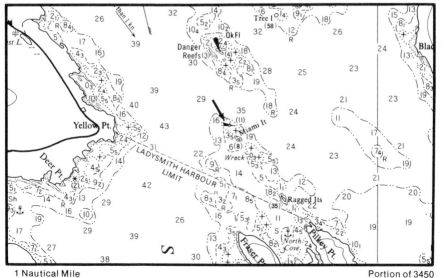

1 Nautical Mile   Portion of 3450

ENTERPRISE REEF **Current Table:** Active Pass
Boat Dive

Skill: Advanced Divers

Why Go: Enterprise Reef combines rich reef life with one of the best drop-offs in the Gulf Islands. Add the swift currents that flow through Active Pass, and you have the ingredients for one of the most exciting dives around.
You'll probably see Puget Sound king crabs, rock scallops, abalones, large lingcod, rockfish, basket stars and cabezons. Beautiful lemon nudibranchs in the kelp. We saw masses of giant red urchins and small green urchins. Work your way around the shallow ledges that look like molten rock flowing southward to go to the drop-off at the southern end of the reef. The wall is a waterfall of white plumose anemones cascading down the sheer side. White fluffy anemones soften the undercut caves and grottoes sheering down to 90 or 100 feet. Swimming scallops rain up around you all down the wall.
Divers have been chased from the water at Enterprise Reef by a pod of killer whales.

Access: Enterprise Reef is less than 1 mile south of the west entry to Active Pass, the way between Galiano and Mayne Islands. Active Pass is one of the busiest and most dangerous passes in the Gulf Islands because it is the main shipping and B.C. Ferry route between Vancouver and Victoria.
Enterprise Reef can be reached by charter from Mayne Island, Galiano Island, Vancouver or Victoria. Or launch at Montague Harbour on Galiano Island and go 4 miles southeast to the marker at Enterprise Reef. Anchor on the north side of the reef in the bull kelp in the shallows, and go down. Do not tie onto marker. It is a federal offense to make fast to a marker or tamper with any aid to navigation.

Bottom and Depths: On the north side of the marker, smooth rock ledges fall in folds at 20 or 30 feet deep. Thick bull kelp. Directly south of the marker the rock wall drops off to 90 or 100 feet.

Hazards: Swift currents, boats and bull kelp. Six- to seven-knot currents sometimes flow through Active Pass. Dive on the slack on a small tidal exchange. Listen for boats and ascend close to the bottom all the way to the surface. Carry a knife and surface with a reserve of air, so that if caught in the kelp you will have time to cut yourself free.

Telephones: 1. Village Bay Ferry Landing, Mayne Island.
2. Montague Harbour Ferry Landing, Galiano Island.

Facilities: None at Enterprise Reef. Charters out of Mayne Island and North Galiano. Camping and launching at Montague Harbour Marine Park on Galiano Island.

Comments: Though Active Pass has both very swift currents and heavy boat traffic, these were not the reasons for its name. It was named after the American survey ship *Active*.

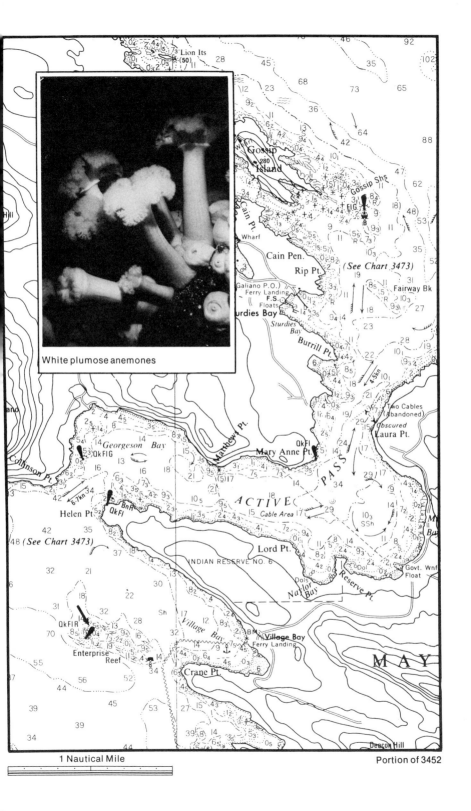

White plumose anemones

1 Nautical Mile

Portion of 3452

Skill: Intermediate and Advanced Divers at point; All Divers in bay.

Why go: I think of castles and caves when I think of Beaver Point. Rocky wall encrusted in castle-like staghorn bryozoans falls in caves, grottoes and overhangs. Some caves are large enough to enter. Hiding places for all kinds of life are scattered along this current-swept, crusty wall. We saw fluffy white plumose anemones under the overhangs. Millions of little crabs poking out of cracks between the staghorn. White encrusting sponges and dahlia anemones add further to this scenic site. Huge sea stars, rockfish, nudibranchs, octopuses, lingcod and giant barnacles. We even saw a prawn and a gorgeous sea pen living in a pocket of sand. Sponges down deeper.

Current-free diving at any time of day for all divers in the shallow cove on the left of the point. And a small reef on the outer edge of the cove near the opposite shore.

But unique to Beaver Point — and why I love it the most — are the overhangs, castles and caves.

Access: Beaver Point is at Ruckle Provincial Park on Saltspring Island, 19 miles from the ferry landing at Long Harbour. From Long Harbour follow signs to Ganges, then Fulford Harbour. Just before Fulford, turn left onto Beaver Point Road and go 6 more miles to Ruckle Park. From the end of the road walk ¼ to ½ mile to the water. Enter and swim around to your right towards Beaver Point.

Bottom and Depths: Rock walls, ledges and overhangs drop to broken rock at 30 or 40 feet. Some bull kelp. The drop-off is progressively deeper at the base of the wall as you move around towards the point.

Hazards: Current and bull kelp. Dive on the slack. Carry a knife and ascend with a reserve of air, so that if caught in the kelp you will have time to cut your way free.

Telephone: Ganges Government Boat Basin parking lot.

Facilities: Ruckle Provincial Park is a spacious, wild park with broad, slightly-wooded grassy slopes rolling down to the water. Being largely undeveloped is part of its charm. Walk-in camping, drinking water and pit toilets at Ruckle Park. Camping, accommodations, boat rentals, and launching at Ganges.

Comments: Locally the area is honoured as an underwater reserve.

Near Beaver Point

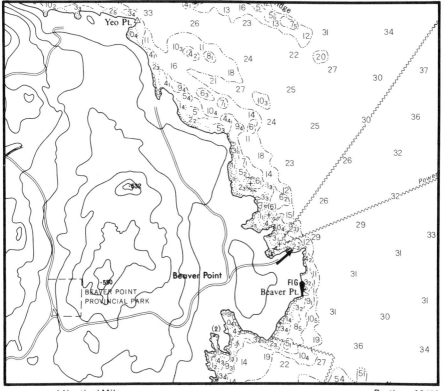

1 Nautical Mile

Portion of 3452

Skill: Intermediate and Advanced Divers and Snorkelers

Why go: All those fish! All that colour! And clean, clean water through which to see it all. Canoe Rock is one of those places where the current never stops. It merely changes direction. And there's a fantastic amount of brilliantly coloured life in only 25 to 40 feet of water. "Carrot tops!" describes the bright orange burrowing cucumbers between the chinks of the rocks. Big bright white boulders tumbled over one another are splattered with purple algae. We saw rock scallops, abalones, giant barnacles, great red urchins, masses of soft white plumose anemones and small orange sea peaches. Cracks and crevices between the rocks are filled with fish. So many huge tiger rockfish I couldn't count them. Large lingcod, cabezons, kelp greenlings and schools of huge black rockfish. Wolf eels under the ledges.

Access: Marked by a light, Canoe Rock is in Moresby Passage 300 yards west of Reynard Point on Moresby Island. It is 3 miles southeast of Beaver Point at Saltspring Island where we launched our inflatable, 15 miles south of Ganges on Saltspring Island, 7 miles west of Bedwell Harbour, Pender Island, or 6 miles northeast of Sidney on Saanich Peninsula. Charter, rent or launch and go to Canoe Rock. Anchor on the inside of the light towards Reynard Point and dive between the rocks and the point.

Bottom and Depths: Boulders, broken and stratified rock with ledges and tables, hollows and crevices and small broken rock lying on top undulates from the marker to 40 feet. Some bull kelp. No silt. A clean-swept bottom.

Hazards: Current and bull kelp. Dive on the slack on a small tidal exchange. A pickup boat is advisable. Carry a knife and ascend with a reserve of air, so that if caught in the kelp you will have time to cut your way free.

Telephone: Ganges Government Boat Basin parking lot, Saltspring Island.

Facilities: None at Canoe Rock. Air fills, camping, accommodations, boat rentals, charters and launching at Ganges, Saltspring Island and Sidney on Saanich Peninsula. Boat rentals and launching at North Pender Island.

Comments: An exceptional dive for those who like shallow reefs.

Tiger rockfish

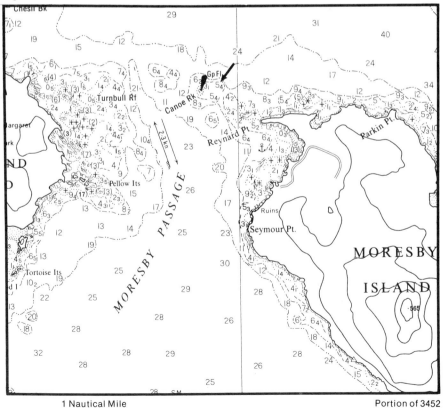

1 Nautical Mile

Portion of 3452

CHAPTER 8
San Juan Islands
including San Juan, Orcas and Lopez

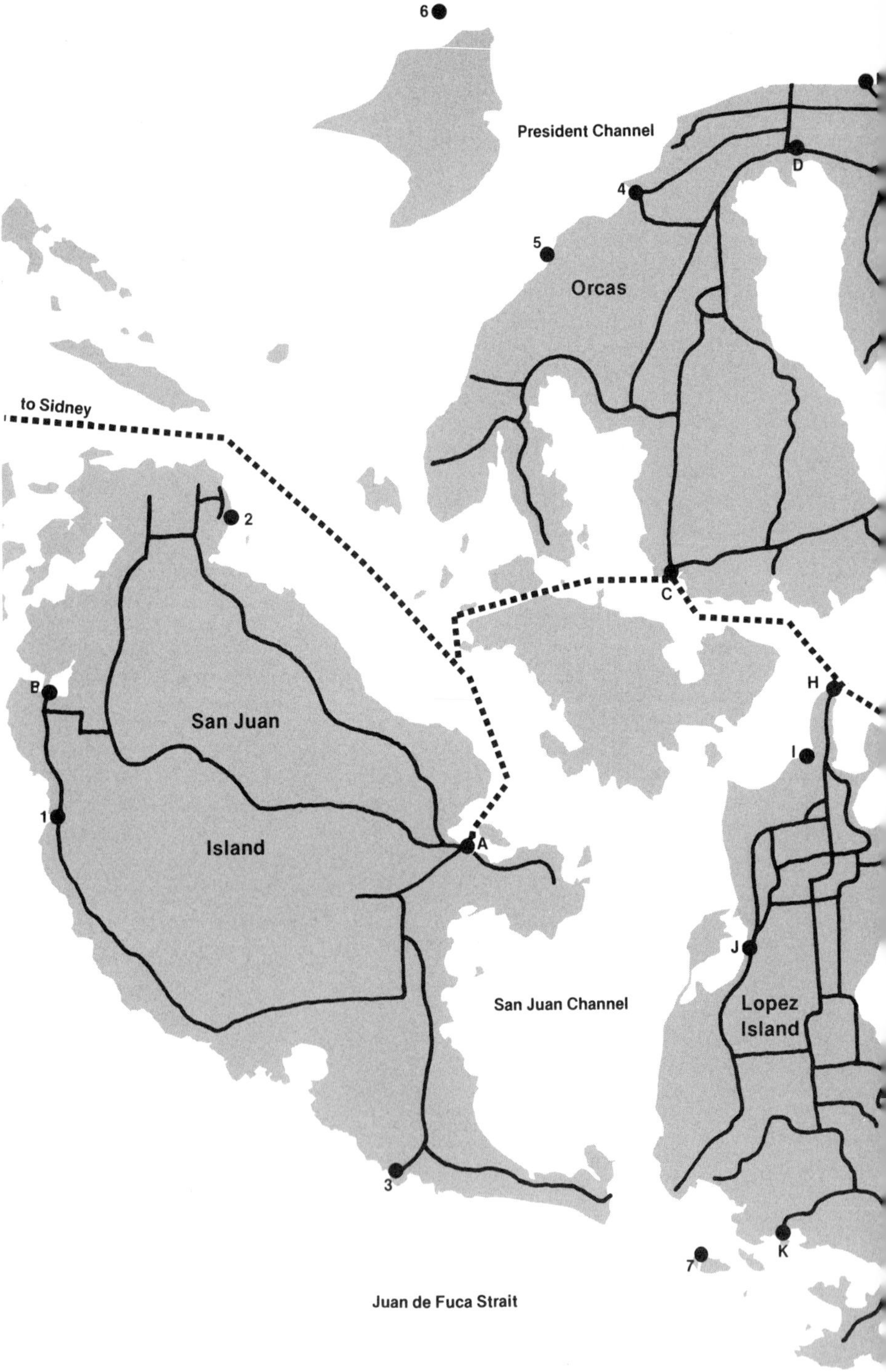

President Channel
Orcas
to Sidney
San Juan
Island
San Juan Channel
Lopez
Island
Juan de Fuca Strait
A
B
C
D
H
I
J
K
1
2
3
4
5
6
7

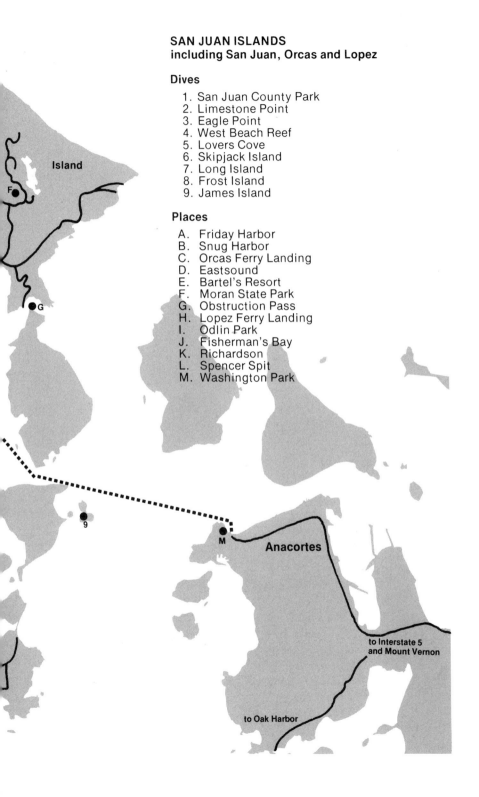

SAN JUAN ISLANDS
including San Juan, Orcas and Lopez

Dives

1. San Juan County Park
2. Limestone Point
3. Eagle Point
4. West Beach Reef
5. Lovers Cove
6. Skipjack Island
7. Long Island
8. Frost Island
9. James Island

Places

A. Friday Harbor
B. Snug Harbor
C. Orcas Ferry Landing
D. Eastsound
E. Bartel's Resort
F. Moran State Park
G. Obstruction Pass
H. Lopez Ferry Landing
I. Odlin Park
J. Fisherman's Bay
K. Richardson
L. Spencer Spit
M. Washington Park

Island

F

G

9

M   **Anacortes**

to Interstate 5
and Mount Vernon

to Oak Harbor

SERVICE INFORMATION*
San Juan Islands
including San Juan, Orcas and Lopez

Charts: United States Department of Commerce NOAA National Ocean Survey Charts

Old System	New System	
●6380	●18421	Strait of Juan de Fuca to Strait of Georgia
●184-SC	●18423	Bellingham to Everett including San Juan Islands

Tide Tables

United States NOAA National Ocean Survey
Tide Tables — West Coast of North and South America
or
Canadian Hydrographic Service
Tide and Current Table, Volume 5

Emergency Telephone Numbers

San Juan Island 378-4141

Orcas Island 376-2207

Lopez Island 468-2333

●Air Stations
Orcas Island
Bartel's Resort
Box 1040
Eastsound, Washington
98245
(206) 376-2242

West Beach Resort
Box 510, Route 1
Eastsound, Washington
98245
(206) 376-2240

San Juan Island
Friday Harbor Hardware
Box 398
Spring Street
Friday Harbor, Washington
98250
(206) 378-4622

San Juan Marina
Box 340
Front Street
Friday Harbor, Washington
98250
(206) 378-2841

San Juan County Park
San Juan Island, Washington
(Summer only.)

Snug Harbor Marina Resort
Friday Harbor, Washington
98250
(206) 378-4762

Anacortes Area (mainland)
Cap Sante Marine
Cap Sante Waterway
Anacortes, Washington
98221
(206) 293-3145

Whidbey Divers Shop
80th NW and 900 W
Oak Harbor, Washington
98277
(206) 675-1112

Bellingham (mainland)
Northwest Divers Inc.
2720 West Maplewood
Bellingham, Washington
98225
(206) 734-1770

Washington Divers
932 North State Street
Bellingham, Washington
98225
(206) 676-8029

•Boat Rentals and Launching Ramps
Orcas Island
Bartel's Resort
Box 1040
Eastsound, Washington
98245
(206) 376-2242

West Beach Resort
Box 510, Route 1
Eastsound, Washington
98245
(206) 376-2240

San Juan Island
San Juan Marina
Box 340
Front Street
Friday Harbor, Washington
98250
(206) 378-2841
(*Boat rentals only.*)

Snug Harbor Marina Resort
Friday Harbor, Washington
98250
(206) 378-4762

Anacortes Area (mainland)
Cap Sante Marine
Cap Sante Waterway
Anacortes, Washington
98221
(206) 293-3145

Washington Park
Anacortes, Washington
(*Launching only.*)

Bellingham (mainland)
Wildcat Cove
Larabee State Park, 2 miles
south off Chuckanut Drive
Bellingham, Washington
(*Launching only.*)

•Charter Boats
Afternoon Delight
Northwest Divers Inc.
2720 West Maplewood
Bellingham, Washington
98225
(206) 734-1770
(*Out of Bellingham.*)

Babnau and *Escort*
Edmonds Diving Center
138 Railroad Avenue
Edmonds, Washington
98020
(206) 775-3483
(*Out of Anacortes.*)

Cap Sante Marine
Cap Sante Waterway
Anacortes, Washington
98221
(206) 293-3145
(*Out of Anacortes.*)

Frolic
Professional Dive Charters
Box 535
Friday Harbor, Washington
98250
(206) 378-4804
(*Out of Anacortes.*)

Hobo
2132 SW 169th
Seattle, Washington
98166
(206) 242-8715
(*Winter only, out of Anacortes.*)

Sea Wolf
Box 413
Anacortes, Washington
98221
(206) 293-7538
(*Out of Anacortes.*)

Snug Harbor Marina Resort
Friday Harbor, Washington
98250
(206) 378-4762
(Out of San Juan Island.)

Teacher's Pet III
5010 North 18th
Tacoma, Washington
98406
(206) 759-9646
(Winter only, out of Anacortes.)

Captain Phil Fusselman
1501 SW 164th Street
Seattle, Washington
98166
(206) 244-2552
(Out of Anacortes.)

•Ferry Information
Washington State Ferries
Seattle Ferry Terminal
Pier 52
Seattle, Washington
98104
(206) 464-6400
(Ferries between Anacortes,
San Juan Islands and Sidney.)

•Tourist Information
Washington State Parks
Public Information
7150 Cleanwater Lane
Olympia, Washington
98504
(206) 753-2027

Chamber of Commerce
Orcas Island
P.O. Box 252
Eastsound, Washington
98245

Chamber of Commerce
San Juan Island
Box 98
Friday Harbor, Washington
98250
(206) 378-4600

How to Go — Go to San Juan Islands via Washington State Ferry from Anacortes, Washington or Sidney, British Columbia. Anacortes is 75 miles north of Seattle and 110 miles south of Vancouver. From Interstate 5 take Exit 230 to Anacortes. Sidney is on Saanich Peninsula 13 miles north of Victoria and 4 miles south of Swartz Bay, 1 mile east of Highway 17 at the end of Beacon Avenue. Follow the signs to Sidney.

*All of this service information is subject to change.

SAN JUAN COUNTY PARK
Shore Dive

Tide Table: Add 30 minutes
onto Port Townsend

Skill: All Divers and Snorkelers

Why go: It's almost too much! Gorgeous seascape — fish and shellfish — plus clean, clear water. Because divers have flocked to San Juan Park for years I can't imagine how this is all still there, unspoilt and virginal and wild. But it is.
And all so accessible. You can walk from your tent to the water.
Beginners and snorkelers can enjoy easy diving in the bay with its shallow sandy bottom rimmed with rock. Even the tidepools hold lots of life. Small pastel green and pink anemones burgeon like flowers. Tufts of orange burrowing cucumbers soften the bright white rocks. Blue starfish, little green urchins, gum boot chitons, kelp greenlings, and giant red urchins decorate the rocky shallows.
Beyond the bay and south around the point you swim into bull kelp and rocky bottom falling away quickly into big-boulder country and rocky overhangs. Shrimp, big black rockfish, lingcod, white plumose anemones, bright yellow encrusting sponges, abalones, and free-swimming scallops are some of the animals you'll see. Look for octopuses, too.
Even more life and good spearfishing are found out at current-swept Low Island less that ¼ mile offshore, but the swim is a tough one through current. Only for advanced divers who are strong swimmers, and divers with paddleboards. There is more good diving from a boat all along the southern shore.

Access: San Juan Island is 2 hours by ferry from Anacortes. From Friday Harbor Ferry Landing at San Juan Island go 12 miles west to San Juan County Park. For diving in the bay or beyond the point, enter easily over sandy beach in front of the campsite office. For Low Island, walk down a short trail.

Bottom and Depths: In the bay the shallow sandy bottom is scattered with eelgrass. Rock rims the bay. Beyond the southern point of the bay where the bull kelp begins, the rocky bottom is 10 or 20 feet deep. From here it falls away fairly quickly in ledges and folds to 40 or 50 feet, to big boulders, small caves and overhangs. Then into very deep water.

Hazards: Current and bull kelp. Beyond the bay, dive on the slack. Carry a knife and surface with a reserve of air, so that if caught in the kelp you will have time to cut your way free.

Telephone: San Juan County Park, outside office.

Facilities: Picnic tables, drinking water, campsites, flush toilets, and launching ramp. Air fills in summer. Accommodation nearby.

Comments: San Juan Island is a comfortable pastoral place where people squeeze fresh apple cider under the trees and where wild rabbits outnumber the people. Even if San Juan Island weren't good diving it would be a pleasant place to go.

Checkout at San Juan County Park

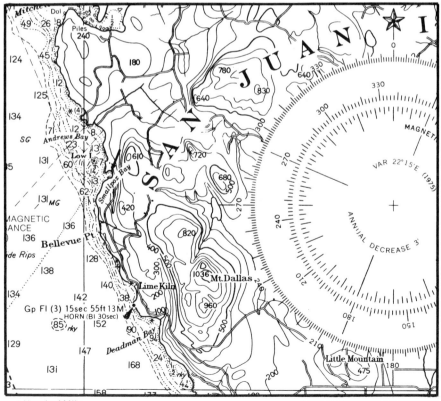

1 Nautical Mile

Portion of 18421 (formerly 6380)

LIMESTONE POINT
Shore Dive

Skill: Intermediate and Advanced Divers and Snorkelers

Why go: A beautiful reef! The sort of reef you usually have to struggle over miles of water to reach. But here it's within a few feet of the rocky beach. Limestone Point has the clean-swept look of a spot with current — and much of the life that goes with it. Bright orange burrowing cucumbers, giant barnacles all over the bottom, lots of rock scallops, a scattering of swimming scallops, rockfish, big sea cucumbers, lingcod, trumpet sponges and strange orange and white encrusting sponges. When diving here I held a red Irish lord. I saw a scarlet blenny with vertical stripes. Spider crabs, hermit crabs and kelp greenlings flashing through the bull kelp. Lots of blue and yellow striped seaperch shimmering in the shallows. Chitons, limpets, bright blue sea stars and giant red urchins stuck to the rocks. It's a good place for available light photography.

Access: San Juan Island is 2 hours by ferry from Anacortes. From Friday Harbor Ferry Landing on San Juan Island go 10 miles to Limestone Point at the northeast corner of the island. Go 8 miles along Roche Harbor Road, then turn right and follow the signs to Limestone Point on San Juan Channel. When the road forks near the top of the island, turn right and go ½ mile to a sign saying Reuben Tarte Picnic Area. Turn left down a steep hill to the beach. Park and walk a few feet to the water. Dive around the point on your right.

Bottom and Depths: White rocky wall with overhangs and crevices drops to 25 or 35 feet, then undulates slowly to 50 or 60 feet and levels off. Big white boulders are scattered around. Bottom kelp and bull kelp are attached to the bright white rocks. Take a light for looking into holes.

Hazards: Very fast current and bull kelp. Dive on the slack. Carry a knife and surface with a reserve of air, so that if caught in the kelp you will have time to cut your way free.

Telephone: San Juan County Park, outside office.

Facilities: Picnic tables, parking for four or five cars. Accommodations nearby.

Comments: Nice wild beach for a picnic. Or, nice beach for a wild picnic!

Hermit crab in Oregon triton shell

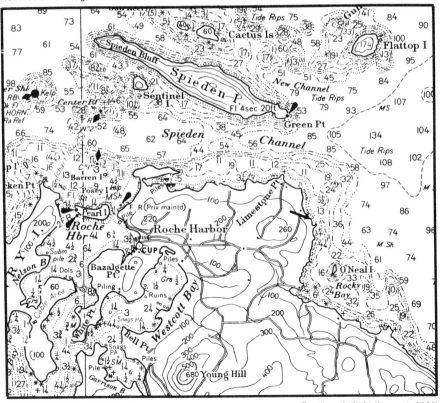

1 Nautical Mile

Skill: Intermediate and Advanced Divers

Why go: More than anywhere else in the San Juan Islands, Eagle Point has a wild, west coast feeling. Untamed wilderness waters crash on the shore. Ankle deep — and you're in surf-dashed tidepools filled with pale green and pink anemones like flowers in a bowl. Ten feet deep — forests of bull kelp, thick, thick, thick, and dense shrubs of green seaweed. Fifteen feet — you can hardly see the rocks for the lacy clumps of mauve coralline algae. Giant urchins tumbled over urchins. Rock scallops, giant barnacles, abalones and hard yellow staghorn bryozoans. Deeper — the bottom falls away fairly quickly. Big boulders and rocky overhangs. Moon jellyfish drift past looking very out of place. A ratfish. And another. We're a long way from anywhere. You expect to see a seal or a whale or something out of fantasy. You feel you're the first one ever to dive here.
A wild place. Not yet tame. And never will be.

Access: San Juan Island is 2 hours by ferry from Anacortes. From Friday Harbor Ferry Landing go 7 miles south to Eagle Point. Follow the signs towards American Camp. Just before reaching American Camp, turn off the paved road onto a gravel road signposted to Eagle Cove. Go 7/10 of a mile to the end of the gravel. There is public access to the water straight down from the end of the road. Climb down the rocks and dive around the point on your right.

Bottom and Depths: The rocky bottom drops off fairly quickly to steeply sloping sand at 70 or 80 feet. Large boulders and overhangs. Bull kelp attached to the rocks. To me, it is prettiest from 20 to 50 feet.

Hazards: Current, bull kelp, wind and surf. Dive on the slack. Carry a knife and surface with a reserve of air, so that if caught in the kelp you will have time to cut your way free. Surf can make entry difficult, and this site is very exposed to southeast wind. Dive here on a still, calm day.

Telephone: Friday Harbor Ferry Landing.

Facilities: None.

Comments: Untamed on land, as well as under water, Eagle Point is strictly for those who don't mind a scramble down the rocks.

Windswept Eagle Point

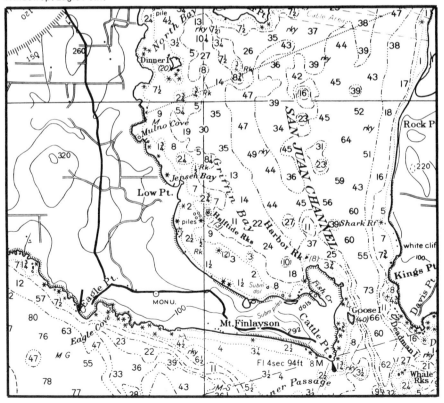

1 Nautical Mile

Portion of 18421 (formerly 6380)

Skill: Intermediate and Advanced Divers

Why go: Good for photography. Good for sightseeing. Good for food. Everything a reef should have. Boulders and bull kelp, irregular overhangs and all the animals to whom these substrates give homes are here. When I first went down, I saw an abalone. Then, soon, a few rock scallops. Plumose anemones, yellow staghorn bryozoans, nudibranchs, trumpet sponges, sea squirts, shrimp and rockfish all over the place, lingcod, pile perch, striped seaperch, painted greenlings or convict fish, and kelp greenlings. My buddy tweaked the tail of a huge cabezon. The local diver with whom we were diving brushed away swimming scallops in a blasé manner. When we surfaced he told me some people consider them to be a nuisance!

The reef is rich in life, has a lot of "shape" to it, boulders, inclines, upthrusts: a real three-dimensional dive. Take a light for looking into crevices and under overhangs.

Access: West Beach Reef is in President Channel 200 yards offshore from West Beach Resort on Orcas Island.

Orcas Island is just over 1 hour by ferry from Anacortes. From Orcas Island Ferry Landing go 8 miles to West Beach. Follow signs north towards Eastsound, turning before you reach Eastsound at the well-signposted turnoff to West Beach. From West Beach Resort go 2 minutes by boat to the point 200 yards to the north. Anchor on the outer kelp bed and go down. The reef is so close that you think you could swim to it, but the current does not allow time. Divers with paddleboards could paddle out and anchor here. All others are well-advised to take a boat.

Bottom and Depths: Rocky reef with bull kelp, boulders and overhangs undulates from 25 to 50 feet deep.

Hazards: Current, bull kelp and broken fishing line. Slack is short-lived at this site. Dive exactly on the slack. Carry a knife and ascend with a reserve of air, so that if caught in kelp or fishing line you will have time to cut your way free.

Telephones: 1. By the telephone company in Eastsound.
2. Orcas Island Ferry Landing.

Facilities: Boat rentals, launching, air fills, hot showers, camping, cabins and trailer hookups. A small fee for day divers.

Comments: Once you've dived West Beach Reef you'll want to return. Just a small sample of the excellent diving on all sides of Orcas Island.

Castanet-like swimming scallops

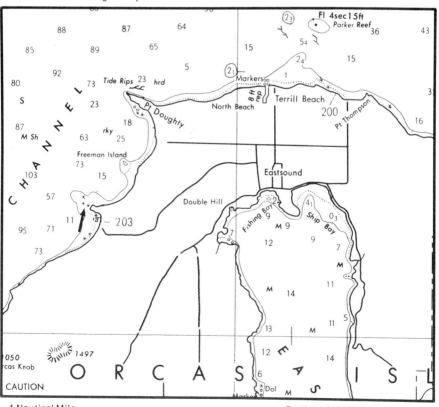

FI 4sec15ft
Parker Reef

Tide Rips 23 hrd
CHANNEL
Pt Doughty
North Beach
Terrill Beach
Pt Thompson
M Sh
rky
Freeman Island
Eastsound
Double Hill
Fishing Bay
Ship Bay
ORCAS
cas Knob
CAUTION
EAST SOUND
Markers
Dol

1 Nautical Mile

Portion of 18423 (formerly 184-SC)

LOVERS COVE
Boat Dive

Tide Table: Add 50 minutes
onto Port Townsend

Skill: Intermediate and Advanced Divers and Snorkelers

Why go: Lovers Cove is the most beautiful spot I've ever seen. Shallow reef and drop-off, all wrapped up in one site. Incredible. Why go? How can you not? Lovers Cove is easily reached by boat and has a sheltered anchorage. The moment you put your face in the water you see abalones and rock scallops. Put your hand on one abalone and find it's clinging to another. Pile perch and striped seaperch light the shallows. Dropping into darker water we saw a large lingcod. And then another. Sinuous fingers of bright pink snakelock anemones flow from the wall. Suddenly we're surrounded with swimming scallops clapping up around us like castanets. We push them away to touch a basket star. It opens its lacy arms like some unearthly flower.
You can go as deep or as shallow as you wish at this incredible site. There's beauty everywhere.

Access: Lovers Cove is in President Channel 2 miles south of West Beach on Orcas Island.
Orcas Island is just over 1 hour by ferry from Anacortes. From Orcas Island Ferry Landing go 8 miles to West Beach. Follow signs north towards Eastsound, turning before you reach Eastsound at the well-signposted turnoff to West Beach. From West Beach Resort go 2 miles by boat to Lovers Cove. Head southwest close along the west shore of Orcas Island which is usually protected from the wind, winter and summer. Go past one point to a small cove where some old pilings project from the water. Past the next point, in another small cove, a rock just barely sticks out of the water. At high tide, only the very top of the rock shows. Half submerged on the channel side is "Lovers" painted on a rock. Anchor near that rock and go down.

Bottom and Depths: Rocky reef from 5 to 15 feet deep slopes off quickly to bull kelp in 20 or 30 feet. North of the reef, a rock wall sheers off to unlimited dark depths.

Hazards: Current, bull kelp and broken fishing line. Dive on the slack. Even then the current never stops completely. It simply changes direction. A pickup boat is advisable. You will encounter less current on a high slack. Carry a knife and ascend with a reserve of air, so that if caught in the kelp or transparent fishing line you will have time to cut your way free.

Telephones: 1. Orcas Island, by the telephone company in Eastsound.
2. Orcas Island Ferry Landing.

Facilities: Boat rentals, launching, air fills, hot showers, camping, cabins and trailer hookups. A small fee for day divers.

Comments: Lovers Cove is just one of the many exciting dives in President Channel. Those who want to explore will find countless more "turn-on" dives along these untouched shores.

!!!

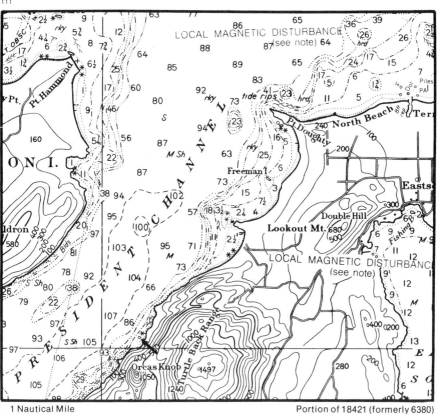

1 Nautical Mile

Portion of 18421 (formerly 6380)

SKIPJACK ISLAND
Boat Dive

Tide Table: Add 50 minutes onto Port Townsend

Skill: Intermediate and Advanced Divers

Why go: Rivers of rock. Underwater hallways. Long narrow channels paralleling the shore. And tassels of bull kelp flowing from the top of this very different reef. For sightseeing, spearfishing, collecting shellfish or taking photographs this is a good place to dive. The shallow bright channels are chock-full of life — both moving and stationary. We saw rock scallops stuck in chinks between rocks. Abalones gliding over them. White encrusting sponges frothing over walls already crusted with mauve algae. Hard yellow fingers of staghorn bryozoans twisting from a crack. And under an overhang, lots and lots of white plumose anemones tilting their tousled heads. Kelp greenlings flash past. A red Irish lord sits while you scratch its back. A swimming scallop claps up to your mask and makes you laugh. Then you see the big lingcod you've wished to see all year. A rewarding dive site.

Access: Skipjack Island is 1 mile north of Waldron Island on the edge of Boundary Pass, midway between Saturna and Orcas Islands. We approached from Orcas Island.
Orcas Island is just over 1 hour by ferry from Anacortes. From Orcas Island Ferry Landing go to West Beach Resort or Bartel's Resort on Orcas Island. Then go 4 miles across the water to Skipjack Island. There is an anchorage sheltered from southeast or west wind near the north shore of Skipjack. Anchor here and swim out to dive the channeled reef near the north shore, or anchor at the reef at the eastern tip of Skipjack. Both reefs are marked with bull kelp.

Bottom and Depths: A series of channeled rocky reefs which run parallel to the north shore of Skipjack Island look as though they have been carved into grooves by giant fingers scraping along the bottom. These channels are 20 or 30 feet deep at the bottom, and 10 or 20 feet deep on the top of the reef where the bull kelp is attached. A scattering of white sand on the bottom. The whole area has a bright clean-swept feeling.

Hazards: Current and kelp. Dive near slack on the north side. Dive on the slack at the eastern tip or else have a pickup boat. The current runs parallel to the shore. Carry a knife and ascend with a reserve of air, so that if caught in the kelp you will have time to cut your way free.

Telephones: 1. Orcas Island, by the telephone company in Eastsound.
2. Orcas Island Ferry Landing.

Facilities: None at Skipjack, but boat rentals, launching, air fills, cabins and hot showers on Orcas Island. Also camping and trailer hookups. A small fee for day divers at West Beach.

Comments: Only one of many boat dives reached from Orcas.

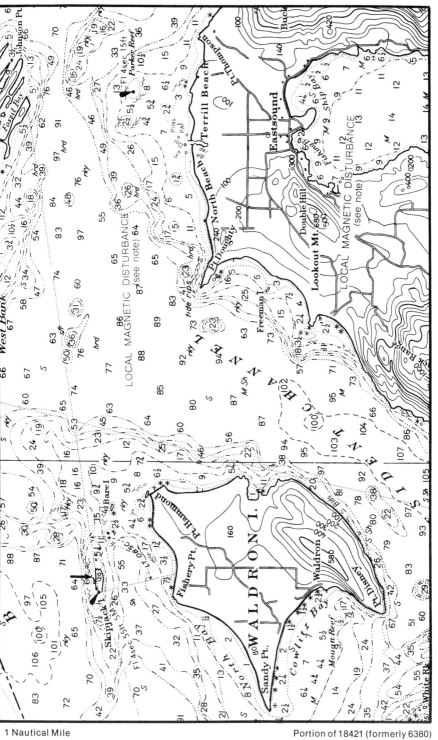

1 Nautical Mile

Portion of 18421 (formerly 6380)

Skill: All Divers and Snorkelers

Why go: Long Island has a couple of good drop-offs. And it'
protected from the southeast wind. All this and abalones, too!
The bright white wall covered with abalones rolls in rounder
globules down the cliff. The rock wall looks melted and poured
Chitons cling to the wall. Small white plumose anemones cluster
under the overhangs. You can easily snorkel for abalones here.
saw some as shallow as five feet.
    The dark wall drops off from clean-swept kelp-covered white
rocks dotted with abalones and lacy bright orange tentacles o
burrowing cucumbers. It falls from 30 feet down to nowhere. You
plummet over the edge. Huge white plumose anemones blanket
ing the wall in froth, cascade down the cliff. The free fall of white
is broken only by a few narrow ledges where giant barnacles
cling in the cracks. Some barnacles are so encrusted with
sponges that you can't see them — only their pink feeding fans
Crimson creeping pedal cucumbers splash the wall with red. A
few small rockfish swim out over the bottomless black. There are
very few fish, but if you like drop-offs, this is a good one.

Access: Long Island is 1 mile offshore southwest of Richardson
on Lopez Island.
    Lopez Island is less than 1 hour by ferry from Anacortes. From
Lopez Ferry Landing head south and west to Fisherman's Bay
where there are boat rentals and launching. Launch and go south
through San Juan Channel to Long Island. Anchor in the small
bay on the north of the island and dive from your boat. East to
the white wall. West to the dark drop-off.

Bottom and Depths: Rocky bottom with bull kelp at 25 or 35 feet,
drops off to 115 or 125 feet.

Hazards: Boats, some current and bull kelp. Listen for boats and
ascend close to the wall all the way to the surface, well out of the
way of those boats. Dive near the slack as there is some current.
Carry a knife and surface with a reserve of air, so that if caught in
the kelp you will have time to cut your way free.

Telephones: 1. Richardson's Store.
                 2. Lopez Ferry Landing.

Facilities: None at Long Island. Camping and accommodations
nearby at Lopez Island.

Comments: A gorgeous site.

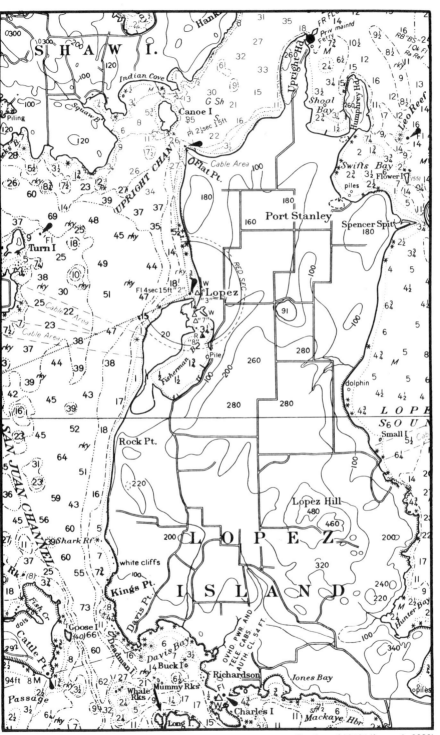

1 Nautical Mile

Portion of 18421 (formerly 6380)

FROST ISLAND
Shore Dive

Skill: All Divers

Why go: San Juan Island dives with easy access from shore are difficult to find. Frost Island is good all-around and suitable for all divers. We saw millions of spider crabs in the kelp. Giant red urchins and small green ones. Lots of little rockfish in crevices of the wall. And a lot of rock scallops. Blennies, a cabezon and pipefish. Some giant barnacles. Sea squirts, shrimp and cucumbers. And crabs in the sand. Just a good all-around dive.

Access: Lopez Island is less than 1 hour by ferry from Anacortes. From Lopez Ferry Landing drive to the northeast corner of Lopez Island to Spencer Spit State Park. Park on the spit and walk across the flat, sandy beach to enter. From here the swim is a long one — 100 yards from the spit to Frost Island. Good diving in the kelp and along the rock wall on the northwest side of Frost Island.

Bottom and Depths: Rock wall drops in crevices, small caves and overhangs to flat sand bottom at 60 or 70 feet. Very silty. Some bull kelp by the wall in 20 or 30 feet. Lots of good flat sand back around the spit — crab country.

Hazards: Long swim, boats and poor visibility. Listen for boats, and ascend close to the wall all the way to the surface, well out of the way of those boats.

Telephone: Lopez Ferry Landing.

Facilities: None at Frost Island. On Lopez, picnic tables, drinking water, campsites and pit toilets at Spencer Spit State Park. Camping at Odlin County Park. Accommodations at Fisherman's Bay.

Comments: Take an underwater light.

Spencer Spit reaching towards Frost Island

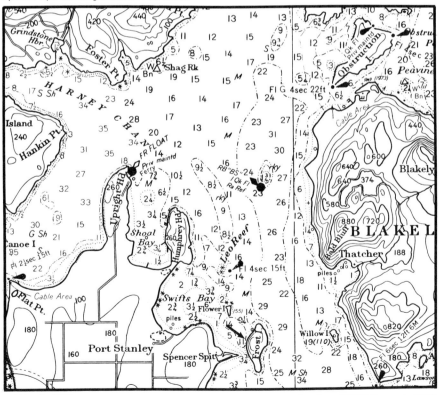

1 Nautical Mile

Portion of 18421 (formerly 6380)

JAMES ISLAND
Boat Dive

Skill: All Divers

Why go: Get away from it all by camping and diving at James Island where there's something for everyone. Beginners will find big rocks covered with anemones in the bay right in front of the campsite. More adventuresome intermediates can look for abalones and octopuses in the rocky cliffs south of the campsite. Advanced divers will find good drop-off diving just north of the campsite. An extraordinary area with some strange invertebrates. Quite barren down to 30 feet. Below 30 feet we saw masses of small white cucumbers and creeping pedal cucumbers with their tentacles withdrawn. The wall looked like a strawberry cake.

Cloud sponges — most unusual for this area — start at 50 feet. Millions of jumping "ants" — my description — or "mosquitoes" — my buddy's. Giant barnacles, lots of swimming scallops and large rock scallops. A blood star and bryozoans. Flamboyant dahlia anemones flame from the wall — small but beautiful. Practically no fish, but fascinating invertebrate life.

Access: James Island is located in Rosario Strait ½-mile east of Decatur Island and 4 miles west of Anacortes.

Charter, rent or launch out of Anacortes or Lopez Island. We launched our inflatable at Spencer Spit Park on Lopez Island. Lopez Island is less than 1 hour by ferry from Anacortes. From Lopez Ferry Landing drive to the northeast corner of Lopez Island to Spencer Spit State Park or south and west to Fisherman's Bay. Go by boat to James Island. Dive from shore in the bay in front of the campsite where there is easy entry over the sand. When diving the points north and south of the bay, anchor in the kelp and dive from your boat.

Bottom and Depths: Big rocks in the bay. North of the bay, bull kelp at the edge. The bottom slopes fairly quickly from 25 to 75 feet, then drops off.

Hazards: Current, boats and bull kelp. Dive on the slack. Be particularly careful of rip currents at the northwest corner of the island. Listen for boats, and ascend along the bottom all the way up to shore, well out of the way of those boats. Carry a knife and ascend with a reserve of air, so that if caught in the kelp you will have time to cut your way free.

Telephone: Lopez Ferry Landing.

Facilities: James Island State Park provides picnic tables, campsites, pit toilets, dock, mooring buoys and hiking trails. No drinking water.

Comments: Both divers and non-divers will enjoy the site for a day or a weekend.

Blood star with bryozoans and ring-top snails

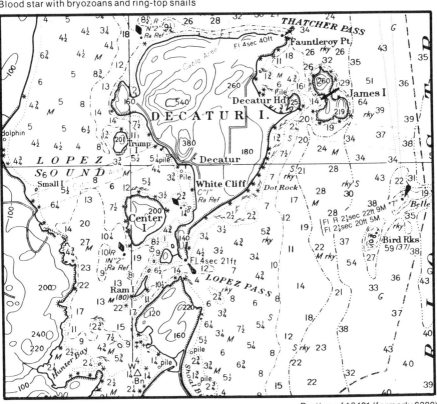

1 Nautical Mile

Portion of 18421 (formerly 6380)

CHAPTER 9
Seattle and Puget Sound
including Fidalgo and Whidbey Islands

Dives

1. Rosario Beach
2. Deception Pass
3. Keystone Area
4. The Wreck at Edmonds
5. Richmond Beach
6. Duwamish Head
7. Alki Beach
8. Blakely Rock
9. Agate Passage
10. Hood Canal Bridge
11. Harper's Abandoned Ferry Wharf
12. Saltwater State Park
13. Tacoma Narrows Bridge
14. Titlow Beach
15. Day Island
16. Fox Island
17. Tolmie State Park
18. Steamboat Island
19. Octopus Hole
20. Union Wharf
21. Point Wilson Reef
22. North Beach

Places

A. Fidalgo Island
B. Skagit River Mouth
C. Whidbey Island
D. Oak Harbor
E. Coupeville
F. Port Townsend
G. Columbia Beach
H. Mukilteo
I. Lynnwood
J. Kingston
K. Fay Bainbridge State Park
L. Space Needle
M. Winslow
N. Lynwood
O. Fort Ward State Park
P. Illahee State Park
Q. Southworth
R. Vashon Island
S. Fauntleroy
T. Tahlequah
U. Gig Harbor
V. Luhr Beach
W. Johnson Point
X. Grapeview
Y. Potlatch
Z. Hoodsport

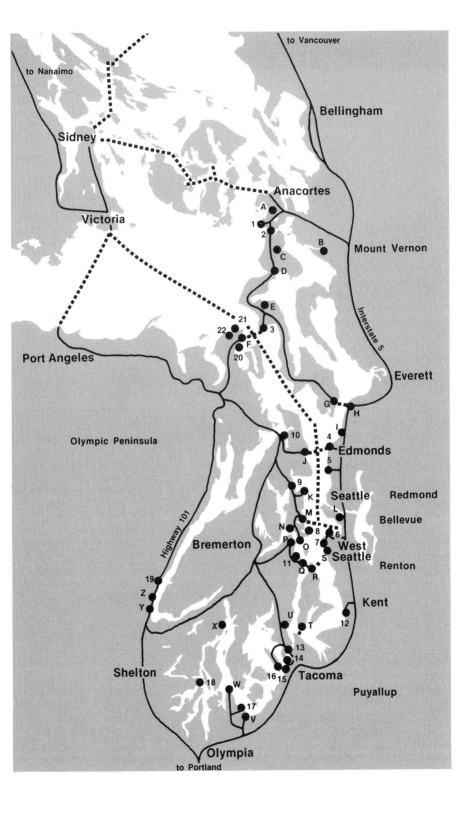

SERVICE INFORMATION*
Seattle and Puget Sound
including Fidalgo and Whidbey Islands

Charts: United States Department of Commerce NOAA National
Ocean Survey

Old System	New System	
●6380	●18421	Strait of Juan de Fuca to Strait of Georgia
●184-SC	●18423	Bellingham to Everett including San Juan Islands
●6450	●18441	Admiralty Inlet and Puget Sound to Seattle
●185-SC	●18445	Puget Sound — Possession Sound to Olympia including Hood Canal
●6445	●18446	Puget Sound — Apple Cove Keyport Agate Passage
●6460	●18448	Puget Sound — Seattle to Olympia
●6446	●18449	Puget Sound — Seattle to Bremerton
●6442	●18450	Seattle Harbor, Elliott Bay and Duwamish Waterway
●6421	●18461	Hood Canal — Port Ludlow to South Point
●6405	●18464	Port Townsend

Tide and Current Tables
United States NOAA National Ocean Survey
Tide Tables — West Coast of North and South America
Tidal Current Tables — Pacific Coast of North America and Asia
or
Canadian Hydrographic Service
Tide and Current Table, Volume 5

Emergency Telephone Numbers
Greater Seattle and Puget Sound
Virginia Mason Hospital
(recompression chamber) 624-1144 ext. 421 or 422

Seattle
Rescue Coordinating Center (U.S. Coast Guard) 442-5886

Emergency 911

Sheriff's Office 344-4080

Tacoma
Sheriff's Office 593-4911

Olympia
Sheriff's Office 753-8111

Port Townsend
Sheriff's Office 385-3831

Whidbey Island
Sheriff's Office 678-5111

Fidalgo Island
Sheriff's Office 336-3666

Other Numbers
Seattle Weather Report 662-1111
State Weather Forecast 285-3710

•Air Stations
Seattle
Lighthouse Dive 'N' Ski
8215 Lake City Way NE
Seattle, Washington
98115
(206) 524-1633

New England Divers, Inc.
11009 - 1st Avenue South
Seattle, Washington
98168
(206) 246-8156

Seattle Skindiving Supply
1661 Harbor Avenue SW
Seattle, Washington
98126
(206) 937-2550

Underwater Sports
10545 Aurora North
Seattle, Washington
98133
(206) 362-3310
(*Compressor rentals also.*)

Greater Seattle — North
Edmonds Diving Center
138 Railroad Avenue
Edmonds, Washington
98020
(206) 775-3483

Scuba Shop
18596 - 76th Avenue West
Edmonds, Washington
98020
(206) 776-4014

Aquarius Skin Diving School
20801 Highway 99 North
Lynnwood, Washington
98036
(206) 776-7706

Underwater Sports North
3515 Broadway
Everett, Washington
98201
(206) 252-7334

Greater Seattle — East
Silent World Divers, Inc.
14444 SE Eastgate Way
Bellevue, Washington
98007
(206) 747-8842

Underwater Sports East
12014 Bellevue-Redmond Rd., NE
Bellevue, Washington
98005
(206) 454-5168

Bremerton — West of Seattle
Divers Hut
4831 Auto Center Way
Bremerton, Washington
98310
(206) 377-9101

Sound Dive Center
2805½ Wheaton Way
Bremerton, Washington
98310
(206) 373-6141

Sound Dive Center
Silverdale Sportsman's Center
P.O. Box 1065
Silverdale, Washington
98383
(206) 692-9758

Greater Seattle — South
Lighthouse Dive 'N' Ski
350 Sunset Blvd. N
Renton, Washington
98055
(206) 772-1415

New England Divers, Inc.,
2507 South 252nd Street
Kent, Washington
98031
(206) 246-3337

Underwater Sports South
31407 Highway 99 South
Federal Way, Washington
98003
(206) 941-1300

Tacoma
Aqua Masters
6605 - 6th Avenue
Tacoma, Washington
98406
(206) 565-0464
(*Compressor rentals also.*)

Northwestern School
of Skindiving
2315 Ruston Way
Tacoma, Washington
98402
(206) 572-6387

Underwater Sports
6132 Motor Avenue SW
Tacoma, Washington
98499
(206) 588-6634

Aqua Masters
1113 River Road
Puyallup, Washington
98371
(206) 845-5350
(*Compressor rentals also.*)

Sea King Dive Shop
4101 Harborview Drive
Gig Harbor, Washington
98335
(206) 858-2115

Olympia
Easons Marine Service
9020 Martin Way East
Olympia, Washington
98506
(206) 491-6899

Hood Canal Area
Mike's Diving
Route 5, Box 916
Potlatch, Washington
98584
(206) 877-9568

Sunrise Motel and Resort
Hoodsport, Washington
98548
(206) 877-5301

Olympic Peninsula
Scuba Supplies Company
104 South Peabody
Port Angeles, Washington
98362
(206) 457-3190

Anacortes Area
Cap Sante Marine
Cap Sante Waterway
Anacortes, Washington
98221
(206) 293-3145

Whidbey Divers Shop
80th NW and 900 W
Oak Harbor, Washington
98277
(206) 675-1112

Bellingham
Northwest Divers Inc.
2720 West Maplewood
Bellingham, Washington
98225
(206) 734-1770

Washington Divers
932 North State Street
Bellingham, Washington
98225
(206) 676-8029

•Boat Rentals and Launching
Seattle
Don Armeni Boat Ramp
1200 Harbor Avenue SW
Seattle, Washington
(*Launching only.*)

Bremerton
Bremerton Boat Service
101 Shore Drive
Bremerton, Washington
98310
(206) 377-2600
(*Rentals and railway
launching. No ramp.*)

Fay Bainbridge State Park
NE end Bainbridge Island
(*Launching only.*)

Fort Ward State Park
Southwest of Winslow
Bainbridge Island
(*Launching only.*)

Illahee State Park
3 miles NE of Bremerton
Highway 306
(Launching only.)

Port of Brownsville
9790 Ogle Road NE
Bremerton, Washington
98310
(206) 692-5498
(Launching only.)

Tacoma
Aqua Masters
6605 - 6th Avenue
Tacoma, Washington
98406
(206) 565-0464
(Inflatable rentals.)

Aqua Masters
1113 River Road
Puyallup, Washington
98371
(206) 845-5350
(Inflatable rentals.)

Olympia
Luhr Beach Launching Ramp
Foot of Meridian Road
Olympia, Washington
(Launching only.)

9's Fairharbor Marina
Box A
Grapeview, Washington
98546
(206) 426-4028
(Launching only.)

Olympia Marina
Foot of Washington Street
Box 143
Olympia, Washington
98507
(206) 352-0411
(Launching only.)

Puget Marina
2 miles south of Johnson Pt
Route 7, Box 638
Olympia, Washington
98506
(206) 491-7388
(Rentals and railway
launching.)

Zittel's Johnson Point Marina
1 mile south of Johnson Pt.
Route 7, Box 549
Olympia, Washington
98506
(206) 491-7196
(Launching only.)

Olympic Peninsula
The Admiralty Resort
Box 75
Port Ludlow, Washington
98365
(206) 437-2222
(Rentals and launching.)

Port of Port Townsend
Mooring Basin
South end of town
Port Townsend, Washington
98368
(206) 385-2355
(Launching only.)

Fort Worden State Park
Port Townsend, Washington
98368
(206) 385-0644
(Launching only.)

Anacortes Area
Fort Casey State Park
3 miles south of Coupeville
Whidbey Island
(Launching only.)

Deception Pass State Park
Cornet Bay
Whidbey Island
(Launching only.)

Deception Pass State Park
Bowman Bay
Fidalgo Island
(Launching only.)

•Charter Boats
Seattle
Divers Hut
4831 Auto Center Way
Bremerton, Washington
98310
(206) 377-9101

Tru-Dive
Edmonds Diving Center
138 Railroad Avenue
Edmonds, Washington
98020
(206) 775-3483

Lighthouse Dive 'N' Ski
8215 Lake City Way NE
Seattle, Washington
98115
(206) 524-1633

Lighthouse Dive 'N' Ski
350 Sunset Blvd. N
Renton, Washington
98055
(206) 772-1415

New England Divers
11009-1st Avenue S
Seattle, Washington
98168
(206) 246-8156
(Winter only.)

Seattle Skindiving Supply
1661 Harbor Avenue SW
Seattle, Washington
98126
(206) 937-2550

Snow Goose
Captain's Quarters
1220 Westlake Avenue N
Seattle, Washington
98109
(206) 283-2100

Underwater Sports
10545 Aurora North
Seattle, Washington
98133
(206) 362-3310

Underwater Sports North
3515 Broadway
Everett, Washington
98201
(206) 252-7334

White Cap
White Cap Inc.
23444 - 10th S
Zenith, Washington
98188
(206) 824-2083
(Winter only.)

Captain Phil Fusselman
1501 SW 164th Street
Seattle, Washington
98166
(206) 244-2552

Tacoma
Aqua Masters
6605 6th Avenue
Tacoma, Washington
98406
(206) 565-0464

Queen Bee
Dogfish Charters
1528 Evergreen Place
Tacoma, Washington
98466
(206) 564-6609

Aqua Masters
1113 River Road
Puyallup, Washington
98371
(206) 845-5350

Olympic Peninsula
Ingenue
Dogfish Charters
1528 Evergreen Place
Tacoma, Washington
98466
(206) 385-3575

Scuba Supplies Company
104 South Peabody
Port Angeles, Washington
98362
(206) 457-3190

•Ferry Information
Washington State Ferries
Seattle Ferry Terminal
Pier 52
Seattle, Washington
98104
(206) 464-6400
(*Ferries from Seattle to
Bremerton and Winslow;
Edmonds to Kingston;
Mukilteo to Columbia Beach;
Port Townsend to Keystone;
Fauntleroy to Vashon and
Southworth; Tahlequah to
Tacoma; Anacortes to San
Juan Islands and Sidney; Port
Angeles to Victoria.*)

B.C. Steamship Company
Pier 69
Seattle, Washington
98121
(206) 623-5560
(*Ferries from Seattle to
Victoria. Summer only.*)

Black Ball Transport, Inc.
106 Surrey Building
10777 Main Street
Bellevue, Washington
98004
(206) 622-2222
(*Ferries from Port Angeles to
Victoria.*)

•Tourist Information
Washington State Parks
Public Information
7150 Cleanwater Lane
Olympia, Washington
98504
(206) 753-2027

Fort Worden State Park
Port Townsend, Washington
98368
(206) 385-0644

Seattle and King County
Visitor's Bureau
1815 Seventh Avenue
Seattle, Washington
98101
(206) 447-7273

*All of this service information is subject to change.

Skill: All Divers

Why go: If you've ever wanted to stroke a fish, Rosario Beach is the place you can probably do so. The bottom is crawling with red Irish lords. Although I wouldn't say they like back scratching, they tolerate it.

Rosario Beach and the waters around are within Deception Pass State Park, an underwater reserve. You must not take any marine life, however the spot is excellent for sightseeing in a wild setting. This is the unique offering of Rosario. Unlike many of the sites in this area, Rosario is a totally natural scene. No man-made pilings to attract animals. No jetty. Just bottom kelp, bull kelp, red and green seaweed feathering up in the water and the most urchins I've seen anywhere — both green ones and giant red ones. The rocks off Rosario Head are well-named Urchin Rocks.

Many other animals live here, too. Millions of little transparent shrimp hop and skitter about like a field of grasshoppers in July. Big frothy white plumose anemones, kelp greenlings, octopuses, Oregon tritons, gum boot chitons and thousands of spider crabs.

But mostly my impression of Rosario is of a tremendous burst of urchins whose spines quiver and glow, and of sluggish slow red Irish lords that I could hold in my hand.

Access: From Seattle go 90 miles by road to Rosario Beach on Fidalgo Island. Heading north on Interstate 5, take Anacortes Exit 230. Go west on Highway 20 until the signs point left to Deception Pass and Whidbey Island. Go south to Deception Pass State Park. Just beyond Pass Lake, turn right and follow signs to Rosario. Walk down a short path past the pavilion to the beach where the entry is very easy over the sand. Walk up the beach to your left and snorkel out to Urchin Rocks.

Bottom and Depths: Shallow sandy bottom in the bay. Around Urchin Rocks, undulating rocky bottom covered with bull kelp and urchins down to 40 or 50 feet. Sand beyond.

Hazards: Current, bull kelp and poor visibility. Dive near the slack. The water is usually silty with debris stirred up by currents through nearby Deception Pass. Water is particularly turbid in spring because of Skagit River runoff. Visibility is best at high slack tide. Carry a knife and ascend with a reserve of air, so that if caught in the kelp you will have time to cut your way free.

Telephones: 1. Bowman Bay Campsite in summer only, 1 mile back.
                2. Harold's Market, 3 miles north towards Highway 20.

Facilities: Parking, pavilion and picnic tables. Restrooms and coin-operated showers. Camping in summer, 1 mile back at Bowman Bay Campsite. Boat launching year-round at Bowman Bay.

Comments: A luxurious place for a winter's dive. With hot showers afterwards!

Urchins

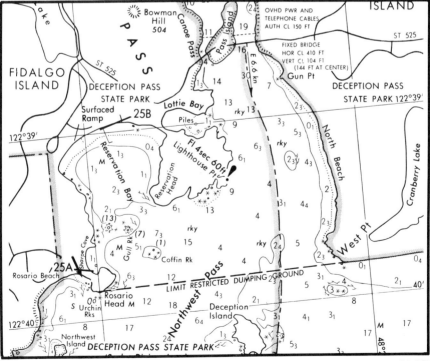

½ Nautical Mile

Portion of 18423 (formerly 184-SC)

Skill: Advanced Divers

Why go: An extravaganza of suspension feeders and fish falls like a surrealistic underwater painting down the steep rock walls of Pass Island.

Purple plume worms burst out along the entire wall in flamboyant bouquets, their purple tufts not even disturbed by divers. Masses of two-inch red, pink and green dahlia anemones carpet the space between. Confetti-like bright red anemones and hot pink brooding anemones are scattered side-by-side in a splash of colour. The brooding anemones spill over onto parchment-like plume worm tubes. Other feather duster tubes are completely encased in yellow sponges. Not enough room for all the life on the rocks!

Strange finger sponges poke out from the most current-washed parts of the wall like flabby pale yellow rubber gloves. We saw urchins, chitons, and white plumose anemones softening the deep crevices. Large lingcod, cabezons and huge kelp greenlings sweeping out of the dark and back again.

But the most striking feature is the splendrous wall of suspension feeders. A grand scenic tour.

Access: From Seattle go 90 miles by road to Deception Pass. Heading north on Interstate 5, take Anacortes Exit 230. Go west on Highway 20 to signs pointing left to Deception Pass and Whidbey Island. Go south following signs to Bowman Bay or Cornet Bay to launch. Then by boat to Pass Island under the bridge. Leave someone in your boat as a pickup while you dive.

Bottom and Depths: Steep rock wall drops off from the island into the pass to 170 or 180 feet. Deep crevices and overhangs. Some bull kelp by Pass Island.

Hazards: Current, down-currents, whirlpools, boats and poor visibility. Very swift currents. Dive on a small incoming tide, precisely on the slack. Arrive on site 45 minutes before predicted high slack. Watch the water and when it slows down, go in. Have a "live" boat ready to pick you up if you are swept away. Listen for boats and ascend close to the steep sides of the island well out of the way of those boats.

Visibility can be poor, particularly when the Skagit River is in flood in springtime. Also, Deception Pass is different from most places. The ebbing tide carries flotsam and jetsam out of the bay into the pass. For best visibility, dive on the tail end of a rising tide.

Telephones: 1. Bowman Bay Campsite in summer only.
　　　　　　　 2. Harold's Market, 2 miles north towards Highway 20.

Facilities: Deception Pass State Park provides excellent facilities: picnicing at North Beach and Rosario Beach; launching at Bowman Bay and Cornet Bay; hot showers at Rosario Beach; and camping at Bowman Bay in summer.

Comments: An underwater reserve as far as Skagit County line. No spearfishing, therefore, at Pass Island.

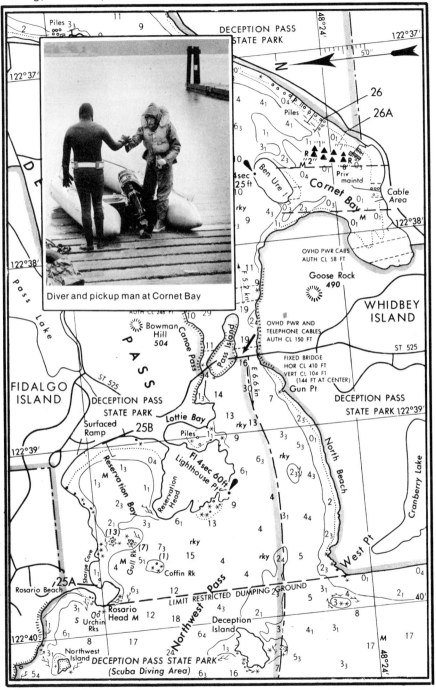

Diver and pickup man at Cornet Bay

½ Nautical Mile

Portion of 18423 (formerly 184-SC)

Skill: All Divers and Snorkelers

Why go: Fort Casey Underwater State Park, better known to divers as Keystone, is a "must" for anyone who wants to dive all the best sites in the northwest. Especially for photographers. Keystone Jetty concentrates life. The fish are fat in this current-washed area. And very tame, too. The fish seem to know that Keystone has been a wildlife reserve for years. Divers actually hand-feed kelp greenlings that live beside the jetty. One photographer says that the painted greenlings are tame to the point of being a nuisance! "They get in the way when you're taking pictures!" Gorgeous white plumose anemones are heaped on the riprap at the base of the jetty like dollops of whipped cream. Other colourful invertebrates, too. Countless rockfish in crevices. An octopus in a dark hole. Life stacked on life. Even divers are accepted as part of this underwater scene.

The abandoned wharf at the left of the jetty provides further shelter for marine life, and the pilings provide some break to the current. I love drifting with schools of seaperch between these piers covered with purple plume worms. Around the wharf is a second good dive.

Keystone Area is shallow and small, but the jetty alone harbours so much life that an underwater photographer can easily use a tank of air before reaching the end of the jetty.

Access: From Seattle go 20 minutes by ferry and 55 miles by road via Mukilteo-Columbia Beach Ferry to Fort Casey on Whidbey Island. Or 106 miles all the way by road. From Interstate 5, take Anacortes Exit 230. Go west on Highway 20 until the signs point left to Deception Pass and Whidbey Island. Then south through Oak Harbor to Coupeville.

Just near a footpath overpass at Coupeville, turn south and follow signs to Keystone Ferry. Park at the beach at the left of the ferry landing. Enter the water at the left of the jetty.

Bottom and Depths: The jetty is 75 yards long. Maximum depth at the tip, 50 or 60 feet. The abandoned wharf harbours life on its 30- or 40-foot deep pilings. Smooth sand between the wharf and jetty.

Hazards: Current, southeast wind, ferry, broken fishing line and bull kelp. Dive on the slack. When current is ebbing, be careful not to be swept around the end of the jetty into the path of the ferry. Stay down, hold onto rocks and pull yourself around the end of the jetty and back towards shore. Do not dive when southeast wind blows surf onto the exposed beach. Carry a knife and ascend with a reserve of air, so that if caught in the kelp you will have time to cut your way free.

Telephone: At Fort Casey Historical Site, 1½ miles back.

Facilities: Picnic tables and restrooms. Campsites, launching ramp and coin-operated showers.

Comments: Walk up the hill to see Fort Casey, the well-preserved fortifications which have guarded the entry to Puget Sound since the 1890's.

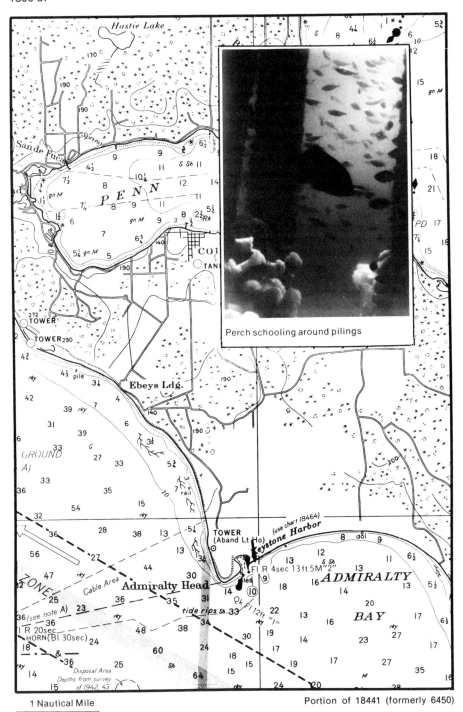

Perch schooling around pilings

1 Nautical Mile

Portion of 18441 (formerly 6450)

Skill: Intermediate and Advanced Divers

Why go: The wreck at Edmonds isn't a wreck at all, but it's the best artificial habitat in the northwest. These three barges have attracted a mass of life. When visibility is good, the place is a mecca for photographers.

Fish life is prolific, and will continue to be, because this is a municipal underwater reserve. Big rockfish, red Irish lords, painted greenlings, often called convict fish, and decorator warbonnets range through the wrecks. I saw a wolf eel here, right out in the open. An octopus, too. Archways of fluff rise around you as you swim through the ribs; the barges are almost smothered in white plumose anemones. A glamourous three-dimensional thing. Everything a wreck should be. Except, no treasure.

Photographers will find best visibility on a weekday in winter when plankton levels are low and fewer divers are stirring the silt.

Access: From Seattle centre go 15 miles to the wreck at Edmonds. Heading north on Interstate 5 take the Edmonds-Kingston Ferry Exit 177 onto Highway 104. Continue 5½ miles west into Edmonds and down Main Street. Just before the water, turn right to Sunset Beach City Park. Entry is easy across a small sliver of beach. To find the wreck, look for two small signs sticking up out of the water. Between the signs and the ferry dock, 170 yards out, is a small float. The sunken barges lie across the bottom between a point just beyond the float and some pilings that stick up at the end of the ferry dock. You see the pilings when you go out in the water. Snorkel to the float, set your compass, go down, and look for the barges.

Bottom and Depths: The barges rest on silty sand at 35 or 45 feet. Between the barges and shore are eelgrass, moon snails, flounders and all the other life associated with a sandy bottom.

Hazards: Long swim, some crosscurrent and close proximity to the ferry dock. Poor visibility in summer. Only dive here if you are very fit. Use a compass. Be aware of current direction as you go down and notice whether you are being swept sideways. Be careful not to stray beneath the ferry slip.

Telephones: 1. Sunset Park and Main Street.
               2. Edmonds Ferry Dock.

Facilities: Restrooms, change rooms and lots of parking.

Comments: Unattractive on the surface, but spectacular under water. For an extra thrill, try diving the wreck at Edmonds at night. Remember it's a reserve.

Sunset Beach and Edmonds Ferry

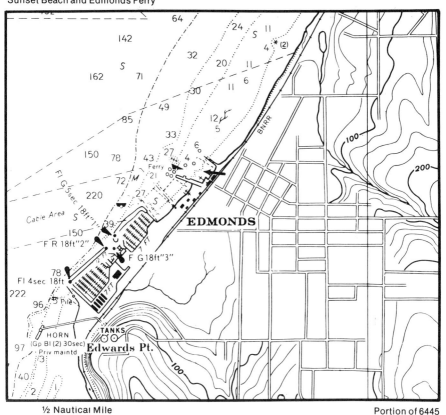

½ Nautical Mile

Portion of 6445
Soundings in feet

Skill: All Divers and Snorkelers

Why go: Lots of the life usually found around pilings and wharves is concentrated here in a more natural setting. The dive is a shallow, relaxed one, with easy access. And Richmond Beach is an attractive place to spend the day. You could walk for miles along the rolling sand dunes.

Under water we saw hermit crabs and moon snails in the eelgrass. Schools of small black rockfish, striped seaperch and pile perch between the bull kelp. Decorator crabs, sea stars and cucumbers. Some large shrimp. Gobies. Plumose anemones. Painted greenlings. Dungeness crabs. Millions of miniature sea pens. And lots of flounders.

An excellent beginner's dive. Good for photography with available light.

Access: From Seattle centre go 13 miles to Richmond Beach. Heading north on Interstate 5, take Exit 176. Go west on 175th Street to the first light. Turn right and go north to 185th Street. Turn left and continue west on 185th Street which changes its name to Richmond Beach Road. At 20th Avenue NW turn left and continue to the lower parking lot at Richmond Beach. From here walk 300 yards over a footbridge to the water. Easy entry over sand directly in front of the bridge. Dive near the kelp.

Bottom and Depths: Bull kelp attached to crumbling metal wreckage and small rocks scattered over the bottom. Most of the life is here, and this is the best place to dive. Kelp, 10 or 20 feet deep, sloping to 30 or 40 feet as you swim north. Beyond the kelp, steeply sloping smooth sand.

Hazards: Boats. Red jellyfish, in the fall. Listen for boats and ascend close to the bottom all the way to shore. If you have seen any red jellyfish, you and your buddy should check one another for stinging tentacles before removing your masks and gloves.

Telephone: At Richmond Beach Road and 20th Avenue NW, on the southwest corner by NW 195th Street.

Facilities: Richmond Beach County Park offers parking space and picnic tables. Restrooms, change rooms and food concessions in summer only.

Comments: Unless changed, park hours are only until 8:00 p.m. As a consequence, no night diving.

Sand at Richmond Beach

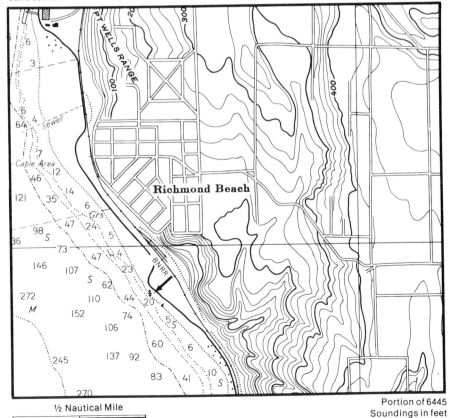

½ Nautical Mile

Portion of 6445
Soundings in feet

Skill: All Divers

Why go: Treasure hunting and a bottom that drops off quickly are two good reasons to dive Duwamish Head. Seattle's first settlement was at this spot back in 1851. Shortly after, many settlers moved into the area of Seattle now called Pioneer Square. They named Seattle after Chief Sealth of the Duwamish Tribe. Later a ferry service connected Seattle and Duwamish Head in West Seattle. For years it was the only way between these two points.

Today a new park occupies this historic strip of land offering excellent access to divers searching for bottles and other valuable old junk from early Seattle days. Even old Indian artifacts. The steep underwater cliff is unstable and periodically whole chunks fall away to reveal new bottom. It is a constantly renewing treasure-hunting ground.

A night dive at the old sawmill at the west end of the park turns up an amazing variety of fish. On one night dive I saw a dozen sailfin sculpins, several painted greenlings, flounders and sturgeon poachers. Look for marine life around the decaying wood of the old sawmill.

Interesting diving — night or day.

Access: From Seattle centre go 8 miles to Duwamish Head. Heading south on Interstate 5, take West Seattle Freeway Exit 163A and go west. From West Seattle Freeway take Harbor Avenue Exit, turn right and continue around the waterfront to the 1600 block Harbor Avenue SW, where old Ferry Avenue came down the hill.

To look for relics, dive anywhere from the east end of the park at 1600 block Harbor Avenue west to Duwamish Head. The old ferry landing was halfway between. Easy entry all along the park to Duwamish Head.

To dive at the old sawmill go west of Don Armeni Boat Ramp, park near the seawall at the west end of the park, and climb a few feet down slippery riprap rocks by the seawall. Once in the water — it's easy! Swim a short way west to pilings which only just project from the water, and go down.

Bottom and Depths: Muddy bottom drops off very steeply at Duwamish Head. Some bull kelp attached to pilings.

Hazards: Boats and broken fishing lines are potential hazards. Listen for boats and ascend up pilings close to the bottom all the way to shore. Carry a knife.

Telephone: Harbor Avenue SW, opposite Don Armeni Boat Ramp.

Facilities: Parking, picnic tables, restrooms and launching ramp at this new grassy park. Café across the road.

Comments: When wind blows at Alki Beach, Duwamish Head is often sheltered.

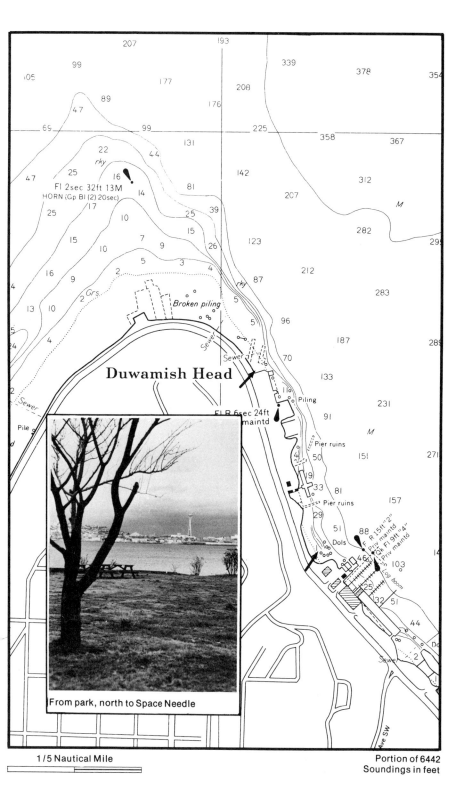

207 193 339 378 354

99 105 177 208 358 367

89 47 176 225

69 99 131 358 367

22 44 142 312

rky 25 16 81 207 M

Fl 2sec 32ft 13M 14 282 295

HORN (Gp Bl (2) 20sec) 17

25 10 25 39

15 15 26 123 283

10 9 9

5 3 4 87 212 187 289

16 9 2 5 Broken piling 96

Grs 5 5 70 133 231

13 10 2 Sewer 110 Piling 91 M

24 4 Sewer Pier ruins 151 271

Fl R 6sec 24ft 50 157

Pile maintd 4

Duwamish Head 9 33 81

Pier ruins

29 51 88 F R 15ft "2" Priv maintd

Dols Ok Fl 9ft "4" Priv maintd

46 103

25 Log boom

32 51

44

Sewer 2

From park, north to Space Needle

1/5 Nautical Mile

Portion of 6442
Soundings in feet

Skill: All Divers

Why go: Popular for good reasons — Alki Beach is a pretty place, easily accessible and easy to dive.

The main attraction is the "tubular reef" or Alki pipeline at 63rd Avenue and Beach Drive. Broken rocks scattered over the pipeline extend in a narrow 3- to 5-foot wide pathway out over the clean white sand. We saw small pink swirls of tube worms, kelp crabs menacing us with their small pincers, sculpins, blood stars, sunflower stars and delicate nudibranchs on and under the long, low row of angular rocks. Orange and white plumose anemones tip their heads over the top of the "reef". There's a profusion of anemones at the apparent end of the pipe about 200 yards offshore.

The pipe reappears and actually ends about 50 yards beyond the apparent end of the pipe. To look for it, follow your compass and continue in a straight line. This area used to have great holes and caves and hid a large octopus in its dark depths under the pipe, but the caves are filling with sand. It is the most beautiful part of the reef and surely the least visited. The end of the pipeline is difficult to find. I missed it altogether.

Finding myself in an orange jungle of sea pens I didn't even mind. And I enjoyed the moon snails, flounders and burrowing anemones on the sand around.

Access: From Seattle centre go 10 miles to Alki Beach. Heading south on Interstate 5, take West Seattle Freeway Exit 163A and go west. Take Harbor Avenue Exit from West Seattle Freeway, turn right and continue around the waterfront to 63rd Avenue SW. Turn left and go less than ½ mile across Alki Point to Beach Avenue and 63rd Avenue SW. Park and walk down the concrete ramp at the end of 63rd Avenue. An easy entry over sand and rocks. Immediately to the left of the ramp you will see a small groin of rocks pointing southwest out into the water. These rocks mark the beginning of the "tubular reef".

Bottom and Depths: Broken rock path, 3 to 5 feet wide, covers the pipeline extending out over clean white sand, gradually sloping to 25 or 35 feet at the end of the pipe. Some bull kelp.

Hazards: Surf. Red jellyfish in the fall. Strong south wind sometimes blows up the surf, making entry difficult at Alki. When windy, check nearby Duwamish Head which is sheltered from most winds. If you have seen any red jellyfish, you and your buddy should check one another for stinging tentacles before removing your masks and gloves.

Telephone: North end of 63rd Avenue SW.

Facilities: Pleasant beach for a picnic.

Comments: I had heard so much about Alki Beach that I felt I didn't want to or need to do the dive. To my surprise I loved it. Now I can't wait to see the sea pens at Alki at night!

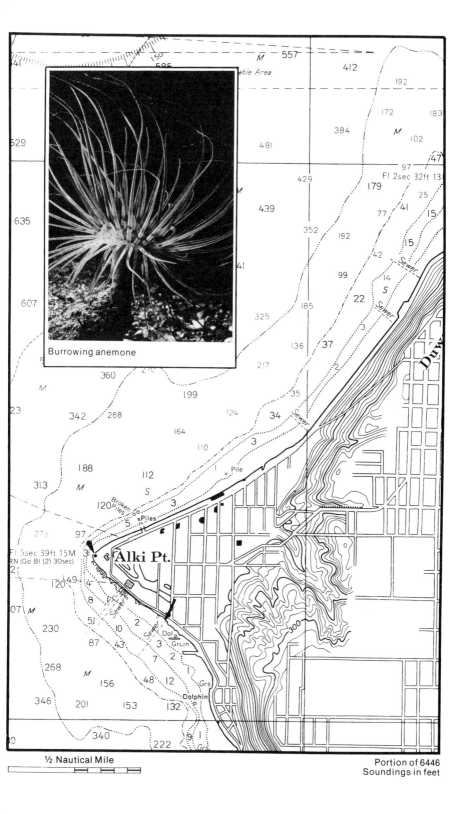

Burrowing anemone

½ Nautical Mile

Portion of 6446
Soundings in feet

BLAKELY ROCK
Boat Dive

Skill: Intermediate and Advanced Divers and Snorkelers

Why go: Blakely Rock must be the most beautiful natural dive site — unassisted by man — in the immediate Seattle area. It is particularly worthwhile for available light photography. Grottoes thick with white plumose anemones in only 10 feet of water. Lots and lots of fish. Like an aquarium. Dusky perch, big black rockfish, silver shiners, striped seaperch, red Irish lords, giant painted greenlings, often called convict fish, and small blennies swim about in the sunny shallows. We saw gorgeous nudibranchs of many varieties, like white ones with white tips, orange ones with white tips and white ones with orange tips. And interesting shells.Leafy hornmouths and Oregon tritons.The area is supposedly good for octopuses, wolf eels, and the occasional lingcod and cabezon which has escaped the hunter up until now, but I saw none of these.
   The unique beauty of Blakely Rock to me is in the shallow grottoes and caves.

Access: Blakely Rock is ½ mile off the east side of Bainbridge Island and 4 miles west of Duwamish Head in West Seattle. Launch from Don Armeni Boat Ramp at Duwamish Head or take Seattle-Winslow Ferry to Bainbridge Island and launch at Fort Ward State Park on the southeast corner of Bainbridge Island or rent a boat in Bremerton. Go around Restoration Point to Blakely Rock which has a marker on it. Anchor south of the rock and dive from the deeper southeast corner around the east side to the shallows on the northern side.
   Bainbridge Island is a ½-hour ferry ride from downtown Seattle.

Bottom and Depths: Silt-covered sedimentary rock and basalt ledges drop in steps to 60 or 70 feet, bottoming out to steeply sloping silty sand off the southeast corner of Blakely Rock. Caves and grottoes from 10 or 20 feet right up to the surface on the eastern and northern side. Very shallow forest of bull kelp on the northwest side of Blakely Rock.

Hazards: Current and bull kelp. Red jellyfish, in the fall. Dive on the slack. Carry a knife and ascend with a reserve of air, so that if caught in the kelp you will have time to cut your way free. If you have seen any red jellyfish, you and your buddy should check one another for stinging tentacles before removing your masks and gloves.

Telephones: 1. By the theatre in Lynwood, Bainbridge Island.
2. Across street from Don Armeni Boat Ramp, Seattle.

Facilities: None.

Comments: Blakely Rock is well worth the effort of taking a boat!

Looking east from Blakely Rock to Seattle

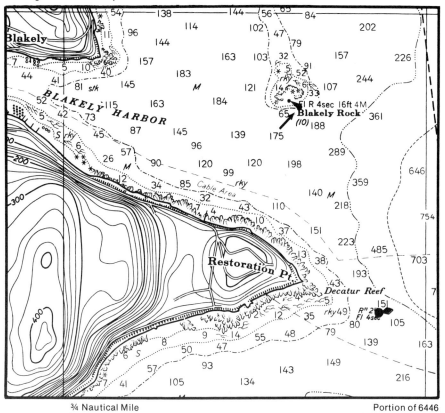

¾ Nautical Mile

Portion of 6446
Soundings in feet

AGATE PASSAGE
Shore or Boat Dive

Current Table: Subtract 45 minutes
from Admiralty Inlet

Skill: Advanced Divers; Intermediate Divers with a pickup boat.

Why go: Tumbling and flying through a fantasy-land of fish and rocks, travel three quarters of a mile through current-swept Agate Pass without kicking a fin. This is the best site for a "drift" dive that I've ever seen.
Access to the water at both ends of the passage makes three dive plans possible: take two cars and leave one at each end; spend the whole day and drift both ways; or take a hand-launchable pickup boat and dive from either access without having to plan the timing. A heady trip however you do it.
Starting the roller-coaster ride we flew through giant pile perch schooling around the piers of the bridge. Sweeping on, you hurtle towards a bright white hedge of horse clams. A gentle push of your hand and you're over it, slowing down, picking up a red Irish lord in your palm. Then off again. Past large rocks crusted over with bright yellow sponges and millions of miniature white anemones. A big rock. You're going to hit it! The current carries you up and over. Looking behind boulders in the lee of the current you see large lingcod staring back at you. A cabezon on eggs. There's no way to stop. You somersault for the sheer joy of it, floating upside down to see where you've been. The motion's enough to make the dive.

Access: From Seattle, Agate Passage is a ½-hour ferry ride and 7½ miles away. Take the Seattle-Winslow Ferry from downtown Seattle to Bainbridge Island and drive north on Highway 305. Just before Agate Pass Bridge turn right down Reitan Road, then left on Spring Road. Park under a large power pole. Gravel steps go 100 feet down to the shore just north of the bridge. We launched our inflatable at the southern end of the passage where you must start if drifting with an ebbing tide.
Reach the northern end of the pass by continuing north across Agate Pass Bridge to the Kitsap Peninsula. Shortly past the bridge turn right down Suquamish Way and go 1 mile towards Suquamish. At signs pointing to Old Man House Park, turn right again. At McKinistry Street, turn left to a small parking spot at the road end. Walk a few feet to the water. A red buoy marks the northern end of Agate Passage.

Bottom and Depths: The bottom is 25 or 35 feet deep through Agate Passage. Mostly sand and gravel. Rocks and boulders north of the bridge. Bull kelp around the bridge piers.

Hazards: Currents and boats. Currents run up to 3.6 knots. Current greater at the southern end of the passage and on flooding tides. Dive on the slack around the piers of the bridge. Plan a "drift" dive carefully according to current and available pickup boats. Listen for boats and ascend with a reserve of air, so that if you hear a boat you can stay down until it passes. When drifting do not take a camera, speargun or goodie bag. Extra gear will be in the way.

Telephone: Fay Bainbridge State Park restroom. Follow signs southeast to the park.

Facilities: Old Man House Park has a small grassy area, parking and pit toilets. No facilities at access on the east side of the bridge. Just a nice wild beach.

Comments: A thrilling flight!

Divers surfacing north of Agate Passage Bridge

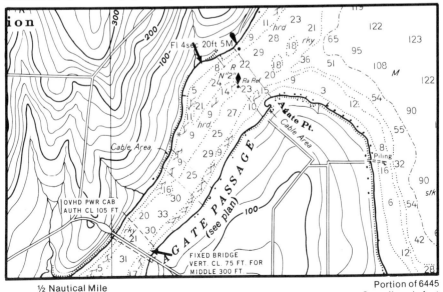

½ Nautical Mile

Portion of 6445
Soundings in feet

HOOD CANAL BRIDGE   **Current Table:** Subtract 25 minutes
Shore Dive   from Admiralty Inlet

Skill: Intermediate and Advanced Divers

Why go: Where else can you dive from shore and see such magnificent feather duster worms?
Fast currents feed these giant purple bouquets. Elegant plumose anemones, countless enormous sea stars and other invertebrates are heaped around the bridge piers. Not an inch of concrete to be seen.
Swimming out to the piers and back, we were fascinated with ranks of sand dollars studding the clean white sand. They feed on fuzzy amber-coloured diatoms hanging quietly in grooves of sand while current rushes over the top of them.

Access: From Seattle take a ½-hour ferry ride and drive 21 miles to Hood Canal Bridge. Take Seattle-Winslow Ferry from downtown Seattle to Bainbridge Island and drive north on Highway 305 across Agate Pass Bridge. Continue north to Highway 3, turn right and go 7 miles further to Hood Canal Bridge. One half mile before the bridge come to Wheeler Road. Turn right down Wheeler and circle back towards the bridge. Two road ends open onto the beach. Enter at the second road end, snorkel south to the bridge, and swim to the first pier. Descend and continue under water to the next pier.

Bottom and Depths: Perfectly smooth silty sand slopes gradually to the bridge piers. At the first pier, 10 or 20 feet deep. At the second, 30 or 40 feet deep.

Hazards: Current. Dive on the slack. Sandy, smooth bottom offers no handholds to grasp to pull yourself along against the current. You cannot, therefore, go far during the very limited slack tide under the bridge. Beyond the second pier, a pickup boat is advisable.

Telephone: No convenient coin telephone. Telephone at Tollgate, east end of Hood Canal Bridge.

Facilities: None.

Comments: A wealth of invertebrate life, but frustrating for the photographer because the current stirs the silt and creates poor visibility.

Entering north of Hood Canal Bridge

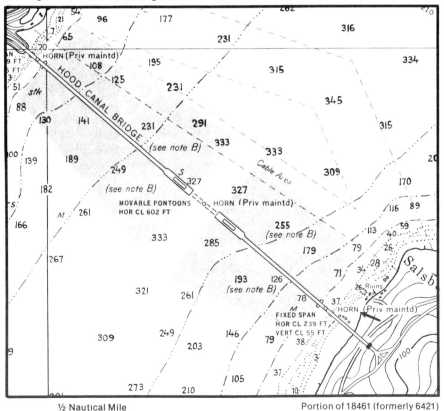

½ Nautical Mile

Portion of 18461 (formerly 6421)
Soundings in feet

Skill: All Divers and Snorkelers

Why go: Nothing sensational in the way of unusual species, but these have to be the most populated pilings around. There's a lot to see at Harper Wharf. It's a quick and easy dive in a quiet place. Uncomplicated. Good for beginners, or anyone who wants to unwind. You can't see the pilings for the plumose anemones. We saw moon snails all around. Horse clams. Schools of slim silvery pipefish spurting forward in unison. Lots of crabs, nudibranchs and all kinds of seaperch. When diving at Harper's, for the first time ever I saw an octopus shoot its ink.
Popularity has not spoiled this spot.

Access: From Seattle centre Harper is 8 miles, a ½-hour ferry ride and 2 more miles. Heading south on Interstate 5 turn off at Exit 163A onto West Seattle Freeway. At the end of the freeway bear left and continue on Fauntleroy Way to Fauntleroy-Southworth Ferry. On the other side, drive off the ferry and head north on Highway 160. Go 2 miles to the centre of the small town of Harper where you will see the abandoned wharf. Two or three cars can park at the roadside. Walk a few steps to the water, snorkel to the pilings beyond the right end of the wharf and go down.

Bottom and Depths: Sand slopes gently to 20 or 30 feet at the last wharf piling. Beyond the end of the wharf and to the right, more pilings which have been cut off beneath the surface.

Hazards: Small boats and fishing lines. Listen for boats and ascend up a piling or follow your compass, swimming close along the bottom all the way back to shore. Be careful of fishing tackle.

Telephone: Southworth Ferry Landing.

Facilities: None.

Comments: A good little dive.

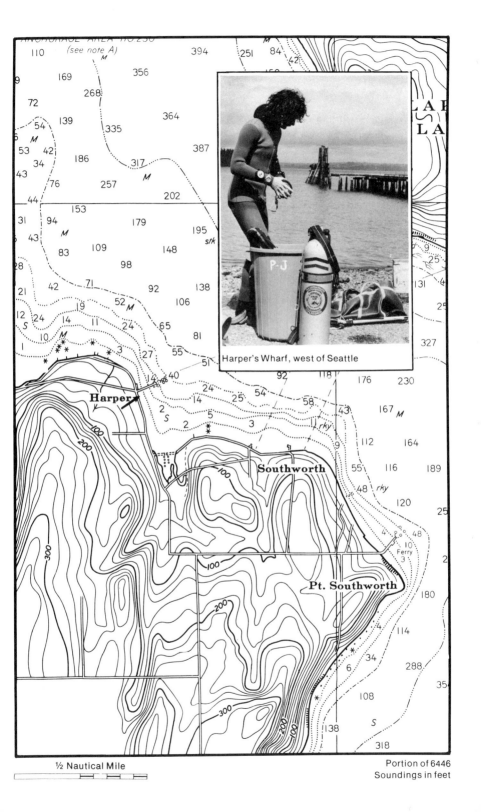

Harper's Wharf, west of Seattle

Harper

Southworth

Pt. Southworth

½ Nautical Mile

Portion of 6446
Soundings in feet

SALTWATER STATE PARK
[SALT WATER]
Shore Dive

Skill: All Divers

Why go: Fish flock to the sunken barge at Saltwater Park. They seem to know they're protected at this underwater reserve. Shallow, with minimal currents and marked with a buoy, the barge is easy for all divers to find. Is it any wonder that Saltwater State Park attracts divers? It's like a goldfish bowl. Striped seaperch, huge shiners, copper rockfish, painted greenlings or convict fish, millions of little sculpins, dusky rockfish and cabezons crowd the interior of the 110-by-40 foot barge. Plumose anemones cling to its walls. Some nudibranchs, too. Sailfin sculpins and an octopus hide under the dark edge of the hull. Flounders, stars and sea pens flourish on the silty sand around.

As the old wooden gravel barge is gradually eaten away by teredos, its shape becomes more interesting. And as it ages it attracts more and more life. Placed here in 1971, this is one of the first intentional man-made underwater habitats in Puget Sound. For years it's been a success, and it's getting better all the time!

Access: From Seattle go 24 miles to Saltwater Park. Heading south on Interstate 5 take Des Moines Exit 149. Go 2½ miles on Highway 516 to Marine View Drive South in Des Moines. Turn left and go 1½ miles farther to the park. Straight out from the point with the flagpole on it you see a white buoy marking the barge. It is 871 feet offshore. This long swim is the only drawback. An inflatable, other small boat, or paddleboard will be useful. No launching ramp, but small boat launching is possible across the sandy log-strewn beach.

Bottom and Depths: The 110-by-40 foot wooden barge rests on silty sand at 45 or 55 feet.

Hazards: Long swim to the barge. Only dive on the barge if you are very fit or if you have a boat.

Telephone: Saltwater Park, by the park concession stand.

Facilities: Kitchen shelter and restrooms year-round. Campground, coin-operated showers and food concession stand in summer only. Plenty of parking space.

Comments: An underwater reserve. Don't take any animals, just take their pictures. And take a light to look for the big octopus under the south end of the hull.

Sailfin sculpin rippling its dorsal fin

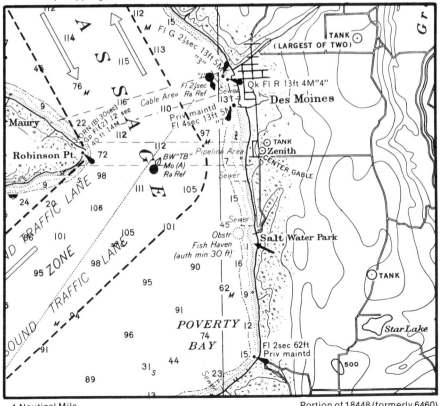

TACOMA NARROWS BRIDGE
Shore Dive

Current Table: Tacoma Narrows
See under The Narrows

Skill: Intermediate and Advanced Divers

Why go: Both beauty and fascination with disaster lure the diver to Tacoma Narrows Bridge.

In November 1940 the first Tacoma Narrows Bridge, "Galloping Gertie", collapsed while cars were crossing. Twisted remains of the original bridge are still under water for divers to explore.

Wildlife is spectacular in The Narrows. Clay ledges carved and undercut by current offer hiding places for red Irish lords, hermit crabs, painted greenlings or convict fish, and buffalo sculpins. The Narrows is well-known for lingcod, octopuses and wolf eels. We found one each living under the huge concrete anchor blocks of the bridge.

Pale pink hydroids that look like powder puffs are scattered over clean-swept rock bottom under the bridge. Near shore, a thicket of bull kelp. South of the bridge, where the bottom is sandy, a forest of sea pens bends in the current.

When I dived The Narrows we did a short "drift" on the ebbing tide. Entering 45 minutes before predicted low slack, we were lucky, and our calculations worked well. Just as we reached the concrete anchor blocks of the bridge, the current slowed and was still, enabling us to stop and explore.

A marvelous way to see The Narrows!

Access: From Seattle go 40 miles to Tacoma Narrows. Heading south on Interstate 5 take Bremerton Exit 132 and follow Highway 16 to Tacoma Narrows Bridge. Highway 16 is Bantz Boulevard, then 6th Avenue, then Olympic Boulevard. Twenty five feet before going onto the bridge turn right into War Memorial Park. Go through the parking lot and down to Western Slopes Treatment Plant. Ask permission to park. Walk 100 yards across the tracks to a concrete slab and steps to the sea. If the tide is outgoing and you plan to drift to the bridge, enter here. Or walk down the beach and dive under the bridge.

The Treatment Plant gate was only open from 9 a.m. till 2 p.m. If the gate is not open, leave your car at War Memorial Park and walk, but the ¼-mile hike down is steep.

Bottom and Depths: Carved undercut clay and conglomerate ledges line The Narrows down to 30 or 40 feet, then smooth sand. Under the bridge, big boulders and concrete anchor blocks the size of a house. Bull kelp by the shore. Depths to 140 feet.

Hazards: Big current and bull kelp. Dive on the slack. Dive on small tidal exchanges only. Carry a knife and ascend with a reserve of air, so that if caught in the kelp you will have time to cut your way free.

Telephone: At 6th Avenue and Howard, 2 miles back where 6th Avenue joins Highway 16.

Facilities: Parking at the Treatment Plant 9 a.m. till 2 p.m., and at War Memorial Park.

Comments: Take a light!

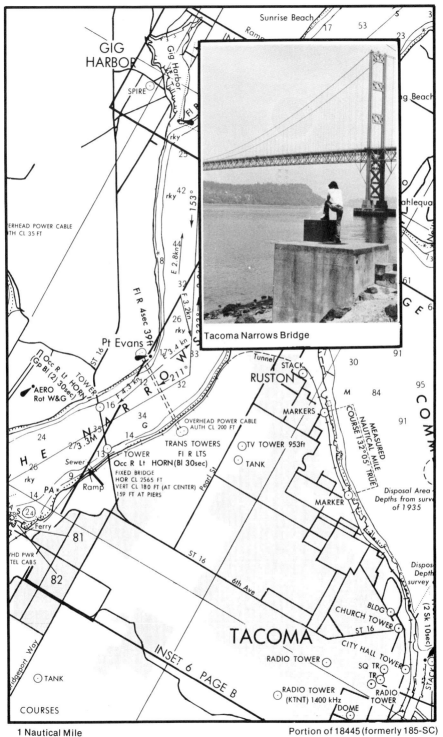

Tacoma Narrows Bridge

1 Nautical Mile

Portion of 18445 (formerly 185-SC)

　　　　TITLOW BEACH　　　**Tide Table:** Add 25 minutes
　　　　　　　　　Shore Dive　　　　　　　onto Seattle

Skill: All Divers

Why go: Octopus, octopus, octopus. And a hallway of plumose-covered piers rising like columns of a Roman temple. Both easily accessible.
If you ever want to look for an octopus, this is a good place. Diving at Titlow, in 20 minutes my buddy and I found five hiding under shallow slit ledges in only 25 to 45 feet of water. Each octopus stirred slightly as we caused vibrations at the den entrance. Probably having a bad dream about some big monster! Octopuses usually hide in the day and hunt at night. We stared into only one wide-awake octopus eye. Take a light for looking under ledges and into holes. Lots of little seaperch and rockfish hide under ledges, too, at this natural part of Titlow.
For those who like a more civilized man-made underwater scene, the white plumose-covered piers of an old landing slip rise like columns of a Roman temple directly in front of the beach. They provide habitat for red Irish lords, cabezons, seaperch, giant sea stars, and much, much more.
A scenic site, both man-made and natural.

Access: From Seattle centre go 40 miles to Titlow Beach. Heading south on Interstate 5 take Bremerton Exit 132 and follow Highway 16 towards Tacoma Narrows Bridge. Highway 16 is Bantz Boulevard, then 6th Avenue. Shortly before The Narrows Bridge, 3 miles after you leave the freeway, the route to The Narrows becomes Olympic Boulevard. At this point you continue on 6th Avenue which veers off to the left and curves down to the water, ending at Titlow Beach. Park at the road end and enter. On your right, pilings of an old abandoned landing slip. On your left, buildings on pilings over the water. Beyond these buildings is a series of shallow rock ledges and small caves.

Bottom and Depths: Abandoned landing slip pilings, 25 or 35 foot sandy bottom. Natural ledges and caves beyond buildings on pilings, 25 to 45 feet deep. Some rocks and bull kelp, flattening out to coarse shell and gravel, at 45 or 55 feet.

Hazards: Current. Red jellyfish, in the fall. Dive near the slack. Fairly strong back eddy from The Narrows. If you see any red jellyfish, you and your buddy should check one another for stinging tentacles before removing your masks and gloves.

Telephone: 6th Avenue and Howard, 2 miles back where 6th Avenue joins Highway 16.

Facilities: Picnic tables and tennis courts. Restrooms in summer.

Comments: Once you've dived here in the day, why not come back and try to find an octopus out and about at night?

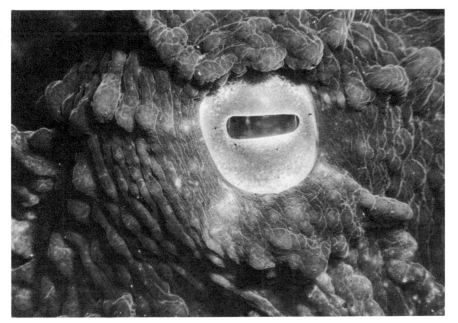

Looking into an octopus eye

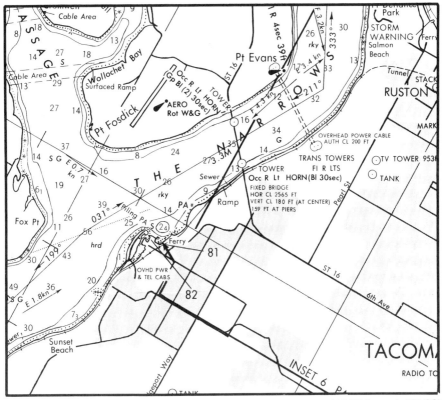

1 Nautical Mile

Portion of 18445 (formerly 185-SC)

DAY ISLAND　　　　**Current Table:** Tacoma Narrows
Shore Dive　　　　　　See Under The Narrows

Skill: Intermediate and Advanced Divers

Why go: Rich marine life in a beautiful natural underwater setting and very easy access are an unbeatable combination to me. This area is especially noted for octopuses and wolf eels and I was not disappointed when diving here. In less than an hour we saw two of each. Many other animals, too. For example, beautiful pink tube worms under every rock in the shallows, moon snails, flounders, sea pens, painted greenlings or convict fish, plumose anemones. Rich in marine life in the shallows and dropping off dramatically into a bare rock canyon, Day Island invites all divers who love a wild underwater seascape.

On the surface it's a civilized scene with homes lining the clean, beautiful pebble beach.

Access: Day Island is easily reached by car alone. No ferries and no major bridges to cross.

From Seattle centre go 42 miles to Day Island. Heading south on Interstate 5 take Bremerton Exit 132. Go west on Highway 16 following signs to Tacoma Narrows Bridge. Highway 16 is Bantz Boulevard, then 6th Avenue and shortly before The Narrows Bridge, 3 miles after you leave the freeway, the route to The Narrows becomes Olympic Boulevard. At this point you continue on 6th Avenue which veers off to the left. At the second light at Jackson, turn left. Continue south on Jackson, which becomes Bridgeport, until you reach 27th. Turn right, following 27th to small bridge on to Day Island and the confluence of five roads. From here, ½ mile to the site. Follow West Boulevard to the 1800 block. You will see a marina on your right and a small open road end on your left. Room for one or two cars at the road end. Walk 100 yards to the water, swim a short way out to your left, and down.

Bottom and Depths: Small broken rock covered with bottom kelp, and some sand between, falls away fairly quickly. Small slit ledges all along where wolf eels live. Starting at 60 or 70 feet, cleanly scooped out clay ledges drop swiftly into a very deep canyon.

Hazards: Current. Very strong current in the canyon. Dive on the slack. Deeper than 60 feet, be very careful of the current.

Telephone: University Place Shopping Centre, 1 mile east of Day Island on 27th Avenue.

Facilities: None. Parking very limited.

Comments: Take a light for looking under ledges. Take a picnic for lunch on the beach at Day Island.

Lunch on pebble beach at Day Island

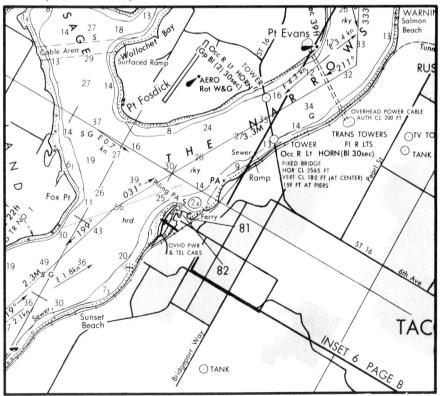

1 Nautical Mile

Portion of 18445 (formerly 185-SC)

Skill: Advanced Divers

Why go: The east wall of Fox Island is the most beautiful wild seascape I've seen in Puget Sound. Canyons and crevices, overhangs and caves within a few feet of shore make marvelous homes for all kinds of life. Rockfish galore, red Irish lords, cabezons, perch, sunflower stars, painted greenlings, giant barnacles, decorator crabs, slime stars, hermit crabs, sea pens, rose stars and flounders. And the list could go on. We were chased by a huge octopus — surely 10 feet across. This is the first time a shy octopus had ever become aggressive with me! The east wall of Fox Island is one of those wild, wonderful places where you feel you might see anything — and do.

Access: From Seattle go 50 miles to the east wall of Fox Island, also known as "The Concrete Dock". Heading south on Interstate 5 take Bremerton Exit 132 to Highway 16 West and follow signs to Tacoma Narrows Bridge. Shortly after crossing Tacoma Narrows, take Fox Island cutoff and follow signs to Fox Island. Once on the island go 3 miles along Fox Island Boulevard. Continue straight past Kamus Drive and 9th and past the dump. At Mowitsh and 14th turn right. Go ½ mile to Ozette Drive and 14th. You will see a small turnaround and room for two or three cars. Park and walk 150 yards down a slippery wooded trail to a coarse shell gravel beach. Concrete dock on your left. Enter, swim a few feet to the bull kelp, and down: work your way south.

Bottom and Depths: Coarse gravel slopes rapidly to bull kelp in 20 or 30 feet. Limestone ledges intricately carved by the current stairstep to 50 or 60 feet, then 100 and on. Not so much a bottom as a quick series of ledges cut by small canyons perpendicular to the shore, current-carved crevices and deep overhangs.

Hazards: Current, current, current. Plus a multitude of small boats and some bull kelp. Dive on the slack on a small tidal exchange. Current is less strong at the east wall on an outgoing tide. Always be ready to pull out of the dive if the current becomes too strong. Fishing boats come very close to the shore. Fly your diver's flag, listen for boats, and hug the bottom all the way up to shore. Carry a knife and ascend with a reserve of air, so that if caught in the kelp you will have time to cut your way free. Best as a morning dive when the sun shines on the east wall: if you can coordinate sun and tides.

Telephone: No convenient telephone. The closest I could find was at 6th and Howard, 2 miles east of Tacoma Narrows Bridge where 6th Avenue joins Highway 16.

Facilities: None. Beautiful wild beach.

Comments: After the dive, signs to Highway 16 point the way back to The Narrows Bridge.

Fox Island's concrete dock

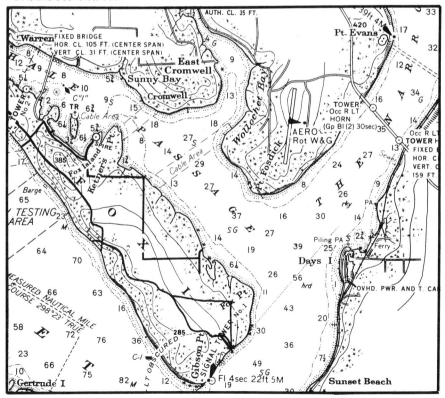

1 Nautical Mile

Portion of 18448 (formerly 6460)

Skill: All divers with a boat. Generally called a shore dive, but this is a shore dive for strong swimmers only.

Why go: Three barges — three dives — at this uncomplicated current-free site. A great place for beginners and for spear fishermen who want to pick up a quick dinner. The barges are loaded with rockfish — some large ones. We stumbled over young cabezons. And it's fun to explore these three old wooden gravel barges. The largest is 110 feet long, is in 40 or 50 feet of water, and has a high picturesque wooden railing. The other two are 90 feet long and rest farther out, at 50 or 60 feet deep. Their metal bins will remain as a habitat for a long, long time. Masses of geoduck clams in the sand all around.

Access: From Seattle go 65 miles to Tolmie State Park which is 8 miles north of Olympia. From Interstate 5 take Yelm-Marvin Road Exit 111. Follow signs 3½ miles north towards Tolmie State Park. Turn right and go another 1½ miles to the park. Walk across a footbridge to the sandy beach and swim out to one of the buoys marking a barge. In summer, when the tide is out, you can walk ⅔ of the way. Still a long swim, but possible. In winter when the tide is in, the swim is over 550 yards. A boat or paddleboard would be a help. There is no current to fight, but the barges are a shore dive for only very strong swimmers.

Bottom and Depths: Smooth sand slopes gently to the barges which are marked with white buoys. The closest barge is in 40 or 50 feet. The other two are 50 or 60 feet deep.

Hazards: Long swim and small boats. Shore dive for very strong swimmers only. All divers with a boat. Listen for boats and ascend with a reserve of air up the chain to the buoy.

Telephone: Interstate 5 and Marvin Road Interchange.

Facilities: Parking, picnic tables and kitchen shelters. Boat rentals and launching nearby. From Tolmie Park go back 1½ miles and turn north towards Johnson Point. Two miles up the road you will find Puget Marina, then Zittel's Marina. Luhr Beach Public Boat Ramp easily reached, too. From Interstate 5 Yelm-Marvin Road Exit 111 go to Martin Way, turn left, proceed to the top of Nisqually Hill and take Meridian Road to Luhr Beach.

Comments: Once you've been here in the day, try diving Tolmie at night. Take a boat and a light!

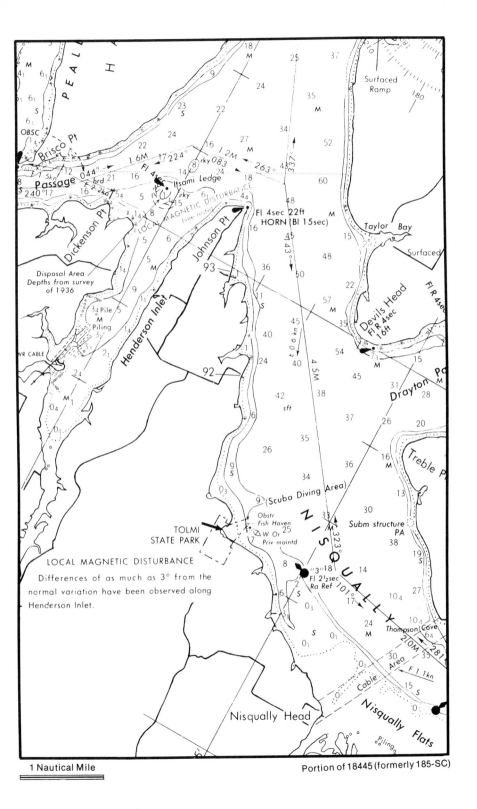

LOCAL MAGNETIC DISTURBANCE

Differences of as much as 3° from the
normal variation have been observed along
Henderson Inlet.

1 Nautical Mile

Portion of 18445 (formerly 185-SC)

STEAMBOAT ISLAND   **Current Table:** Subtract 35 minutes
Boat Dive   from Tacoma Narrows
                                                    See under The Narrows

Skill: Intermediate and Advanced Divers

Why go: Dropping quickly in steep giant steps, Steamboat Island's sheer clay corrugated cliffs with narrow ledges carved by the current make a most unusual dive for this area where gently sloping sand is the norm.
The beautiful nooks and crannies carved in the clay offer hiding places for all kinds of animals. When diving here we found whole pockets of life stashed here and there. In one, half a dozen red Irish lords. In another, a handful of painted greenlings or convict fish. But my biggest thrill was seeing a six-foot wolf eel lying right out in the open. Usually you see dogfish at Steamboat Island and always a mass of peculiar invertebrates.
A different and interesting site. Well worth the bother of taking a boat.

Access: Steamboat Island is 7 miles northwest of Olympia at the northern entry to Squaxin Passage. Boat rentals and launching available in Olympia and south of Johnson Point which is 6 miles by water from Steamboat Island. Public boat launching available at Luhr Beach. From Interstate 5 Yelm-Marvin Road Exit 111 go to Martin Way, turn left, proceed to the top of Nisqually Hill and take Meridian Road to Luhr Beach. Go to Steamboat Island via Dana Passage, anchor near the north end and go down.

Bottom and Depths: Clay cliffs drop in steep steps down to 100 or 110 feet. Some big boulders at 30 or 40 feet. Narrow, scooped-out undercut ledges all the way down. Visibility often limited because of silt. A dark dive. Take a light.

Hazards: Current and whirlpools. The current is weird at Steamboat Island, probably because of the unusual bottom. Dive on the slack.

Telephone: Interstate 5 and Marvin Road Interchange.

Facilities: None at Steamboat Island. No place to land; all private property. Beautiful park for a picnic back at Tolmie State Park. More diving, too!
Rentals and launching at Johnson Point and Olympia. Launching at Luhr Beach.

Comments: For me, a real "turn-on" dive.

Corrugated clay cliff

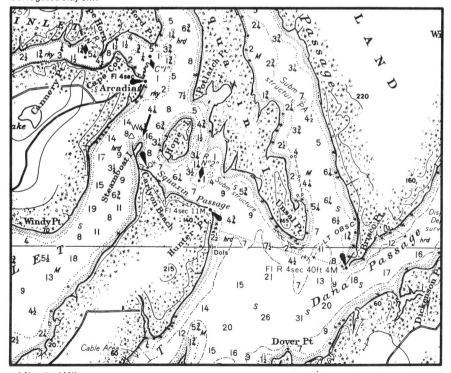

1 Nautical Mile

Portion of 18448 (formerly 6460)

Skill: All Divers

Why go: Easy access, minimal currents, and an attractive rock wall dropping from 30 to 60 feet make this a popular checkout site. "Octopus Hole" is excellent for beginners. We saw rockfish in crevices, lots of bright orange encrusting sponges splashed over the wall, rocks capped with picturesque white plumose anemones, an octopus and sunflower stars. One weird animal I have seen nowhere else, except a couple of miles farther up the Hood Canal — a galatheid crab. Another slightly unusual animal sometimes seen in Hood Canal that looks more like a giant tarantula than anything else, the hairy lithode crab.

Octopuses are, of course, plentiful at "Octopus Hole", but you have to look hard to find one of these shy creatures because so many divers scatter along this shore. To find an octopus, look in holes and under ledges. And look for small piles of bits and pieces of crabs, telltale signs of the entrance to an octopus's lair.

Access: From Seattle "Octopus Hole" is 94 miles away. Heading south from Seattle on Interstate 5 just past Olympia, turn off at Exit 104 and head north on Highway 101. Go 35 miles to Hoodsport. Three miles past Hoodsport pass through an even smaller town, one that seems to have no name. And 2/10 of a mile past this town that has no name you come to "Octopus Hole". You will know you have reached "Octopus Hole" when the road curves down close to the water. Roadside parking for three or four cars just before road curves down close to the water. Park, climb down a few feet over rocky shore and enter. The rock wall starts slightly southeast of this point. To find the wall, snorkel south 100 yards before going down.

Bottom and Depths: Rocky beach gives way to silty sand bottom which slopes rapidly to 20 or 30 feet where the rock wall drops to 50 or 60 feet. The wall parallels the shore. Slightly farther offshore the bottom drops off quickly again. Very deep water in Hood Canal.

Hazards: Red jellyfish, in the fall. If you see any, you and your buddy should check one another for stinging tentacles before removing your masks and gloves.

Telephone: South ½ mile, just past the small unnamed town.

Facilities: Air fills at Hoodsport and Potlatch. Camping at Potlatch State Park, 3½ miles south of Hoodsport. Boat launching ½ mile north of campsite near the power plant.

Comments: Great place for beginners or anyone wanting to see an octopus.

Galatheid crab

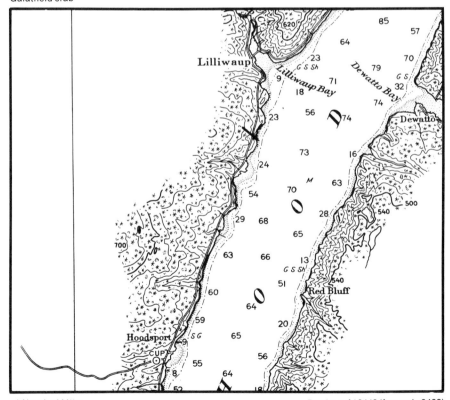

1 Nautical Mile

Portion of 18448 (formerly 6460)

Skill: All Divers

Why go: Paradise for treasure hunters! Stories of the area are bigger-than-life. But, peculiarly, they're true. Gold coins and hundred-year-old soda pop bottles have been gleaned from the muddy bottom. Union Wharf at Port Townsend is said to be the location of the first incorporated business in Washington Territory. There used to be a tavern on the old dock, too. A lot of stuff has been thrown in over the years. Current comes around the shore and back eddies near the wharf, continually turning up a new supply.

Beautiful for sightseeing in the still waters at the end of the wharf where the submerged pilings are smothered in white plumose anemones and purple plume worms. Masses of small rockfish and seaperch and the occasional large cabezon swim between. Flounders on the sand around. From the pilings we followed the shallow clay ledge around to the right to look for an octopus.

A good dive, day or night, and popular for checkouts.

Access: Port Townsend is a ½-hour ferry ride and 50-mile drive northwest from Seattle. Take the Seattle-Winslow or Edmonds-Kingston Ferry, cross Hood Canal Bridge and follow the signs to Port Townsend. Union Wharf is just south of the ferry terminal at Water and Taylor. You can drive right down onto the dock, gear up, and jump off.

Heading south take the Keystone Ferry from Whidbey Island to Port Townsend. To reach Keystone from Interstate 5, take Anacortes Exit 230, and go west on Highway 20 to signs pointing left to Deception Pass and Whidbey Island. Then south through Oak Harbor to Coupeville. Just near a footpath overpass at Coupeville, turn south and follow signs to Keystone Ferry and cross to Port Townsend.

Bottom and Depths: At the base of the dock, silty sand bottom 20 or 30 feet deep. Submerged pilings 80 feet straight out from the righthand corner of the dock in 25 or 35 feet of water. Beyond the pilings a shallow clay ledge leads off to the right, paralleling the shore. Bottles and antiques have been found in the shallow muddy waters close around the wharf, only 8 to 10 feet deep.

Hazards: Boats. Listen for boats and ascend up the pilings or use a compass and stay close to the bottom all the way back to shore.

Telephone: Surf Restaurant, Union Wharf, inside.

Facilities: Parking and restaurant on the wharf. Camping, vacation housing, coin-operated showers and launching ramp 1 mile north at Fort Worden State Park. Air fills at Oak Harbor or Port Angeles.

Comments: After the dive walk around historical old Port Townsend, one of the oldest settlements in Washington State. Each Victorian home is as well-painted as the day it was built. Signs on over 200 homes indicate the date of building and name of the original owner.

Bottles

½ Nautical Mile

Portion of 18464 (formerly 6405)

POINT WILSON REEF
Boat Dive

Current Table: Subtract 1 hour
from Admiralty Inlet

Skill: Advanced Divers

Why go: Spearfishing is good on the few days of the year you can dive this current-swept, kelp-covered reef at Point Wilson. Big lingcod are all over the place. Some say divers have seen 60 and 70 pound lingcod at Point Wilson, particularly in the fall when the salmon are around. We saw schools of big black rockfish, kelp greenlings, copper, and brown rockfish on the reef. Loads of flounders between the reef and shore.

Sightseeing is good, too. White rocks make a bright background for pale lavender anemones, dark red sculpins, hot pink and yellow-and-white striped dahlia anemones. Boulders crusted over with chitons and giant barnacles and capped with small white plumose anemones make good hiding places for wolf eels. Mauve encrusting algae, large yellow bath-like sponges and big rock scallops fill any space that's left.

A rich dive.

Access: From Seattle, Port Townsend is a ½-hour ferry ride and 50-mile drive northwest. Take the Seattle-Winslow or Edmonds-Kingston Ferry, cross Hood Canal Bridge and follow signs to Port Townsend. Point Wilson is 1 mile north of Port Townsend at Fort Worden State Park. Launch and go to the north shore of Point Wilson where bull kelp marks two reefs. The kelp is most easily seen at low tide. The best reef is 300 yards offshore under the kelp bed closest to the red buoy. Do not anchor. Dive from your "live" boat, leaving a pickup person to follow if you are swept away by the current.

Heading south, take Keystone Ferry from Whidbey Island to Port Townsend. To reach Keystone from Interstate 5, take Anacortes Exit 230, and go west on Highway 20 to signs pointing left to Deception Pass and Whidbey Island. Then south through Oak Harbor to Coupeville. Just near a footpath overpass at Coupeville, turn south, follow signs to Keystone Ferry and cross to Port Townsend.

Bottom and Depths: The bright white rock reef is clean-swept with no silt, 25 or 35 feet deep. Some big boulders, scattered white sand, and thick bull kelp.

Hazards: Current and bull kelp. Dive on the slack. All the water going into Puget Sound pours past Point Wilson. The reef can only be dived on a small tidal exchange and exactly on slack. Rip tides are vicious and could sweep you out into the big shipping lanes in Admiralty Inlet. Dive from a "live" boat at Point Wilson Reef. Carry a knife and ascend with a reserve of air, so that if caught in the kelp you will have time to cut your way free.

Telephone: Fort Worden State Park, by the old train.

Facilities: Beautiful natural beach. Camping, trailer hookups and vacation housing in old Victorian homes which were once officer's quarters. Launching ramp, kitchen shelter, picnic tables, restrooms and coin-operated showers. Plus historical remains of Fort Worden.

Comments: Approach Point Wilson Reef with respect and have a good dive.

At Fort Worden Park, preparing to dive Point Wilson Reef

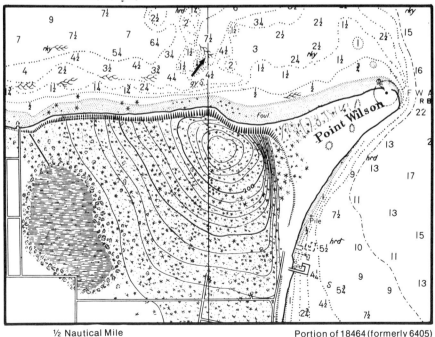

½ Nautical Mile

Portion of 18464 (formerly 6405)

Skill: All Divers and Snorkelers

Why go: If looking for a beautiful natural underwater setting you'll find that North Beach is a little gem. A miniature west coast scene.

Centred around one rock which sticks up out of the water 75 yards offshore is a sampling of life not typical of Puget Sound. It has a subtle west coast look. Thick, thick shrubs of green algae crowd the rock. Rocky overhangs hide flamboyant yellow dahlia anemones. Small white plumose anemones and giant barnacles are under the rock. As we descended something flashed away. You may find an octopus, abalones and rock scallops hiding in the cracks of the rock. The area is small, but complete. A good cross-section of life.

After a circuit of the rock we still had a lot of air left, and therefore drifted through eelgrass and kelp, pipefish and purple plume worms, back to North Beach Park where we had left our car. The current is not especially treacherous near North Beach because it parallels the shore. And the sensation of drifting is fun. When the tide is coming in, drift back to North Beach Park.

Access: From Seattle, North Beach is a ½-hour ferry ride and 55-mile drive to the northwest. Take the Seattle-Winslow or Edmonds-Kingston Ferry, cross Hood Canal Bridge and follow signs to Port Townsend. From Port Townsend go north 1 mile to Fort Worden, west 1 mile and down an angled road to the top of a high bluff overlooking the sea. Look down on the rock to see where you are going. Then go a short way back to the lagoon. Turn towards the sea and drive past the lagoon to North Beach. Park and walk up the beach 15 minutes to the rock. Swim 75 yards to the rock and go down.

Heading south take Keystone Ferry from Whidbey Island to Port Townsend. To reach Keystone from Interstate 5, take Anacortes Exit 230 and go west on Highway 20 to signs pointing left to Deception Pass and Whidbey Island. Then south through Oak Harbor to Coupeville. Just near a footpath overpass at Coupeville, turn south and follow signs to Keystone Ferry and cross to Port Townsend.

Bottom and Depths: Around the rock, only 10 or 15 feet deep. Small cave-like overhangs surround the rock. Algae and eelgrass grow from the sand around. Kelp forests, farther offshore.

Hazards: Some current and bull kelp. Dive near the slack. If drifting back to North Beach, dive on the end of a rising tide that will carry you. Carry a knife and ascend with a reserve of air, so that if caught in the kelp you will have time to cut your way free. Kelp is thickest in summer.

Telephone: Fort Worden State Park, 1 mile east, by the old train.

Facilities: A small grassy area. Picnic tables, fireplaces and pit toilets. No camping. In front of the park, unspoilt beach stretches for miles in both directions.

Comments: Legends surround the rock. One is that an Indian woman was taken out by canoe and left on the rock till she'd had her vision. Probably one from fear and hunger!

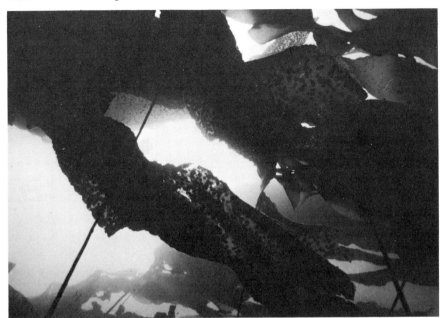

Bull kelp in the current

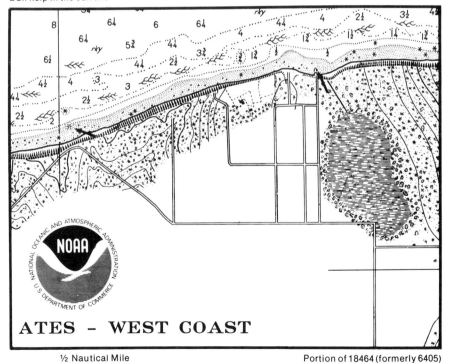

ATES – WEST COAST

½ Nautical Mile   Portion of 18464 (formerly 6405)

METRIC CONVERSION TABLE

Miles	Kilometres
1	1.609
2	3.219
3	4.828
4	6.437
5	8.047
6	9.656
7	11.265
8	12.875
9	14.484
10	16.093
10	16.09
20	32.19
30	48.28
40	64.37
50	80.47
60	96.56
70	112.65
80	128.75
90	144.84
100	160.93

All photographs are by the author except for those listed below.

Cover photograph: Lou Lehmann
Foreword photograph: Alisen Brown
Photographs to illustrate text:
Lou Lehmann, pages 29, 71, 81, 169, 199, 247, 281, 289
Ocean Images: Neil McDaniel, pages 43, 53, 63, 65, 73, 75, 77, 85, 89, 99,
109, 115, 125, 129, 131, 143, 153, 175, 187, 217, 219, 221, 231, 245,
257, 265, 299, 303, 315, 319, 329, 341, 353, 363, 377, 383
Lloyd Gomez, page 61
Jim Willoughby, pages 95, 113, 367
Phil Edgell, page 141
George Crawshaw, page 205
John Pratt-Johnson, page 293
Harry Truitt, page 345

Editorial Assistant: Gordon R. Elliott
Printed and bound in Canada.

●**Everywhere in British Columbia**
R.C.M.P. Dial "0".
Ask for Zenith 50,000

●**Vancouver, Indian Arm and Howe Sound**
Rescue Coordination Centre
(Vancouver) 732-4141

Van. General Hospital
recompression chamber
876-3211 ext. 2739

Marine Rescue 732-4242

●**Sechelt Peninsula**
R.C.M.P. Dial "0".
Ask for Zenith 50,000

Rescue Coordination Centre
(Vancouver) 732-4141

●**Powell River and North**
R.C.M.P. Dial "0".
Ask for Zenith 50,000

General Hospital 483-3211

●**Campbell River to Kelsey Bay**
R.C.M.P. Dial "0".
Ask for Zenith 50,000

R.C.M.P.
(Campbell River) 286-6221
Ask for staff member.

●**Nanaimo, Hornby Island, and South to Sansum Narrows**
R.C.M.P. Dial "0".
Ask for Zenith 50,000

Rescue Coordination Centre
(Victoria) 388-1543

R.C.M.P. (Nanaimo) 754-2345

R.C.M.P. (Duncan) 746-4125

●**Victoria and Saanich Inlet**
Rescue Coordination Centre
(Victoria) 388-1543

●**Southern Gulf Islands including Gabriola, Galiano and Saltspring**
R.C.M.P. Dial "0".
Ask for Zenith 50,000

Rescue Coordination Centre
(Victoria) 388-1543

Rescue Coordination Centre
(Vancouver) 732-4141

●**San Juan Islands including San Juan, Orcas and Lopez**
San Juan Island 378-4141

Orcas Island 376-2207

Lopez Island 468-2333

●**Seattle and Puget Sound including Fidalgo and Whidbey Islands**

Seattle
Rescue Coordinating Center
(U.S. Coast Guard) 442-5886

Va. Mason Hospital
recompression chamber
624-1144 ext. 421

Emergency 911

Sheriff's Office 344-4080

Tacoma
Sheriff's Office 593-4911

Olympia
Sheriff's Office 753-8111

Port Townsend
Sheriff's Office 385-3831

Fidalgo Island
Sheriff's Office 336-3666

Whidbey Island
Sheriff's Office 678-5111